Dynamics of Social Institutions

DYNAMICS OF SOCIAL INSTITUTIONS

Dr Shweta

MD PUBLICATIONS PVT LTD
NEW DELHI
www.mdppl.com

Published by :

MD Publications Pvt Ltd
"MD House", 11, Darya Ganj,
New Delhi - 110 002
Phone : +91-11-41563325 (Customer Service)
+91-11-41562846 (Editorial)
E-mail (orders): order@mdppl.com
Website: www.mdppl.com

ISBN: 978-81-7533-221-8

Published and Printed by Mr. Pranav Gupta on behalf of **MD Publications Pvt Ltd** at Times Press, New Delhi.

PREFACE

The term, "social institution" is somewhat unclear both in ordinary language and in the philosophical literature. However, contemporary sociology is somewhat more consistent in its use of the term. Typically, contemporary sociologists use the term to refer to complex social forms that reproduce themselves such as governments, the family, human languages, universities, hospitals, business corporations, and legal systems.

It is convenient to conceive of social institutions as possessed of three dimensions, namely, structure, function and culture. While the structure, function and culture of an institution provide a framework within which individuals act, they do not fully determine the actions of individuals. There are a number of reasons why this is so. For one thing, rules, norms and ends cannot cover every contingency that might arise; for another, rules, norms and so on, themselves need to be interpreted and applied. Moreover, changing circumstances and unforeseeable problems make it desirable to vest individuals with discretionary powers to rethink and adjust old rules, norms, and ends, and sometimes elaborate new ones.

Barriers to the progress of analysis of the individual stem from the powerful taboo of social prohibition. Conversely, barriers to insight into social process emerge from the depths of intrapersonal collusion. The last bastions to yield to analysis are inevitably those shared most deeply and in common between most people. The residual blind-spots of social and intra-personal analysis are the commonly shared neuroses and psychoses holding behind their defences the most deep, most primitive, most painful and most common trauma.

The study of psychosocial analysis has other criteria of significance. It takes as its field the 'normal' zone of behaviour distribution. The most significant phenomena are the most common dynamics of the highest aggregation social systems. In this it affirms the criteria of the sociologist and inverts the criteria of the therapist. On the other hand, the discipline of psychosocial analysis seeks to break through the collusional repression of both sociology and psychoanalysis by affirming the psychoanalytic approach to normal phenomena. It understands common social processes as energised by unconscious material, just as are the less common neuroses and psychoses of social sub-sector or individual deviation. It is committed to the analysis of those deeply repressed areas of common psychotic anxiety, defence against which constitutes the driving dynamic of normal institutional process.

I am very grateful to Mr. Pranav Gupta, Director of MD Publications Pvt Ltd, New Delhi, for his kind cooperation and support for this book.

Dr Shweta

CONTENTS

1

Dynamics of Social Institutions

An Introduction

The term, "social institution" is somewhat unclear both in ordinary language and in the philosophical literature. However, contemporary sociology is somewhat more consistent in its use of the term. Typically, contemporary sociologists use the term to refer to complex social forms that reproduce themselves such as governments, the family, human languages, universities, hospitals, business corporations, and legal systems.

A typical definition is that proferred by Jonathan Turner: "a complex of positions, roles, norms and values lodged in particular types of social structures and organising relatively stable patterns of human activity with respect to fundamental problems in producing life-sustaining resources, in reproducing individuals, and in sustaining viable societal structures within a given environment." Again, Anthony Giddens says: "Institutions by definition are the more enduring features of social life." He goes on to list as institutional orders, modes of discourse, political institutions, economic institutions and legal institutions.

The contemporary philosopher of social science, Rom Harre follows the theoretical sociologists in offering this kind of definition: "An institution was defined as an interlocking double-structure of persons as role-holders or office-bearers and the like, and of social practices involving both expressive and practical aims and outcomes." He gives as examples schools, shops, post offices, police forces, asylums and the British monarchy. In this entry the above-noted contemporary sociological usage will be followed and doing so has the virtue of grounding philosophical theory in the most salient empirical discipline, namely, sociology.

At this point it might be asked why a theory of social institutions has, or ought to have, any philosophical interest; why not simply leave such theorising to the sociologists? One important reason stems from the normative concerns of philosophers. Philosophers, such as John Rawls, have developed elaborate normative theories concerning the principles of justice that ought to govern social institutions. Yet they have done so in the absence of a developed theory of the nature and point of the very entities (social institutions) to which the principles of justice in question are supposed to apply. Surely the adequacy of one's normative account of the justice or otherwise of any given social institution, or system of social institutions, will depend at least in part on the nature and point of that social institution or system. The entry has five sections. In the first section various salient accounts of social institutions are discussed. Accounts emanating from sociological theory as well as philosophy are mentioned.

Here, as elsewhere, the boundaries between philosophy and non-philosophical theorising in relation to an empirical science are vague. Hence, it is important to note the theories of the likes of Durkheim and Talcott Parsons as well as those of John Searle and David Lewis. In the second section a teleological account of social institutions is presented. Teleological explanation is out of fashion in many areas of philosophy. However, it remains influential in contemporary philosophical theories of social action. In the third section, the so-called agent-structure question is addressed. At bottom, this issue concerns the apparent inconsistency between the autonomy (or alleged autonomy) of individual human agents, on the one hand, and the ubiquity and pervasive influence of social forms on individual character and behaviour, on the other. In the fourth section the normative character of social institutions is outlined in general terms. This normativity is multifaceted.

For example, it includes the human goods realised by institutions as well as the rights and duties that attach to institutional roles. In the fifth and final section the more specific normative issue of the justice of social institutions is explored. This section includes a discussion of intra-institutional justice, e.g. the justice or injustice of the reward system within an institution, as well as extra-institutional justice, e.g. the justice or injustice of a power relationship between a government and refugees.

Accounts of Social Institutions

Any account of social institutions must begin by informally marking off social institutions from other social forms. Unfortunately, as noted above, in ordinary language the terms "institutions" and "social institutions" are used to refer to a miscellany of social forms, including conventions, rituals, organisations, and systems of organisations. Moreover, there are a variety of theoretical accounts of institutions, including sociological as well as philosophical ones. Indeed, many of these accounts of what are referred to as institutions are not accounts of the same phenomena; they are at best accounts of overlapping fields of social phenomena. Nevertheless, it is possible, firstly, to mark off a range of related social forms that would be regarded by most theorists as being properly describable as social institutions; and, secondly, to compare and contrast some of the competing theoretical accounts of the "social institutions" in question.

Social institutions need to be distinguished from less complex social forms such as conventions, social norms, roles and rituals. The latter are among the constitutive elements of institutions. Social institutions also need to be distinguished from more complex and more complete social entities, such as societies or cultures, of which any given institution is typically a constitutive element. A society, for example, is more complete than an institution since a society—at least as traditionally understood—is more or less self-sufficient in terms of human resources, whereas an institution is not. Thus, arguably, for an entity to be a society it must sexually reproduce its membership, have its own language and educational system, provide for itself economically and—at least in principle—be politically independent.

Social institutions are often organisations. Moreover, many institutions are *systems* of organisations. For example, capitalism is a particular kind of economic institution, and in modern times capitalism consists in large part in specific organisational forms—including multinational corporations—organised into a system. Further, some institutions are *meta-institutions*; they are institutions (organisations) that organise other institutions (including systems of organisations). For example, governments are meta-institutions. The institutional end or function of a government consists in large part in organising other institutions (both individually and collectively); thus governments regulate and coordinate economic systems, educational institutions, police and military organisations and so on largely by way of (enforceable) legislation.

Nevertheless, some institutions are not organisations, or systems of organisations, and do not require organisations. For example, the English language is an institution, but not an organisation. Moreover, it would be possible for a language to exist independently of any organisations specifically concerned with language. Again, consider an economic system that does not involve organisations, e.g. a barter system involving only individuals. An institution that is not an organisation or system of organisations comprises a relatively specific type of agent-to-agent interactive activity, e.g. communication or economic exchange that involves:

- Differentiated actions, e.g. communication involves speaking and hearing/understanding, economic exchange involves buying and selling, that are;
- Performed repeatedly and by multiple agents;
- In compliance with a structured unitary system of conventions, e.g. linguistic conventions, monetary conventions, and social norms, e.g. truth-telling, property rights.

In this entry the concern is principally with social institutions (including meta-institutions) that are also organisations or systems of organisations. However, it should be noted that institutions of language, such as the English language, are often regarded not simply as institutions but as more fundamental than many other kinds of institution by virtue of being presupposed by, or in part constitutive of, other institutions.

Searle, for example, holds to the latter view. A case might also be made that the family is a more fundamental institution than others for related reasons, e.g. it is the site of sexual reproduction and initial socialisation. Note also that uses of the term "institution" in such expressions as "the institution of government" are often ambiguous. Sometimes what is meant is a particular token, e.g. the current government in Australia, sometimes a type, i.e. the set of properties instantiated in any actual government, and sometimes a set of tokens, i.e. all governments.

Restricting the notion of an institution to organisations is helpful in this regard; the term "organisation" almost always refers to a particular token. On the other hand, the term "institution" connotes a certain gravity not connoted by the term "organisation"; so arguably those institutions that are organisations that have a central and important role to play in or for a society. Being central and important to a society, such roles are usually long lasting ones; hence institutions are typically transgenerational. Having informally marked of social institutions from other social forms, let us turn to a consideration of some general properties of social institutions.

Here there are four salient properties, namely, structure, function, culture and sanctions. Roughly speaking, an institution that is an organisation or system of organisations consists of an embodied (occupied by human persons) structure of differentiated roles. These roles are defined in terms of tasks, and rules regulating the performance of those tasks.

Moreover, there is a degree of interdependence between

these roles, such that the performance of the constitutive tasks of one role cannot be undertaken, or cannot be undertaken except with great difficulty, unless the tasks constitutive of some other role or roles in the structure have been undertaken or are being undertaken. Further, these roles are often related to one another hierarchically, and hence involve different levels of status and degrees of authority. Finally, on teleological and functional accounts, these roles are related to one another in part in virtue of their contribution to (respectively) the *end(s)* or *function(s)* of the institution; and the realisation of these ends or function normally involves interaction between the institutional actors in question and external non-institutional actors. (The assumption here is that the concept of an end and of a function is distinct concepts.) The constitutive roles of an institution and their relations to one another can be referred to as the *structure* of the institution.

Note that on this conception of institutions as *embodied* structures of roles and associated rules, the nature of any institution at a given time will to some extent reflect the personal character of different role occupants, especially influential role occupants, e.g. the British Government during the Second World War reflected to some extent Winston Churchill's character. Moreover, institutions in this sense are dynamic, evolving entities; as such, they have a history, the diachronic structure of a narrative and (usually) a partially open-ended future.

Aside from the formal and usually explicitly stated, or defined, tasks and rules, there is an important implicit and informal dimension of an institution roughly describable as institutional *culture*. This notion comprises the informal attitudes, values, norms, and the ethos or "spirit" which pervades an institution. Culture in this sense determines much of the activity of the members of that institution, or at least the manner in which that activity is undertaken. So while the explicitly determined rules and tasks might say nothing about being secretive or "sticking by one's mates come what may" or having a hostile or negative attitude to particular social groups, these attitudes and practices might in fact be pervasive; they might be part of the culture.

Naturally, there can be competing cultures within a single organisation; the culture comprised of attitudes and norms that is aligned to the formal and official complex of tasks and rules might compete with an informal and "unofficial" culture that is adhered to by a substantial subelement of the organisation's membership. It is sometimes claimed that in addition to structure, function and culture, social institutions necessarily involve sanctions.

It is uncontroversial that social institutions involve informal sanctions, such as moral disapproval following on non-conformity to institutional norms. However, some theorists, e.g. Jon Elster argue that formal sanctions, such as punishment, are a necessary feature of institutions. Formal sanctions are certainly a feature of many institutions, notably legal systems; however, they do not seem to be a feature of all institutions. Consider, for example, an elaborate and longstanding system of informal economic exchange between members of different societies that have no common system of laws or enforced rules.

Again, a spoken language such as Pidgin English is presumably an institution; yet breaches of its constitutive norms and conventions might not attract any formal sanctions.

Thus far we have informally marked off social institutions from other social forms, and we have identified a number of general properties of social institutions. It is now time to outline some of the main theoretical accounts of social institutions. Notwithstanding our understanding of social institutions as complex social forms, some theoretical accounts of institutions identify institutions with relatively simple social forms—especially conventions, social norms or rules. (By stipulative definition, a rule is a formal species of norm governing action.) At one level this is merely a verbal dispute; contra our procedure here, such simpler forms could simply be termed "institutions". However, at another level the dispute is not merely verbal, since what we are calling "institutions" would on such a view consist simply of sets of conventions, social norms or rules. Let us refer to such accounts as *atomistic* theories of institutions. Schotter is a case in point.

Here the "atom" itself typically consists of the actions of individual human persons, e.g. conventions as regularities in action that solve coordination problems. The individual agents are not themselves defined in terms of institutional forms, such as institutional roles. Hence atomistic theories of institutions tend to go hand in glove with atomistic theories of all collective entities, e.g. a society consists of an aggregate of individual human persons. Moreover, atomistic theories tend to identify the individual agent as the locus of moral value. On this kind of view, social forms, including social institutions, have moral value only derivately, i.e. only in so far as they contribute to the prior needs or other requirements of individual agents. The regularities in action or rules made use of in such atomistic accounts of institutions cannot simply be individual regularities in action or individual rules for action; rather there must be interdependence of action such that, for example, agent *A* only performs action *x*, if other agents, *B* and *C* do likewise. Moreover, some account of the interdependence of action in question is called for, e.g. that it is not the sort of interdependence of action involved in conflict situations.

Assume that the conventions, norms or rules in question are social in the sense that they involve the required interdependence of action, e.g. the parties to any given convention, or the adherent to any such norm or rule, conform to (respectively) the convention, norm or rule on the condition that others do.

Nevertheless, such interdependence of action is not sufficient for a convention, norm or rule, or even a set of conventions, norms or rules, to be an institution. Governments, universities, corporations etc. are structured, unitary entities. Accordingly, a mere *set* of conventions (or norms or rules) does not constitute an institution. For example, the set of conventions comprising the convention to drive on the left, the convention to utter, "Australia", to refer to Australia, and the convention to use chopsticks does not constitute an institution. Accordingly, a problem for atomistic accounts of social institutions is the need to provide an account of the structure and unity of social institutions, and an account that is faithful to atomism, e.g. that the structure is essentially aggregative in nature.

Some theorists, notably Searle, have sought to identify institutions with a particular species of rule, namely, so called constitutive rules. Constitutive rules have the form, "Doing *X* counts as *Y* in circumstances *C*". (They are often also held to be self-referential and/or self-validating, e.g. by Bloor). No doubt many such constitutive rules are an integral element of larger structures of rule-governed activity that are in fact institutions. (Constitutive rules also raise the issue of constructivist, e.g. collective acceptance, accounts of institutional properties—an issue taken up in the final section of this entry.) However, the mere fact that some regularity in action has the form of a constitutive rule does not make it an institution per se.

Consider a child who collects pebbles on the beach, and counts or treats them as money by causing his mother to give him a lolly for each pebble. He has not thereby established an institution, even an institution which is only derivative from, or a pale reflection of, a monetary institution. Nor would it make any difference if a number of children engaged in this practice, and if each did so only on condition the others did.

By contrast with atomistic accounts of social institutions, *holistic*—including *structuralist-functionalist*—accounts stress the interrelationships of institutions (structure) and their contribution to larger and more complete social complexes, especially societies (function). Thus according to Barry Barnes: "Functionalist theories in the social sciences seek to describe, to understand and in most cases to explain the orderliness and stability of entire social systems. In so far as they treat individuals, the treatment comes after and emerges from analysis of the system as a whole.

Functionalist theories move from an understanding of the whole to an understanding of the parts of that whole, whereas individualism proceeds in the opposite direction". Moreover, "such accounts list the "functions" of the various institutions. They describe the function of the economy as the production of goods and services essential to the operation of the other institutions and hence the system as a whole."

Such theorists include Durkheim, Radcliffe-Brown and Parsons. Of particular concern to these theorists was the moral decay consequent (in their view) upon the demise of strong, mutually supportive social institutions. Durkheim, for example, advocated powerful professional associations. He said: A system of moral morals is always the affair of a group and can operate only if the group protects them by its authority. It is made up of rules which govern individuals, which compel them to act in such and such a way, and which impose limits to their inclinations and forbid them to go beyond.

Now there is only one moral power - moral, and hence common to all - which stands above the individual and which can legitimately make laws for him, and that is collective power. To the extent the individual is left to his own devices and freed from all social constraint, he is unfettered by all moral constraint. It is not possible for professional ethics to escape this fundamental condition of any system of morals. Since, then, the society as a whole feels no concern in professional ethics, it is imperative that there be special groups in the society, within which these morals may be evolved, and whose business it is to see that they are observed.

Moreover, here the meta-institution of government obviously has a pivotal directive and integrative role in relation to other institutions and their interrelationships, albeit government is itself simply one institution within the larger society.

Further, holistic accounts of institutions lay great stress on institutional roles defined in large part by social norms; institutional roles are supposedly largely, or even wholly, constitutive of the identity of the individual human agents who occupy these roles. (Individuals participate in a number of institutions and hence occupy a number of institutional roles; hence the alleged possibility of their identity being constituted by a number of different institutional roles.)

Many such holistic accounts deploy and depend on the model, or at least analogy, of an organism. A salient historical figure here is Herbert Spencer. On this holistic, organicist model, social institutions are analogous to the organs or limbs of a human body. Each organ or limb has a function the realisation of which contributes to the wellbeing of the body as a whole, and none can exist independently of the others.

Thus the human body relies on the stomach to digest food in order to continue living, but the stomach cannot exist independently of the body or of other organs, such as the heart. Likewise, it is suggested, any given institution, e.g. law courts, contributes to the wellbeing of the society as a whole, and yet is dependent on other institutions, e.g. government. Here the "wellbeing" of the society as a whole is sometimes identified with the stability and continuation of the society as it is; hence the familiar charge that holistic, organicist accounts are inherently politically conservative. This political conservatism transmutes into political authoritarianism when society is identified with the system of institutions that constitute the nation-state and the meta-institution of the nation-state—the government—is assigned absolute authority in relation to all other institutions. Hence the contrasting emphasis in political liberalism on the separation of powers between for example, the executive, the legislature and the judiciary.

Holistic accounts of social institutions often invoke the terminology of internal and external relations. An internal relation is one that is definitive of, or in some way essential to, the entity it is a relation of; by contrast, external relations are not in this way essential. Thus being married to someone is an internal relation of spouses; if a man is a husband then necessarily he stands in the relation of being married to someone else. Likewise, if someone is a judge in a court of law then necessarily he stands in an adjudicative relationship to defendants. Evidently, many institutional roles are possessed of, and therefore in part defined by, their internal relations to other institutional roles. However, the existence of institutional roles with internal relations to other institutional roles does not entail an holistic account of social institutions. For the internal relations in question might not be relations between institutional roles in different institutions; rather they might simply be internal relations between different institutional roles in the same institution. On the other hand, the existence of institutional roles with internal relations does undermine the attempts of certain forms of atomistic individualism to reduce institutions to the individual human agents who happen to constitute them; ex hypotheses, the latter are not qua individual human persons in part defined in terms of their relations to institutional roles.

Here it is important to distinguish the plausible view that institutions are not reducible to the individual human persons who constitute them from the controversial view that institutions are themselves agents possessed of minds and a capacity to reason. French is an advocate of the latter view (French 1984).

If we ascribe intentions to organisations, e.g. ascribe to Gulf Oil the intention to maximise profits, then we are apparently committed to ascribing to Gulf Oil a whole network of sophisticated propositional attitudes concerning economic production, the workings of markets, and so on. Moreover, a being with such a network of propositional attitudes would be capable of high level thought, and therefore be possessed of a language in which to do this thinking. Further, this agent's thought processes would include planning for its future and doing so on the basis of its past mistakes, and the likely responses of other corporations. Such a corporate agent is self-reflective; it not only distinguishes its present from both its past and its future, and itself from other corporations, it reflects on itself for the purpose of transforming itself. Such a being has higher order propositional attitudes, including beliefs about its own beliefs and intentions, and conceives of itself as a unitary whole existing over time. In short, it looks as though we now have a fully conscious, indeed self-conscious, being on our hands. Nor do matters rest here. For if we are prepared to grant Gulf Oil a mind, then why not all its subsidiaries, as well as all other companies and subsidiaries worldwide. Indeed how can we stop at corporations? Surely governments, universities, schools, supermarkets, armies, banks, political parties, trade unions, English soccer teams' supporters' clubs (at least) now all have minds, albeit in some cases smaller minds (so to speak). Not only do we have a self-conscious mind, but apparently we have an ever expanding community of self-conscious minds; or so it could be argued.

Thus far we have discussed atomistic and holistic accounts of social institutions. However, there is a third possibility, namely, (what might be termed) *molecularist* accounts. Roughly speaking, a *molecularist* account of an institution would not seek to reduce the institution to simpler atomic forms, such as conventions; nor would it seek to define an institution in terms of its relationships with other institutions and its contribution to the larger societal whole. Rather, each institution would be analogous to a molecule; it would have constitutive elements ("atoms") but also have its own structure and unity. Moreover, on this conception each social institution would have a degree of independence vis-à-vis other institutions and the society at large; on the other hand, the set of institutions might itself under certain conditions form a unitary system of sorts, e.g. a contemporary liberal democratic nation-state comprised of a number of semi-autonomous public and private institutions functioning in the context of the meta-institution of government.

A general problem for holistic organicist accounts of social institutions—as opposed to molecularist accounts—is that social institutions can be responses to *trans-societal* requirements or needs. Accordingly, an institution is not necessarily a constitutive element of some given society in the sense that it is both in part constitutive of that society and wholly contained within that society. Examples of such trans-societal institutions are the international financial system, the international legal system, the United Nations and some multinational corporations. Indeed, arguably any given element of such a trans-societal institution stands in some *internal* relations to elements of other societies.

This raises the question as to whether or not the category of social institution might be *conceptually* independent of the category of society in the sense that it might be conceptually possible for there to be an institution without there being a society. This is consistent with the impossibility of there being a society without institutions. That is, perhaps societies presuppose social institutions, but not *vice-versa.*

Here we need to distinguish conceptual (or logical) impossibility from *practical* impossibility. For example, it might well be that no society and no system of institutions can exist, practically speaking, without the meta-institution of government; absent government, societies and social institutions tend to disintegrate. However, it would not follow from this that the institution of government is logically necessary for the existence of societies and (non-government) institutions. The claim that institutions are conceptually independent of societies goes hand in glove with the proposition that human social life is dependent on institutions, but not necessarily on societies as such. The picture here is of human beings who are members of many different social groups, e.g. academic philosophers, EU citizens, speakers of the Spanish language, each of which group is sustained by one or more social institutions; however, there are no societies as such. For those who lived, or are living, in traditional tribes or clans this picture might be incomprehensible. However, it does have some resonance for those living in contemporary cosmopolitan settings.

In response to this claim of the independence, and perhaps priority, of institutions *vis a vis* society it can be pointed out that trans-*societal* institutions presuppose societies. This is true enough. However, this would not rescue the holistic organicist conception; for such trans-societal institutions are not generally—and certainly not necessarily—constitutive "organs" of some larger society. Moreover, international institutions presuppose only nation-states, and the latter might be conceived of in narrowly political terms. Contemporary nation-states are not, it might be insisted, complete and self-sufficient societies, such as traditional tribes or clans might have been. In this section atomistic and holistic accounts of institutions have been presented and found to be problematic.

Atomistic accounts focus on the elements of institutions, and thereby fail to provide an adequate account of the structure or "glue" that might transform a mere set of conventions or rules into an institution. Holistic accounts focus on the whole societies of which institutions are typically a part, and seek to explain the part in terms of the whole; in so doing they fail to offer an account of institutions that sufficiently respects their distinctive character and relative ontological independence of society conceived as a unitary whole. Let us now turn to an account of institutions that treats institutions, so to speak, on their own terms. The account in question is consistent with institutional molecularism, broadly conceived.

Teleological Account of Institutions

Teleological accounts of social action in general, and of social institutions in particular, fall well within the rationalist, individualist, philosophy of action tradition that has its roots in Aristotle, Hume and Kant and is associated with contemporary analytic philosophers of social action such as Michael Bratman, John Searle and Raimo Tuomela. However, this way of proceeding also has a place outside philosophy, in sociological theory. Broadly speaking, it is the starting point for the voluntaristic theory of social action associated with the likes of Max Weber and (the early) Talcott Parsons. Consider, for example, the following idea in relation to social action expressed by Parsons: Actions do not take place separately each with a separate, discrete end in relation to the situation, but in long complicated 'chains' ... [and] the total complex of means-end relationships is not to be thought of as similar to a large number of parallel threads, but as a complicated web (if not a tangle).

The central concept in the teleological account of social institutions is that of *joint action*. Joint actions consist of the intentional individual actions of a number of agents directed to the realisation of a collective end. (Note that intentions are not the same things as ends, e.g. an agent who intentionally and *gratuitously* raises his arm *ex hypothesei* has no end or purpose in doing so.) A collective end—notwithstanding its name—is a species of individual end; it is an end possessed by each of the individuals involved in the joint action. However it is an end, which is not realised by the action of any one of the individuals; the actions of all or most realise the end. Examples of joint action are two people lifting a table together, and two men jointly pushing a car so joint actions can be analysed in terms of individualist notions. Collective ends can be unconsciously pursued, and have not necessarily been at any time explicitly formulated in the minds of those pursuing them; collective ends can be *implicit* in the behaviour and attitudes of agents without ceasing to be ends as such.

Further, in the case of a collective end pursued over a long period of time, e.g. by members of an institution over generations, the collective end can be *latent* at a specific point in time, i.e. it is not actually being pursued, explicitly or implicitly, at that point in time. However, it does not thereby cease to be an end of that institution—which is to say, of those persons—even at those times when it is not being pursued. These individualist notions of joint actions and collective ends do not necessarily bring with them a normative dimension, other than the minimal normativity of instrumental rationality. By the term, "instrumental rationality" is meant the rationality of undertaking an action which is the means to one's end; one ought to do *x* for the reason that *x* is the means to one's end, *e.* accordingly, it is concluded that joint actions do not necessarily have a normative dimension (other than in this minimal sense).

We can further distinguish between different, albeit connected and overlapping, *generic* kinds of joint action and activity, including communicative, economic, educative, sexual and religious activity. The repetition over time and duplication in space, of any one of these different kinds of generic joint activity can give rise to a more or less connected, and more or less continuous, stretch of joint activity which can be termed a *sphere of activity*. So the ongoing series of economic transactions across Germany constitutes a sphere of activity. Spheres of activity (by stipulative definition) are regulated by *conventions*. They thereby take on different specific forms according to the specific conventions which structure them. Often, though not necessarily, they are also regulated by explicit rules, including laws. And they are also often—but again, not necessarily—regulated by social norms. Here we need to distinguish between rules, conventions and social norms.

A *rule* is a (typically explicitly formulated) directive issued by some authority or other to undertake a certain course of action in certain circumstances. So laws are a species of rule enacted by governments. A convention is regularity in action performed by a set of individual agents and directed to a collective end. More precisely, conventions are *joint procedures*, where a procedure is (roughly speaking) a habit; the automatic repetition of an action in a recurring situation. So a joint procedure is a procedure which is jointly followed because it realises a collective end. Moreover, on these conception conventions *qua conventions* are normatively neutral—other than in the minimal sense involved in instrumental rationality. Conventions are normatively neutral notwithstanding the fact that agents can be held to have failed to conform to any given convention. On this account a conventional regularity in action does not constitute a *standard of behaviour* to which agents *ought* to conform. Naturally, an agent by not conforming might fail to realize the collective end that he has; the end which is realized by conformity to the convention. However, that would be a mere failure of instrumental rationality.

The conventional actions are not necessarily the content of directives issued by authorities. Nor are they necessarily explicitly formulated anywhere. Thus driving on the left hand side is a convention in Australia, though not in Germany; it is regularity in action among Australians, which secures the collective end of avoiding car collisions. As it happens, this convention is also a law, though it might not have been. Social norms are regularities that are also norms; agents believe that they have a duty to conform or that they otherwise *ought* to conform. Such norms include ones respecting and enforcing rights. Here the "ought" is not that of mere instrumental rationality; it is not simply a matter of believing that one ought to conform because it serves one's purpose. Some conventions and most rules are also norms in this strong sense. For example, the convention and the law to drive on the left is a norm; people feel that they ought to conform. This strong (and wide) sense of "ought" *includes*—but is not exhausted by—the so called *moral* "ought".

Perhaps, for example, members of some social group feel strongly about aesthetic requirements. Organisations consist of an (embodied) formal *structure* of interlocking roles. These roles can be defined in terms of tasks, procedures (in the above sense) and conventions. Moreover, unlike social groups, organisations are individuated by the kind of activity that they undertake, and also by their characteristic *ends*. So we have governments, universities, business corporations, armies, and so on.

Perhaps governments have as an end or goal the ordering and leading of societies, universities the end of discovering and disseminating knowledge, and so on. Here it is important to reiterate that these ends are, firstly, collective ends and, secondly, often the latent and/or implicit (collective) ends of individual institutional actors.

A further defining feature of organisations is that organisational action typically consists in, what has elsewhere been termed, a *layered structure of joint actions*. One illustration of the notion of a layered structure of joint actions is an armed force fighting a battle.

Suppose at an organisation level a number of "actions" are severally necessary and jointly sufficient to achieve some collective end. Thus the "actions" of the mortar squad destroying enemy gun emplacements, the flight of military planes providing air-cover and the infantry platoon taking and holding the ground might be severally necessary and jointly sufficient to achieve the collective end of defeating the enemy; as such these "actions" constitute a joint action. Call each of these "actions" level two actions. Suppose, in addition, that each of these level two "actions" is itself—at least in part—a joint action whose component actions are severally necessary and jointly sufficient for the performance of the level two "action" in question. Call these component actions, level one action.

So the collective end of the level one action is the performance of the level two "action". Thus the individual members of the mortar squad jointly operate the mortar in order to realise the collective end of destroying enemy gun emplacements. Each pilot, jointly with the other pilots, strafes enemy soldiers in order to realise the collective end of providing air-cover for their advancing foot soldiers.

Finally, the set of foot soldiers jointly advance in order to take and hold the ground vacated by the members of the retreating enemy force. The actions of each of the individual foot soldiers, mortar squad members and individual pilots are level one action. It is important to note that on this (stipulative) definition of organisations they are, *qua organisations,* non-normative entities.

In this respect they are analogous to conventions, as we have defined conventions. So being an organisation is not of itself something that is ethically good or bad, any more than being a convention is in itself ethically good or bad. This can be consistently held while maintaining that organisations, as well as conventions, are a pervasive and necessary feature of human life, being indispensable instruments for realising collective ends. Collective ends are a species of individual ends; but merely being an end is in itself neither, say, morally good nor morally bad, any more than being an intention or a belief are in themselves morally good or morally bad.

While this definition of an organisation does not include any reference to a normative dimension, most organisations do as a matter of contingent fact possess a normative dimension. As was the case with conventions, this normative dimension will be possessed (especially, though not exclusively) by virtue of the particular moral/immoral ends (goods) that an organisation serves, as well as by virtue of the particular moral (or immoral) activities that it undertakes. Further, most organisations possess a normative dimension by virtue (in part) of the *norms* governing the constitutive organisational roles.

More specifically, most organisations consist of a hierarchical role structure in which the tasks and procedures that define the individual roles are governed by norms. It is not simply that an employee in fact undertakes a particular set of tasks, or tends to comply with the directives of his employer. Rather the employee undertakes those tasks, and obeys the directives of his employer, by virtue of the social and other norms governing the employee's (and employer's) roles.

The employee believes that someone in his position has a duty to perform the tasks in question, and believes that the employer has a right to issue directives to his employees. Moreover, this belief is shared and acted upon by the other employees (and employers), and is held by each conditionally on its being held by the others. In short, the behaviour of the employees and employers is governed by *social norms*. It should also be noted that the social norms governing the roles and role structures of organisations are both formal and informal.

If formal, then they are typically enshrined in explicit rules, regulations and laws, including laws of contract. For example, an employee not only believes that he ought to undertake certain tasks and not others, but these tasks are explicitly set forth in his contract of employment. As mentioned above, informal social norms to a greater or lesser extent comprise the *culture* of an organisation.

Organisations with the above detailed normative dimension are *social institutions*. So—and as already mentioned—institutions are often organisations, and many systems of organisations are also institutions. As has also been mentioned, arguably some social institutions are not organisations, or systems of organisations, notably human languages. While it is self-evident that, say, the English language is governed by a structure of conventions and social norms, it is perhaps less clear what purposes or ends it serves *qua institution*. Obviously, at the micro-level individual speakers and hearers have collective ends, e.g. the speaker, *S*, and the hearer, *H*, at spatio-temporal point, *P*, both have as a collective end that *H* understand what it is that *S* is intending to communicate.

However, there are a number of collective ends that all or most or many speaker-hearers of English have, and that constitute *institutional* ends. For example, each speaker-hearer has as an end that each be able—at least in principle—to communicate with each of the other speaker-hearers, e.g. *A* wants to be able to communicate with *B* and *C*, but *A* also wants *B* to be able to communicate with *C* (and similarly for *B* and *C*). Moreover, each speaker-hearer has as an end that each be able—at least in principle—to understand what has been communicated in the past, including by at least some speaker-hearers who are no longer present, e.g. present "audiences" want to be able to understand the information directories, autobiographies, and the Bible produced by past "speakers". Further, each speaker-hearer has as an end that the communications of each be able—at least in principle—to be understood in the future, including by some not yet existing speaker-hearers, and by some not yet existing speaker-hearers in circumstances in which they themselves are no longer in existence, e.g. past "speakers" want the information directories, autobiographies, and the Bible that they produced to be understood by future "audiences".

A feature of many social institutions, whether they are of the organisational or non-organisational variety, is their use of *joint institutional mechanisms*. Examples of joint institutional mechanisms are the device of tossing a coin to resolve a dispute and voting to elect a candidate to political office. Joint institutional mechanisms consist of:

- A complex of differentiated but interlocking actions (the

input to the mechanism);

- The result of the performance of those actions (the output of the mechanism), and;
- The mechanism itself. Thus a given agent might vote for a candidate. He will do so only if others also vote. But further to this, there is the action of the candidates, namely, that they present themselves as candidates. That they present themselves as candidates is (in part) constitutive of the input to the voting mechanism. Voters vote *for candidates*. So there is interlocking and differentiated action (the input). Further there is some result (as opposed to consequence) of the joint action; the joint action consisting of the actions of putting oneself forward as a candidate and of the actions of voting.

The result is that some candidate, say, John Howard is voted in (the output). That there is a result is (in part) constitutive of the mechanism. That to receive the most number of votes is to be voted in, is (in part) constitutive of the voting mechanism. Moreover that Howard is voted in, is not a collective end of all the voters. (Although it is a collective end of those who voted for Howard.) However, that the one who gets the most votes—whoever that happens to be—is voted in, is a collective end of all the voters, including those who voted for some candidate other than Howard. Human languages are institutions that appear to consist in part of joint institutional mechanisms. Assume that there are the following joint procedures in a community of speaker-hearers: utter "Sydney" when you have as an end reference to Sydney; utter "Paris" when you have as an end reference to Paris; utter "is a city" when you have as an end ascription of the property of being a city; utter "is frequented by tourists" when you have as an end ascription of the property of being frequented by tourists.

Then there might be the resultant joint action to utter, "Paris is a city", when you have as an end ascription to Paris of the property of being a city; and there might be the second, and different, resultant joint action to utter, "Sydney is frequented by tourists", when you have as an end ascription to Sydney of the property of being frequented by tourists. It is easy to see how by the inclusion of a conjunctive operation indicated by "and" additional linguistic combinations might yield multiple additional resultant actions, e.g., the communication effected by uttering "Paris is a city and Paris is frequented by tourists". This is a final point concerning the teleological account of social institutions. As is the case with other kinds of account of social institutions, teleological accounts can be either descriptive or normative. Slavery is a morally objectionable social institution mobilising physical force and ideology in the economic interests of the slave-owners at the expense of the human rights of the slaves; in the case of many such institutions the real end of the institution might need to be masked by the ideology, if the institution is to survive. Perhaps many asylums are likewise morally objectionable institutions.

On a descriptive teleological account, such institutions will turn out to be institutions; their nature as institutions will not be denied. However, in the context of such a descriptive account of institutions the question of their morally objectionable institutional activities and ends will simply not arise. However, by the lights of a *normative* teleological account of social institutions, the end(s) of any given institution to be some social or human *good* and there ought to be moral constraints on institutional activities. Accordingly, on a normative teleological account a morally objectionable institution such as slavery will turn out to be defective *qua institution*. Nevertheless, on the normative account such morally objectionable collectivities are institutions; the normative teleological account needs to be consistent with the descriptive teleological account. In this section the teleological account of social institutions has been elaborated. In the following section the so-called agent-structure question is addressed.

Agency and Structure

It is convenient to conceive of social institutions as possessed of three dimensions, namely, structure, function and culture. However, it needs to be kept in mind that this is potentially misleading since, as we saw above, there are conceptual differences between functions and ends. On some accounts, function is a quasi-causal notion, on others it is a teleological notion, albeit one that does not necessarily involve the existence of any mental states. While the structure, function and culture of an institution provide a framework within which individuals act, they do not fully determine the actions of individuals.

There are a number of reasons why this is so. For one thing, rules, norms and ends cannot cover every contingency that might arise; for another, rules, norms and so on, themselves need to be interpreted and applied. Moreover, changing circumstances and unforeseeable problems make it desirable to vest individuals with discretionary powers to rethink and adjust old rules, norms, and ends, and sometimes elaborate new ones. Inevitably, the individuals who occupy institutional roles are possessed of varying degrees of discretionary power in relation to their actions.

These discretionary powers are of different kinds and operate at different levels. For example, senior and middle level public servants have discretion in the way they implement policies, in their allocations of priorities and resources, and in the methods and criteria of evaluation of programs. Indeed, senior public servants often exercise discretion in relation to the formulation of policies. Consider that Gordon Chase, the New York Health Services Administrator, conceived, developed and implemented the methadone program in New York in the early 1970s, notwithstanding political opposition to it. Lower echelon public servants also have discretionary powers. Police officers have to interpret rules and regulations, customs officers have the discretionary power to stop and search one passenger rather than another, and so on. Traditionally, members of the so-called professions, such as doctors, lawyers, members of the clergy, engineers and academics, have enjoyed a very high degree of individual autonomy, notwithstanding their membership of, and regulation by professional associations. In recent times they have increasingly been housed in large bureaucratic organisations in which their professional autonomy has evidently diminished somewhat.

So certain categories of individual institutional actors have discretionary powers and a reasonable degree of autonomy in the exercise of their institutional duties. However, it is not only the individual actions of institutional actors that are not fully determined by structure, function and culture. Many joint or cooperative actions that take place in institutions are not determined by structure, function or culture. For example, a senior public servant might put together a team of like minded people and they might pursue a specific agenda which is not one determined by the prevailing institutional structure, function or culture, and is even in part inconsistent with them. It should also be noted that legitimate individual or collective discretionary activity undertaken within an institution is typically facilitated by a rational internal structure—including role structure—by rational policy and decision making procedures, and by a rational institutional culture. By rational, it is here meant internally consistent, as well as rational in the light of the institution's purposes.

Arguably, the corporate culture in many contemporary corporations, e.g. Enron, is not rational in this sense. In particular, a culture of greed, recklessness and of breaking the rules is—from the standpoint of this rationality, as opposed to the rationality of some self-interested factions within these organisations—inconsistent with a hierarchical organisational structure preoccupied with accountability. Accordingly, it is likely that many (individual and collective) discretionary judgments will be ones that do not contribute to the realisation of the institution's purposes, even if they do facilitate the narrow self-interest of individuals and factional elements. Aside from the internal dimensions of an institution, there are its external relationships, including its relationships to other institutions. In particular, there is the extent of the independence of an institution from other institutions, including government. One thinks here of the separation of powers between the legislative, executive and judicial institutions in the United States of America and elsewhere.

It should be noted that, strictly speaking, independence is not the same thing as autonomy, but is rather a necessary condition for it. An institution possessed of independence from other institutions might still lack autonomy, if it lacked the kinds of rational internal structure and culture noted above. Indeed, internal conflicts can paralyse an institution to the point where it becomes incapable of pursuing its institutional purposes. A university, for example, might enjoy independence from outside institutions, including government, but might be paralysed by internal conflict between staff and students. Such conflict might take the form (in part) of ongoing demonstrations that disrupt classes, and thereby prevent lectures and tutorials from being held. Granted that institutional actors have a degree of discretionary power, nevertheless, they are constrained by institutional structure, and specifically the role structure, of the role that they occupy. As is often pointed out, institutional structure also enables the action of institutional actors. Police officers, for example, have significant powers not possessed by ordinary citizens.

However, a question arises as to the nature of the relationship between institutional structure and the agency of institutional actors. More specifically, a question arises as to whether or not one of these is logically prior to the other (or whether neither is). Thus some theorists, e.g. Emile Durkheim are held to conceive of structure as *sui generis* in relation to individual agency; and indeed, at least in the case of structuralists such as Althusser, explanatory of human 'agency'. The proposition of structuralists such as Althusser is that institutional structures (in the sense of a structure of social roles and social norms) are a basic, non-reducible feature of the world and the actions, values, self-images and the like of individual human agents must conform to these structures because individual agency, properly understood, is in fact constituted by such structures. An individual human agent is simply the repository of the roles and values of the institutions in which the 'agent' lives his or her life.

Other theorists, e.g., arguably Max Weber and methodological individualists, conceive of institutional structure as simply an abstraction from the habitual and interdependent actions of individual human beings actors. Social reality is wholly compromised of individual human agents and their ongoing, patterned interactions; there is no structure as such. (Theorists such as Durkheim occupy a mid-position in which there is both sui generis structure and non-reducible agency; such theorists now confront the problem of conflict between structure and individual agency - Which overrides which?) In relation to this issue Anthony Giddens has attempted to reconcile the felt reality of individual agency with the apparent need to posit some form of institutional structure that transcends individual agency.

According to Giddens, structure is both constituted by human agency and is the medium in which human action takes place. This seems to mean, firstly, that structure is nothing other than the repetition over time of the related actions of many institutional actors. So the structure consists of:

- The habitual actions of each institutional agent;
- The set of such agents; and
- The relationship of interdependence between the actions of any one agent and the actions of the other agents. But it means, secondly, that this repetition over time of the related actions of many agents provides not just the context, but the framework, within which the action of a single agent at a particular spatio-temporal point is performed. Structure qua framework *constrains* any given agent's action at a particular spatio-temporal point. (In addition, and as Giddens is at pains to point out, structure qua framework *enables* various actions not otherwise possible, e.g. linguistic structure enables speech acts to be performed.)

This seems plausible as far as it goes; however, we are owed an account of the *interdependence* between the actions of different agents. On a teleological account of institutions this interdependence is in large part generated by the *ends* of the institutions. Here we need to remind ourselves of a characteristic feature of institutions, namely, their reproductive capacity. Institutions reproduce themselves, or at least are disposed to do so. On the teleological account of institutions, this is in large part because the members of institutions strongly identify with the institutional ends and social norms that are definitive of those institutions, and therefore make relatively long term commitments to institutions and induct others into those institutions.

However, it has been suggested by, for example, Roy Bhaskar that this reproduction of institutions is the unintended result of the free actions of institutional actors in institutional settings. By way of support for this proposition Bhaskar claims that people do not marry to reproduce the nuclear family or work to reproduce the capitalist system. The first point to be made by way of response to Bhaskar is that even if the *reproduction* of an institution was an unintended consequence of the intentional participation of agents in that institution it would not follow that those agents did not have various other institutional outcomes as an end. For example, members of a business might have the maximisation of profit as an explicit collective end, even if the reproduction of the company was not intended by anyone.

The second point is that having an outcome as an *implicit* and/or *latent collective end* is not equivalent to individually explicitly intending to bring about that outcome. But it is the former, and not the latter that is in question. What is the evidence for the former in relation to Bhaskar's chosen examples? It is plausible to assume that in the typical case of a nuclear family in a contemporary western setting the couple married in order to, i.e. having as a collective end to, establish and maintain a single nuclear family; indeed, such a couple tries also to ensure that their adult children in turn establish and maintain nuclear families. Moreover, in their interaction with members of other families and with potential fathers, mothers, husbands and wives, let us assume that the married couple in question express—often explicitly—not only their own commitment to their own nuclear family, and to the present or future nuclear families of their adult children, but to nuclear families in general. Further, where appropriate and possible, such a married couple—let us assume—often assists members of other families to establish and maintain their own nuclear families.

Arguably, these fairly plausible assumptions, if they obtain, taken in combination constitute empirical evidence that each member of the large set of such typical married individuals has—jointly with each or most of the other members of the set—an implicit and (much of the time) latent collective end to reproduce the institution of the nuclear family. Similarly, assume that the owners and managers of a company work to maintain the existence of their company and—through training, recruitment and so on—to ensure that it continues beyond their retirement or resignation. Moreover, assume that in their ongoing interaction with customers and with other businesses, they knowingly—and in the case of sales and marketing personnel, intentionally—establish and maintain specific economic relationships. More generally—let us assume—they express, often explicitly, not only their commitment to their own business, but to the market system in general. Further, let us assume that where appropriate and possible, they assist in the maintenance and further development of that system, e.g. by voting for a market oriented political party. Now consider a set of such companies.

Arguably—given these fairly plausible assumptions—each of owner and manager of any of these companies has—jointly with the others—an implicit and (much of the time) latent collective end to reproduce the market system. Further, there are institutions, such as schools and churches, and policymaking bodies, such as governments, that are *explicitly* engaged in the enterprise of reproducing a variety of social institutions other than themselves. They contribute to the reproduction of various social institutions by propagating the "ideology" of these institutions, but also by advocating and, in the case of government, by implementing specific policies to ensure the reproduction of these institutions.

Doubtless, unintended consequences—or, more precisely, consequences not aimed at as an end—have an important role in the life and for that matter, the death, of institutions. Such consequences might include ones produced by evolutionary style causal mechanisms, or ones involved in so-called "hidden hand" mechanisms. (Albeit, as we saw above, "hidden hand" mechanisms are often the product of deliberate institutional design, and so their consequences are in a general sense aimed at by the designers, if not by the participating institutional actors themselves.)

More specifically, habitual action is a necessary feature of individual and collective—including institutional—life; and each single action performed on the basis of a habit, contributes in turn, and often unintentionally, to the maintenance and reinforcement of that habit. So the fact that institutional actors necessarily act in large part on the basis of habit means that many of their actions unintentionally contribute to the reproduction of the institution. However, this is consistent with a teleological account of social institutions—since, as noted above, there are outcomes other than institutional reproduction, and many of these are outcomes that are clearly aimed at.

Moreover, it is consistent even with a teleological explanation of the reproduction of social institutions, since the establishment and *periodic* justificatory review of habits are themselves susceptible to teleological explanation. Arguably, many social institutions produce collective goods; indeed, on teleological (and, for that matter, functional) accounts institutions exist to do so. Let us now turn to a closer consideration of the normative character of social institutions. In so doing we will deploy the teleological model of institutions adumbrated above.

Normative Character of Institutions

Social institutions have a multifaceted normative dimension. Moral categories that are deeply implicated in various social institutions include human rights and duties, contract based rights and obligations and rights and duties derived from the production and consumption of collective goods. Take police institutions. Police are typically engaged in protecting someone from being deprived of their human right to life or liberty, or their institutional right to property. Moreover, a distinctive feature of policing is the use, or threatened use, of coercive force. Here the institution of the police is different from other institutions that are either not principally concerned with protecting moral rights, or that do not necessarily rely on coercion in the service of moral rights. Take welfare institutions. There is a human right to a subsistence living, and aiding the deprived is a fundamental purpose of welfare institutions. However, aiding the deprived does not necessarily or routinely involve the use, or threat of the use, of coercive force. Thus welfare institutions are different in kind from policing institutions, but both centrally involve human rights.

Now consider business. Many business organisations do not have the protection of human rights or the aiding of the deprived as a primary purpose; nor should they. On the other hand, moral rights are an important *side constraint* on business activity. Business organisations should not engage in activities that violate the human rights of workers or other members of the community. So *some* institutions have as their principal end the protection of human rights or the aiding of those deprived of their human rights; but many institutions do not. On the other hand, human rights constitute an important side constraint on the activities of *all* institutions.

Notice that when the protection of a human right or the aiding of those deprived of a human right is the end of an institution it is a collective end. Each member of a community has an individual human right to, say, welfare, if they need it. However, it is only when a certain threshold of need exists that the establishment of an institution takes place; a welfare institution is not created because a single person's right to a subsistence living has not been realised. When such a threshold of need exists, what is required is collective or joint action on the part of many persons. Accordingly, a cooperative enterprise or institution is established that has as a collective end the provision of welfare to the needy many by means of the joint activity of members of the welfare institution so much for the relationship between social institutions and human rights per se.

However, there are a range of moral rights that might be termed "institutional moral rights". These are moral rights that depend in part on rights generating properties possessed by human beings qua human beings, but also in part on membership of a community or of a morally legitimate institution, or occupancy of a morally legitimate institutional role. Such institutional moral rights include the right to vote and to stand for political office, the right of legislators to enact legislation, of judges to make binding judgments, of police to arrest offenders, and of patients to sue doctors for negligence. Here we need to distinguish between:

- Institutional rights that embody human rights in institutional settings, and therefore depend in part on rights generating properties that human beings possess as human beings (these are institutional *moral* rights), and;
- Institutional rights that do not embody human rights in institutional settings (these are not necessarily institutional *moral* rights, but rather might be *mere* institutional rights).

The right to vote and the right to stand for office embody the human right to autonomy in the institutional setting of the state; hence to make a law to exclude certain people from having a vote or standing for office, as happened under apartheid in South Africa, is to violate a moral right. But the right to make the next move in a game of chess, or to move a pawn one space forward, but not (say) three spaces side wards, is entirely dependent on the rules of chess; if the rules had been different, e.g. each player must make two consecutive moves or pawns can move side wards, then the rights that players have would be entirely different. In other words these rights that chess players have are *mere* institutional rights; they depend entirely on the rules of the "institution" of the game of chess.

Likewise, (legally enshrined) parking rights, such as reserved spaces and one hour parking spaces in universities are *mere* institutional rights, as opposed to institutional *moral* rights. Let us now focus on institutional moral rights. There are at least two species of institutional (moral) rights. There are individual institutional (moral) rights and there are *joint* moral rights. Joint moral rights are moral rights that attach to individual persons, but do so jointly. For example, in the context of some institution of property rights the joint owners of a piece of land might have a joint right to exclude wouldbe trespassers.

Take another example, the right to political secession. Arguably, the Kurds in Iraq have a right to secede. But, if this is a right, it is not a right that some Kurdish person has as an individual, even an individual qua member of the Kurdish people. After all, an individual person cannot secede. The right of the Kurds to secede—if it exists—is a right which attaches to the individual members of the Kurdish social group, but does so jointly. Roughly speaking, two or more agents have a joint moral right to some good, if they each have an individual moral right to that good, if no-one else has such a moral right to that good, and if the individual right of each is dependent on the individual rights of the others. Let us assume that participation in the institution of the government of Canada is a good. Let us further assume that: each Canadian citizen has a moral right to participate in political institutions in Canada; non-Canadians do not have a right to such political participation in Canada; and the right to political participation of each Canadian is dependent on the possession of the right to political participation in Canada of all the other Canadians. In that case Canadians have a joint moral right.

Such joint rights need to be distinguished from universal individual human rights. Take the right to life as an example of a universal individual human right. Each human being has an individual human right to life. However, since one's possession of the right to life is wholly dependent on properties one possesses as an individual, it is not the case that one's possession of the right to life is dependent on someone else's possession of that right. However, notice that joint rights can be based in part on properties individuals possess as individuals. The right to participate in political institutions is based in part on membership of a political and legal community, and in part on possession of the property or right of autonomy. Sometimes the end realised in joint action is not merely a collective end, it is also a collective *good*.

If so, then a joint right may well be generated. It is easy to see why these agents, and not other agents, would have a right to such a good; they are the ones responsible for its existence, or continued existence. In this connection consider the managers and workers in a factory that produces cars that are sold for profit. Managers and workers in the factory—but not necessarily others—have a joint right to be remunerated from the sales of the cars that they jointly produced. It is also clear that if one participating agent has a right to the good, then—other things being equal—so do the others. That is, there is interdependence of rights with respect to the good. Let us look a little closer at this joint right. Firstly, what is the basis of this right? Perhaps the basis of this joint right is simply the fact that each of the participants performed some individual action and the result of their actions was the coming into existence of some good. This is not quite correct. One does not have a joint right in virtue of performing an action which is describable independently of the actions of other agents.

For example, one does not have a right to use a house that a number of persons jointly built simply in virtue of the fact that one built one of the walls. Rather one has a right in virtue of having *contributed* to the building of the house by building the wall in question. One's wall building considered by it would not give rise to a right in respect of the house for there might not be a house, but only a single wall. Secondly, what is the relationship, if any, between joint rights and collective goods? The good is a realised collective end to which the participants possess a joint right. Accordingly, even if the good considered in it is not intrinsically a *collective* good, each of the individual (jointly held) rights to it is a right to it qua collective good. For example, two mining companies might work together to enable the buying of land and the mining of ore on the land. Assume that the deposit is too large and too inaccessible for it to be profitable for one company to go it alone.

By prior agreement the two companies might each possess an individual right to sell 50% of the ore produced. But this agreement is something additional to the joint right to the land bought and the ore produced, and indeed presupposes this joint right. Imagine that, contra expectations, the ore produced could not be parceled out in the manner envisaged in the agreement. Perhaps there turns out to be only one large buyer who will not accept two separate suppliers. If so, each individual mining company could still claim an individual (jointly held) right to the ore produced, and therefore legitimately insist on making some different agreement in relation to selling it (or perhaps no agreement). It has been argued that social institutions are in part defined in terms of their collective ends. It has been further argued that when such collective ends are also collective goods then this gives rise to joint moral rights to those goods. That is, "functional" properties (collective ends) give rise to deontic properties (joint rights) under certain conditions—especially the condition that the collective end in question is also a human good.

Let us now give more detailed attention to the sources of deontic properties that attach to institutional roles. Such deontic properties comprise both rights and duties. The sources of deontic properties, such as rights and duties, include the following ones. Firstly, as we have just seen, collective ends—that are also collective goods—generate joint moral rights under certain conditions. So the normative dimension of institutions involves more than deontic properties and some deontic properties are presupposed by this normative dimension. Specifically, it involves the ethical or moral worth of the ends or purposes of institutions, i.e. the kinds of human goods that institutions produce or fail to produce. Accordingly, the definition of an institution will typically include a description of the human good that it purports to produce. For example, universities purport to produce knowledge and understanding, language enables the communication of truths, marriages facilitate the caring and moral development of children, economic systems ought to produce material wellbeing, and so on.

Secondly, explicitly formulated directives issued by properly constituted authorities can give rise to duties to perform certain kind of actions under certain circumstances, e.g. a military officer instructs a subordinate to undertake a military task. That said, it does not follow that general policies or habits necessarily generate *standards* of conduct—as opposed to mere regularities in behaviour—and therefore deontic properties. Thirdly, promises generate obligations to perform the promised actions. This is relevant to institutional actors in so far as they undertake oaths of office and the like. Moreover, part of the moral and/or legal basis of some institutions, such as corporations and governments, might consist in part in contracts or quasi-contracts, e.g. the so-called social contract between an elected government and its citizens. Fourth, various natural properties that persons have, e.g. human needs, generate moral rights, namely, human rights and correlative duties. Typically, human rights act as side constraints on the actions of institutional actors. However, sometimes—as we saw above—the end or function of an institution is the realisation of human rights.

This multiplicity of sources of deontic properties suggests a pluralist explanatory account of the deontic properties of institutional actors. Moreover, on a teleological account of social institutions, participants in an institution pursue a collective good and this gives rise to deontic properties. However, this (normative) teleological explanation of deontic properties needs to be supplemented by recourse to the other above-mentioned sources of deontic properties, e.g. promises, human rights. Theorists subscribing to a *collective acceptance* account of social institutions argue that the collective imposition of functional, including teleological, properties on persons or objects can in and of itself generate deontic properties. But it is a non sequitur to move from individual or collective imposition of functional or teleological properties to deontic properties.

For it is perfectly possible for a person or an object to have a set of ends or functions—and be treated as having those ends or functions—without any associated (non-instrumental) deontology. For example, a set of individuals might use a certain sort of relatively rare shell as a medium of exchange, and do so notwithstanding the fact that no-one had any desire to possess these shells independent of the fact that they could be used as a medium of exchange. In this scenario all that is required is that each exchanges shells for goods, and goods for shells, intends to continue to do so, and believes that all the others do and intend likewise. Of course it would add greatly to the stability of this arrangement if these shells were somehow authorised as an official medium of exchange, and if a (rule constituted) system of rights and duties in relation to the exchange of these shells was introduced and enforced. However, such a deontological structure is not a necessary feature of the system of exchange.

Moreover, even where a deontological framework has been adopted, the relevant deontic powers do not subsume, take the place of, provide the basis for, or go hand in hand with, the substantive functions (or ends) of the objects or persons in question. Here by *substantive* functions it is meant the functions which are *central* and necessary to the object or person being the kind of thing that it is. Consider an incompetent surgeon who is incapable of performing a successful operation on anybody, and who largely avoids doing so, or when he absolutely has to, always ensures that he is part of a team comprised of other competent surgeons and nurses who actually do the work. By virtue of being a fully accredited surgeon this person has a set of deontic powers, including the right to perform surgery, and others have deontic powers in relation to him, including the right that he performs operations competently and with due diligence. Moreover, these deontic powers are maintained in part by, say, the Royal College of Surgeons, his colleagues and the community. However, the surgeon simply does not possess the substantive functions of a surgeon.

The deontology is there but the substantive functionality is not. Accordingly, it is simply false to claim that he is a surgeon. If someone cannot perform, and knows nothing about surgery, he cannot be a surgeon, irrespective of whether he has the highest professional qualification, there is treated as if he were a surgeon, and indeed is widely believed to be the finest surgeon in the land. It might be thought that this kind of example suits the foregoing argument by virtue of the physical character of the role of surgeon. But the point can be made in relation to non-physical roles and objects. Consider a philosophical article published in a leading journal. This is an institutional fact. Now recall the recent notorious Sokal hoax. Alan Sokal, a physicist decided to write a piece of gibberish and submit it to a learned journal specialising in postmodernist writings. The journal, *Social Text*, accepted his piece, and published it.

So the piece of writing was institutionally certified as being a very high quality philosophical article. Moreover, many who read it believed this to be the case. In reality, however, it was nothing of the kind; it was gibberish and intentionally created by Sokal as such. So the "article" possessed the relevant collectively imposed deontic properties. However, this piece was not a philosophical article; for it lacked the intellectual properties necessary for it to be so. Accordingly, the collective imposition of deontic properties was not sufficient to generate the relevant institutional fact. Institutional authorisation and collective intentionality cannot turn entirely incompetent surgeons into real surgeons; nor can they turn gibberish into real philosophical articles. Naturally, whether or not deontic properties, including rights, are *respected* might ultimately turn on the attitude of the community. So general community "acceptance" of deontic properties, including rights—in a weak sense of acceptance, i.e. non-resistance—is necessary for the *maintenance* of the deontological framework in that community. So much is trivially true.

However, are there other cases of deontic properties—especially those involved in *authority* relations—which might be ontologically dependent on collective intentionality? Consider Peter Sellars in the movie, *Being There*. Sellars plays the role of a gardener who for various reasons begins to be treated by the staff of the President, and ultimately by everyone, as if he was the President of the USA. Eventually, he might even have run for office and been elected. Unfortunately, he has no understanding of the political system, or of relevant policies, and has no leadership qualities whatsoever. Nevertheless, it seems to be the case that the gardener is, or has become the President by virtue of collective acceptance.

Institutional authorities are vulnerable to a degree that other institutions, such as language, are not. As Searle points out, the communist government of USSR turned out to have clay feet. Once people chose not to obey its directives, it was finished; it simply ceased to function or exist as a government. However, it is difficult to see how the English language could go out of existence in such spectacular fashion; for it depends on millions of often disconnected communicative interactions between millions of different people. There is a reason for the vulnerability of institutional authorities, including political authorities. In the special case of institutional authorities deontic properties are *ontologically dependent* on collective acceptance; no collective acceptance, no deontic properties. The point here is not simply that, say, rulers cannot *exercise* their right to rule if their right to rule is not collectively accepted.

Rather a ruler does not even possess a *right* to rule unless she is able to exercise authority over her subjects. This seems to be a general feature of the deontic properties of those in authority in general, and of political authorities in particular. Having explored in general terms the normative character of social institutions let us now turn in the final section of this entry to a more specific normative aspect of institutions, namely their conformity or lack of it with principles of distributive justice.

Social Institutions and Distributive Justice

Justice is an important aspect of many, if not all, social institutions. Market economies, salary and wage structures, and tax systems, judicial systems, prisons, and so on are all in part to be evaluated in terms of their compliance with principles of justice. Here it is important to distinguish the concept of justice from, on the one hand, the related concept of a right—especially a human right—and from goods, such as wellbeing and utility, on the other hand. Self-evidently, wellbeing is not the same thing as justice. However, there is a tendency to conflate justice and rights. Nevertheless, arguably the concepts are distinct; or at least justice in a narrow relational sense should be distinguished from the concept of a right. Genocide, for example, is a violation of human rights—specifically, the right to life—but it is not necessarily, or at least principally, an act of injustice in a relational sense. A person's rights can be violated, irrespective of whether or not another - or indeed everyone - has suffered a rights violation. However, injustice in the relational sense entails unfairness as between persons or groups; injustice in this sense consists in the fact that someone has suffered or benefited but others have not (and there is no adequate justification for this state of affairs).

Although the concept of a right and the concept of justice (in this sense) are distinct, violations of rights are typically acts of injustice (and *vice-versa*). Moreover, the concept of justice is itself multidimensional. Penal justice (sometimes referred to as retributive justice), for example, concerns the punishment of offenders for their legal and/or moral offences, and is to be distinguished from distributive justice. Thus it is a principle of penal justice, but not distributive justice, that the guilty be punished and the innocent go free. Distributive justice is essentially a relational phenomenon to do with the comparative distribution of benefits and burdens as between individuals or groups, including the distribution of rights and duties but not restricted to the distribution of rights and duties, e.g. the injustice of excluding blacks (but not whites) from voting in elections to determine the national government in apartheid South Africa or of lower wages being paid to women than those paid to men for the same work. (These are also instances of rights violations.)

On the view of distributive justice being propounded here, justice is but one moral value and distributive justice but one dimension of justice. Accordingly, it is always an open question whether or not some action or policy required by the principles of distributive justice is morally required *all things considered*. Distributive justice is an important aspect of most, if not all, social institutions; the role occupants of most institutions are the recipients and providers of benefits, e.g. wages, consumer products, and the bearers of burdens, e.g. allocated tasks and, accordingly, are subject to principles of distributive justice. Moreover, arguably some institutions, perhaps governments, have as one of their defining ends or functions, to ensure conformity to principles of distributive justice in the wider society. However, distributive justice does not appear to be a *defining* feature, end or function of *all* social institutions. By this I do not mean that some social institutions are unjust, e.g. the institution of slavery; though clearly many are. Rather I am referring to the fact that a number of social institutions, such as the English language or even the institution of the university, are not *defined*—normatively speaking—in terms of justice, but rather by some other moral value(s), e.g. truth.

Communication systems, such as human languages, are arguably defined in part in terms of the end of truth, but not in terms of justice; hence, a communicative system would cease to be a communication system if its participants never attempted to communicate the truth, but not if its participants failed to respect principles of distributive justice, e.g. in terms of the number of occasions on which particular speakers were allowed to speak. The principles of distributive justice can be applied at an individual level, at an intra-institutional level, at a societal level and at a global level. If principles of distributive justice are applied at an individual level then the questions arises as to the scope of the application: Is it, for example, the individuals who happen to occupy a neighbourhood, the individuals who comprise a society, the individuals who comprise the human race, or some other demarcated set of individuals?

Moreover, if the principles of distributive justice are applied at an institutional level then an analogous question arises in relation to the scope of the application: Is it, for example, a particular institution or a structure of institutions? If the latter, Is it the institutional structure of a society or the global institutional structure? Famously, John Rawls addressed and privileged the question of the distributive justice of the structure of institutions in a given (liberal democratic) society. Arguably, this is a somewhat narrow focus, whatever one thinks of the specific account of distributive justice that Rawls elaborated in relation to the structure of institutions at the societal level. Why is it not, for example, important to focus on the application of principles of distributive justice in relation to the global structure of, say, political and economic institutions? At any rate, our concern here is with the application of the concept of distributive justice at the institutional level (though not necessarily only with respect to the structure of institutions within a given society, let alone liberal democratic society).

The contrast here is between the institutional level and the individual level. However, it is important to determine what this distinction consists in. Justice is a moral (relational) property and as such, I suggest, is only properly applied either to the actions of *individual* human beings or to the relations between *individual* human beings, including their relative wealth, status and power. More specifically, a social entity or relation between social entities is not per se just or unjust, notwithstanding that in ordinary speech social entities and their relations to one another are said to be just or unjust, e.g. the USA is sometimes said to be an unjust society. Rather claims ascribing justice or injustice to social entities and/or their relations are translatable into claims regarding the actions of, and relations between, individual human beings, e.g. the distribution of income between the individual citizens of the USA is unjust.

Given this individualistic conception of justice (and of moral properties more generally) how is a distinction to be maintained between the application of principles of distributive justice at an institutional level, on the one hand, and at an individual level, on the other? Quite simply by helping ourselves to an institutional role the occupant (and the relations, actions and effects on role occupant's quasi role occupants). Institutional role occupants are individual human persons. However, they are individual human persons who happen to occupy one or more institutional roles, including in contemporary nation-states the role of citizen. As such, they have certain institutional rights and duties, in the manner adumbrated in earlier sections of this entry. Accordingly, an institution is in some respect or on some occasion unjust in one of two main ways, intrainstitutionally unjust and externally institutionally unjust.

An institution is in some respect or on some occasion *intra-institutionally* unjust if a role occupant(s) of this institution qua role occupant(s) of this institution:

- Stands in an unjust relation to some other role occupant(s) within this institution qua role occupant(s) of this institution or
- Performs an action(s) that is unjust to some role occupant(s) of this institution qua role occupant of this institution. For example, a company in which the CEO's salary is 50 times the wage of the lower echelon workers is prima facie unjust in respect of its system of rewards. An institution is in some respect or on some occasion *externally unjust* if a role occupant(s) of this institution qua role occupant of this institution:
- Stands in an unjust relation to some other non role occupant(s) of this institution; or
- Performs an action(s) that is unjust to some non role occupant of this institution, e.g. the members of a parliamentary cabinet jointly decide to remove the minimum wage level in the interests of economic growth and notwithstanding that this policy will further impoverish the least well-off.

Accordingly, the unjust actions of, and unjust relations between, ordinary human beings are actions and relations at the individual *non-institutional* level by virtue of not being acts of, and relation between, individuals qua institutional role occupants. Thus if a group of wealthy entrepreneurs buy a large (but allowable) number of tickets to soccer matches in some national league and then sell them at grossly inflated prices to wealthy soccer fans (again, this is allowable) then arguably there has been an injustice to the relatively impoverished soccer fans who would otherwise have been able to afford these tickets and attend the matches of their beloved home teams.

However, these are not acts of injustice at the institutional level, since there are no institutional actors involved in this injustice.

Notice that on the account of the distinction between the institutional and the individual levels of just/unjust actions and relations, if a role occupant (acting qua role occupant) treats some *non-role occupant* unjustly then this is, nevertheless, an injustice at the institutional level. So if the members of an apartheid government refuse to enact legislation giving the vote to (currently unenfranchise) blacks then this is an institutional injustice. Note also that on this way of drawing the distinction it does not matter whether the institution in question is an intra-societal institution, e.g. an institution within a nation-state or an extra-societal, including global institution, e.g. the United Nations.

On the other hand, this way of drawing the distinction between the individual and the institutional level of the application of principles of distributive justice assumes that some relevant institution has been established. However, it is possible that there are in fact no institutions designed to deal with some pressing issue of distributive justice and, therefore, no institutional role occupants to rectify the injustice. Surely, it might be argued, such an injustice is an injustice at the institutional level. I suggest that such cases are not cases of the injustice of institutions per se, but rather of the injustice of *the absence* of institutions. Such cases point to the need to make a threefold, rather than a merely twofold, distinction in this area:

- Injustice at the individual level;
- Injustice at the institutional level;
- Injustice at the individual level that is of such magnitude as to warrant the establishment of an institution.

It might further be argued that a crucial factor in all this has been ignored, namely, *groups* of individuals, e.g. socio-economic classes, ethnic and gender-based groups. The application of principles of distributive justice at the institutional level is, or ought to be, in large part the application of such principles not so much to individuals per se, but to groups whose members are known to be, say, systemically discriminated against.

Doubtless, much injustice is group-based. To the extent that institutional actors are themselves guilty of group-based injustice, e.g. politicians whose policies discriminate against indigenous people, employers who exploit young workers in terms of pay and conditions, then this is a matter of injustice at the institutional level, as this notion has been characterised above. However, there is a further point at issue here.

Group-based injustices can exist primarily at the individual level rather than primarily at the institutional level. Some groups of individuals might have significant advantages in the competition for scarce goods, such as wealth, power and status, by virtue of their greater initial wealth, their access to social networks etc. and so on. That is, they have no *formal* institutional advantages. Moreover, it is not self-evident that a given institution, e.g. corporation, university, medical or legal profession etc., is unjust simply by virtue of the fact that some groups enjoy informal and highly generic advantages in relation to the competition for access to and progress within the institution in question; surely it is too much to insist that every institution must ensure complete equality of opportunity if it wants to avoid the charge of injustice.

However, it might be argued that this line of argument

fails to accommodate group-based injustices of the kind in question. Indeed, the Rawlsian difference principle might be invoked at this point; the system of institutional arrangements within a society taken as a whole should work to the advantage of the least advantaged. In response to this, I suggest that such group-based injustices, if injustices they be, are not necessarily injustices at the institutional level, but rather might well be injustices at the individual level. Nevertheless, they might be injustices at the individual level that are of such a magnitude that they need to be addressed institutionally. However, they are not injustices in respect of which there is no relevant remedial institution in existence. Rather existing institutions, especially governments, are presumably obliged to formulate appropriate policies to deal with such group-based injustices. Such policies might include death duties and/or tax scales with very high marginal rates of taxation at the top end of the scale.

On the other hand, if such group-based injustices are in fact the result of the practices or structures of institutions (taken individually or collectively) within the society then they would constitute injustices at the institutional level. For example, if the quality of educational preparation necessary to become a doctor or lawyer was in fact only available to the very rich, then arguably the educational institutions themselves are unjust, i.e. there is injustice at the institutional level. In many societies socio-economic group-based injustices exist at both the individual and the institutional level. That is, relevant institutions are both failing to take steps to redress prior group-based injustices at the individual level and further exacerbating those injustices by adding another layer of injustice at the institutional level.

There is a category of institutions in respect of which the distinction between group-based individual injustices and injustices at the institutional level collapses, namely, institutions that have as a defining purpose to redress large-scale distributive injustices in the wider society, i.e. governments. The assumption here is that the institutional end of government goes beyond protecting human rights to, for example, life and liberty, and providing necessary means to the realisation of those rights, e.g. basic health, education and conditions of law and order that enable citizens to pursue their various individual and collective projects. For, as we have seen, the concept of a right, especially a human right, needs to be distinguished from the concept of justice, including distributive justice; and the realisation of human rights is a more pressing moral imperative than compliance with the principles of distributive justice.

On the other hand, minimalist conceptions of the institution of government might stop short of advocating a major role for government in applying principles of distributive justice in the wider society. A further question that arises here pertains to the putative obligation of governments to protect the human rights of citizens of other states (or for that matter, non-citizens). Arguably, all individuals and institutions, including governments, have a moral obligation to protect human rights, e.g. not to violate the right to life or liberty. And some of these human rights evidently include positive rights to security and the provision of basic necessities, such as food and water. Some have argued that there are no such obligations on the part of governments, other than to their own citizens.

This view might prove difficult to sustain, given that the principle not to infringe a human right applies universally, and given that the notion of a human right cannot easily be restricted to so-called negative rights, i.e. cannot easily be restricted to rights not to be interfered with. Perhaps ironically, a conception of the institution of government that is minimalist in respect of the *nature* of its obligations, i.e. government exists only to protect the human rights of its citizens, might generate (presumably unwittingly) maximalism in respect of the *scope* of those obligations, i.e. other things being equal, the government has an obligations to protect the human rights of all, whether they be its citizens or not.

Naturally, other things are not equal, e.g. there are practicalities and a certain division of labour in respect of the protection of the human rights of different groups. Australia, for example, cannot presumably be expected to protect the human rights of the Tibetans, given the relative power of China *vis a vis* Australia. On the other hand, Australia might be reasonably expected to intervene to protect the human rights of the East Timorese.

Some have argued:

- That a liberal democratic government has a moral obligation to ensure respect for the human rights of its own citizens and others alike, but only has moral obligations to ensure that its own citizens comply with principles of distributive justice (specifically, the (controversial) Rawlsian difference principle), and
- That the reason for this is that its own citizens alone are legitimately subject to the coercive authority of the government. The latter claim is open to question. No doubt citizens subject to the coercive authority of a government have a moral right to political rights, e.g. a right to vote and to stand for political office; they relinquish a degree of their individual autonomy in favour of a degree of jointly held autonomy (as well as (at least) protection of their human rights, and law and order). However, it is difficult to see why citizens being subject to the coercive authority of a government (willingly or, for that matter, unwillingly) generates a moral obligation on the part of the government in question to apply principles of distributive justice—specifically, the controversial Rawlsian difference principle—to the interactions between the citizens.

On the other hand, arguably, the coercive authority of government does generate a moral obligation on the part of government to enforce respect for contracts between citizens that are freely entered in to. For the latter are expressions of the autonomy of citizens, and in accepting the coercive authority of the government, citizens have relinquished a further aspect of their individual autonomy, namely their individual rights to enforce the contracts that they freely enter in to. In conclusion, a final point about liberal democratic governments and distributive justice. There is at least one important and uncontroversial principle of distributive justice that arises in the context of collective enterprises (joint action); namely that, other things being equal, the benefits produced by joint actions should flow back to those who performed the joint action. Let us assume that inevitably citizens of a given polity participate in collective enterprises; whereas this is not necessarily the case for individuals who are not citizens of the same polity. (In the contemporary globalising world this assumption is increasingly implausible; but let us grant it for the sake of argument.)

Surely this principle of distributive justice, if any, should be enforced by governments in relation to their own citizens but not in relation to non-citizens. Perhaps at any rate, one key test of this proposition is whether or not individuals would be morally entitled to enforce such a principle of distributive justice in the absence of government. If the answer is in the affirmative, i.e. individuals have a "natural" right to enforce this principle of distributive justice, then presumably governments have a right to enforce it; after all, as we have seen above, according to liberal democratic theory individuals relinquish to government whatever pre-existing moral rights to enforcement they might have had. What if the answer to our question is in the negative; does it follow that the government has no moral right to enforce this principle of distributive justice? Not necessarily. For one thing enforcement of such a principle of distributive justice is not necessarily the violation of a human right; if it were, this would be a moral constraint on governmental action in this regard.

For another thing, in the context of a liberal democratic state citizens can make legitimate joint decisions—via their representative governments—that are simply unavailable to them when they are functioning as lone individuals; and one of these joint decisions might well be to enforce such a principle of distributive justice in their society on the grounds that it is a weighty moral principle the enforcement of which is morally required. Now consider—as is in fact the case—a world in which many joint economic enterprises are in fact trans-societal, e.g. a multinational corporation. Naturally, the citizens of different societies (polities)—or at least their representative governments—might also make a joint decision to (jointly) enforce this principle of distributive justice in relation to trans-societal joint economic enterprises involving citizens from both polities, e.g. wages in a poor society would need to reflect the contribution of the wage-earner to the overall benefits produced by the multinational corporation. And if the citizens are committed on moral grounds to the enforcement of this principle of distributive justice in relation to *intra*-societal economic interactions, it is difficult to see why they should not be likewise committed to it in *trans*-societal economic interactions.

2

Elements of Socialization

As socialization is a fundamental sociological concept, there are a number of components to this concept that are important to understand. While not every sociologist will agree which elements are the most important, or even how to define some of the elements of socialization, the elements outlined below should help clarify what is meant by socialization.

Goals of Socialization

Arnett, in presenting a new theoretical understanding of socialization, outlined what he believes to be the three goals of socialization:

- Impulse control and the development of a conscience
- Role preparation and performance, including occupational roles, gender roles, and roles in institutions such as marriage and parenthood
- The cultivation of sources of meaning, or what is important, valued, and to be lived for.

In short, socialization is the process that prepares humans to function in social life. It should be reiterated here that socialization is culturally relative - people in different cultures are socialized differently. This distinction does not and should not inherently force an evaluative judgment. Socialization, because it is the adoption of culture, is going to be different in every culture. Socialization, as both process and an outcome, is not better or worse in any particular culture.

Primary and Secondary Socialization

Socialization is a life process, but is generally divided into two parts: *Primary socialization* takes place early in life, as a child and adolescent. *Secondary socialization* refers to the socialization that takes place throughout one's life, both as a child and as one encounters new groups that require additional socialization. While there are scholars who argue that only one or the other of these occurs, most social scientists tend to combine the two, arguing that the basic or core identity of the individual develops during primary socialization, with more specific changes occurring later - secondary socialization - in response to the acquisition of new group memberships and roles and differently structured social situations. The need for later life socialization may stem from the increasing complexity of society with its corresponding increase in varied roles and responsibilities.

Jaskiran - Socialization in childhood is thought to be concerned with the regulation of biological drives. In adolescence, socialization is concerned with the development of overarching values and the self-image. In adulthood, socialization involves more overt and specific norms and behaviours, such as those related to the work role as well as more superficial personality features.

Jassan - In earlier periods, the *socializee* (the person being socialized) more clearly assumes the status of *learner* within the context of the family of orientation, the school, or the peer group. Also, relationships in the earlier period are more likely to be affectively charged, i.e., highly emotional. In adulthood, though the socializee takes the role of student at times, much socialization occurs after the socializee has assumed full incumbency of the adult role. There is also a greater likelihood of more formal relationships due to situational contexts (e.g., work environment), which moderates down the affective component.

Neetu - The child and adolescent may be more easily malleable than the adult. Also, much adult socialization is self-initiated and voluntary; adults can leave or terminate the process at any time.

Socialization is, of course, a social process. As such, it involves interactions between people. Socialization, as noted in the distinction between primary and secondary, can take place in multiple contexts and as a result of contact with numerous groups. Some of the more significant contributors to the socialization process are: parents, friends, schools, siblings, and co-workers. Each of these groups includes a culture that must be learned and to some degree appropriated by the socializee in order to gain admittance to the group.

Total Institutions

Not all socialization is voluntary nor is all socialization successful. There are components of society designed specifically to resocialize individuals who were not successfully socialized to begin with. For instance, prisons and mental health institutions are designed to resocialize the people who are deemed to have not been successfully socialized. Depending on the degree of isolation and resocialization that takes place in a given institution, some of these institutions are labeled *total institutions*. In his classic study of total institutions, Erving Goffman gives the following characteristics of total institutions:

- All aspects of life are conducted in the same place under the same authority,
- The individual is a member of a large cohort, all treated alike,
- All daily activities (over a 24-hour period) are tightly scheduled,
- There is a sharp split between supervisors and lower participants,
- Information about the member's fate is withheld.

The most common examples of total institutions include mental hospitals, prisons, and military boot camps, though there are numerous other institutions that could be considered total institutions as well. The goal of total institutions is to facilitate a complete break with one's old life in order for the institution to resocialize the individual into a new life. Mortimer and Simmons note a difference in socialization methodologies in different types of institutions. When the goal of an institution is socialization (primary or secondary), the institution tends to use normative pressures. When the goal of an institution is resocialization of deviants, coercion is frequently involved.

Broad and Narrow Socialization

Arnett proposed an interesting though seldom used distinction in types of socialization. Arnett distinguishes between broad and narrow socialization:

- Broad socialization is intended to promote independence, individualism, and self-expression; it is dubbed *broad* because this type of socialization has the potential of resulting in a broad range of outcomes,
- Narrow socialization is intended to promote obedience and conformity; it is dubbed *narrow* because there is a narrow range of outcomes.

These distinctions correspond to Arnett's definition of socialization, which is:

- The whole process by which an individual born with behavioural potentialities of enormously wide range, is led to develop actual behaviour which is confined with a much narrower range; the range of what is customary and acceptable for him according to the standards of his group.

Arnett explains that his understanding of socialization should not be understood as having just two options, broad or narrow. Instead, the author argues that socialization can be broad or narrow within each of the seven socializing forces he outlines (e.g., family, friends, etc.). Because each force can be either broad or narrow, there is a wide variety of possible broad/narrow socialization combinations. Finally, Arnett notes two examples where his distinction is relevant. First, Arnett argues that there are often differences in socialization by gender.

Where these differences exist, argues Arnett, socialization tends to be narrower for women than for men. Arnett also argues that Japanese socialization is narrow as there is more pressure toward conformity in that culture. Arnett argues that this may account for the lower crime rates in Japan.

Importance of Socialization

One of the most common methods used to illustrate the importance of socialization is to draw upon the few unfortunate cases of children who were, through neglect, misfortune, or willful abuse, not socialized by adults while they were growing up. Examples of such children can be found here.

Theoretical Understandings of Socialization

Socialization, as a concept in social scientific research, has evolved over time. While the basic idea outlined above has been a component of most understandings of socialization, there has been quite a variety of definitions and theories of socialization. Some of these approaches are presented here as definitional variety is often informative.

Symbolic Interactionism - the self develops as a result of social interactions; as a result, socialization is highly dependent on the situations in which the actor finds him/herself; this approach also argues that socialization is a continuous, lifelong process.

Role Theory - socialization is seen as a process of acquisition of appropriate norms, attitudes, self-images, values, and role behaviours that enable acceptance in the group and effective performance of new roles; in this framework, socialization is seen as a conservative force, permitting the perpetuation of the social organization in spite of the turnover of individual members through time.

Reinforcement Theory - the self develops as a result of cognitive evaluations of costs and benefits; this understanding assumes that the socializee, in approaching new roles, is an independent and active negotiator for advantages in relationships with role partners and membership groups.

Internalization Theory - socialization is a series of stages in which the individual learns to participate in various levels of organization of society; this theory contends that the child internalizes a cognitive frame of reference for interpersonal relations and a common system of expressive symbolism in addition to a moral conscience; this approach was advocated by Talcott Parsons.

Socialization as Joining Groups

The concept of socialization has traditionally addressed the problem of individual adjustment to society. In all of the approaches outlined above, socialization has, in one way or another, referred to the idea that society shapes its members toward compliance and cooperation with societal requirements. In order to reduce confusion, develop a research methodology for measuring socialization, and potentially lead to the comparability of research findings from different studies, Long and Hadden proposed a revised understanding of socialization. Rather than referring to a vague adoption or learning of culture, Long and Hadden reframed socialization as "the medium for transforming newcomers into bona fide members of a group." Before discussing some of the specifics of this approach, it may be useful to outline some of the critiques Long and Hadden present of earlier approaches to socialization.

According to Long and Hadden, many earlier approaches to socialization extended socialization to every part of human social life. As a result, everyone becomes both a socializing agent (socializer) and a novice (socializee) in all encounters with others.

This conceptualization leaves socialization without a social home; it is all around but no place in particular. Another criticism of previous approaches is that they allowed socialization to include anything, and anything which is part of the process at one time may be excluded at another. With this conceptualization, any phenomenon may shift its status in the socialization process without changing its own composition or expression. In other words, socialization includes virtually everything, excludes almost nothing, and shifts with circumstance and outcomes. Additionally, previous approaches to socialization lacked specificity about the nature of socialization activity.

Defining socialization by its outcomes made it unnecessary to stipulate the nature of the process conceptually. Socialization could be attributed to *this or that* but in order to truly understand what is taking place it is necessary to go beyond just pointing to socializing agents and specify what it is about those agents that is doing the socializing. Another serious drawback of earlier approaches is that they disregard the *process* component of socialization. Doing so limits the socialization concept to employment primarily as a post hoc interpretive category that is used to lend significance to findings defined and developed in other terms. As a result of these criticisms, Long and Hadden found themselves presented with a two-fold task:

- Locate socialization and its social boundaries more precisely specify the distinctive properties which distinguish it from related phenomena.

To accomplish this, Long and Hadden developed a new understanding of socialization, "socialization is the process of creating and incorporating new members of a group from a pool of newcomers, carried out by members and their allies". Under this understanding, the principal agents of socialization are certified and practicing members of the group to which novices are being socialized. It should be noted that *certified* here is only a shortened way of saying "a socially approved member of the group." Thus, Long and Hadden's revised understanding of socialization sees it as both the process and outcome of joining groups.

Research Examples

Numerous examples of research on socialization could be presented in this section. One important area of socialization research involves differences in gender socialization, but much of that research is summarized in the chapter on gender. The following three research examples are interesting in that they explore both primary and secondary socialization and do so from varying perspectives.

Socialization and Social Class

Ellis, Lee, and Peterson, developing a research agenda begun by Melvin L. Kohn, explored differences in how parents raise their children relative to their social class. Kohn found that lower class parents were more likely to emphasize conformity in their children whereas middle-class parents were more likely to emphasize creativity and self-reliance. Ellis et. al. proposed and found that parents value conformity over self-reliance in children to the extent that conformity superseded self-reliance as a criterion for success in their own endeavors. In other words, Ellis et. al. verified that the reason lower-class parents emphasize conformity in their children is because they experience conformity in their day-to-day activities. For example, factory work is far more about conforming than innovation.

Another study in this same area explored a slightly different component of this relationship. Erlanger was interested in a correlation between social class and physical violence. While he did not find a strong correlation indicating lower class individuals were more likely to employ physical violence in punishing their children, he did present evidence concerning several outdated propositions. Erlanger's findings include:

- Physical punishment *does not* lead to *working class authoritarianism,*
- Childhood punishment experiences *do not* explain the greater probability that working class adults, as opposed to middle class adults, will commit homicide,

- General use of corporal punishment *is not* a precursor to child abuse,
- Use of corporal punishment *is not* part of a sub-cultural positive evaluation of violence.

It should be noted that this is an older study and that more recent findings may have shed more light on these issues. It should also be noted that Erlanger readily points out when his findings are strongly supported or weakly supported by his data. It behooves the interested party to read his paper directly rather than rely on the summary above for the specific nuances.

Socialization and Death Preparation

Marshall interviewed a number of retirement home residents to explore how their environment influenced their thinking about death. In essence, Marshall was examining secondary socialization concerning mortality. Marshall found that a combination of relationships, behavioural changes, and retirement home culture contributed to a conception of death that was both accepting and courageous. Residents of this particular retirement home found themselves with more time on their hands - to think about death - because they no longer had to care for their own homes. Additionally, they found themselves surrounded by people in a situation similar to their own: they were basically moving into the retirement home to prepare for death.

The prevalence of elderly people facilitated discussions of death, which also helped socialize the residents into their acceptance of mortality. Finally, the retirement home community encouraged a culture of life and fulfillment in part to counter-act the frequency of death. Some residents calculated there was one death per week in the retirement home. In light of such bad numbers, it was important to the success of the community to maintain a positive culture that embraced life yet accepted death. In summary, Marshall found that numerous factors contributed to the socialization of residents into a positive lifestyle that was also accepting of and preparatory for their impending deaths.

Rosenbaum was interested in the effects of high school tracks on IQ. High school tracks are the different levels or types of courses students can take; for instance, many high schools now include college preparation tracks and general education tracks.

Rosenbaum's theory was that students who followed the lower tracks (non-college preparation) would score lower on IQ tests over time than would students who followed the higher tracks (college preparation). Considering that school is one of the primary contributors to socialization, it makes sense that participation in a given track can also result in the adoption of the norms, values, beliefs, skills, and behaviours that correspond to that track.

In other words, tracks can turn into a type of self-fulfilling prophecy: you may start out at the same level as someone in a higher track, but by the time you have completed the lower track you will have become like the other students in your track.

To reduce confounding variables and ensure notable test effects, Rosenbaum selected a homogeneous, white, working class public school with five different, highly stratified classes. Rosenbaum then compared IQ scores for individuals in the different tracks at two time points. As it turns out, *tracking* does have a significant effect on IQ. People in lower tracks can actually see a decline in IQ compared to a possible increase among those in the upper track. In other words, tracks socialize their students into their corresponding roles.

A Case of the Southwestern Highlands of Uganda

The policy environment for natural resource management (NRM) is changing dramatically from centralized top-down conservation approaches, to community-based livelihood approaches, which are increasingly seen as offering pro-poor alternative to resources management.

In Uganda, recent decentralization efforts have reinforced pluralism in property regimes with porous boundaries both of regimes, stakeholders, and uses, and complex relationships among a wide range of social actors and resource users.

The intensively cultivated and densely populated southwestern highlands of Uganda are characterized by fragile agro ecology, with a combination of uses, users, resources, and rules that govern resource use. In this context, NRM can be typically described as a "commons" with overlapping combinations of porous boundaries both of regimes and stakeholders, and when actions by individuals or groups often generate offsite effects. In such fragile environments, people compete for the natural resources they need to ensure or enhance their livelihoods. NRM is in many ways a form of conflict management.

These conflicts are intensifying and if continued to be ignored, they can escalate and result into further degradation of natural resources, erosion of social and human capital, and pose significant challenges to sustainable rural livelihoods. Therefore, the management of the inevitable conflicts in NRM is important as public good, and merit policy support. Any policy support must rely on a detailed and systematic understanding of the nature, types, dimensions, and implications of conflicts and their management mechanisms. Much of the literature on conflict management emphasizes social institutions as mediating factors that govern the relationship between a society or community and the natural resources on which it depends, and therefore emphasizes the relationship between social and natural capital. Most of this research has shown the importance of social capital foundations for sustainable management of natural resources, successful policy interventions, and community development. Its reinforcement and continued deployment in a society is what maintains both the existence of particular institutions and the process of institutional innovations within the society.

The emphasis on social capital is based on the assumption that communities are more efficient than state structures in the management of common-pool resource conflicts. However, although literature on social capital has emerged in the last decades, there is still limited empirical information on the role of the different dimensions of social capital in managing conflicts. The central hypothesis of this chapter is that presence of social capital is a necessary precondition for the management of NRM conflicts, and for sustainable management and use of common pool resources at the local level. This examines the different types of conflicts over the use and management of natural resources, and determines the role, strengths, and limits of social capital in managing NRM conflicts. The rest of this chapter starts with the description of status of natural resources in Kabale and their different property regimes. Then, we examine the prevalence and the different types of conflicts over the use and management of natural resources. The sections that follow examine the role, strengths, and limits of social capital mechanisms for managing conflicts. The concluding section suggests a framework for strengthening synergy between social capital and policy, and building local capacity for alternative conflict management.

Natural Resources Management Regimes in the Highlands of Kabale, Uganda

The study was conducted in Kabale district in the southwestern highlands of Uganda. Kabale district has an estimated population of 461,785. Population density exceeds 350 inhabitants/km^2 in areas making Kabale, one of the highest densely populated rural districts in Uganda. Population pressure has continued to increase resulting in fragmented small farms, i.e., 0.25–1.0 ha for an average family of six, and steep cultivated slopes (1500–2700 masl). Several scholars have extensively documented the status of natural resources management (NRM) and technologies for reversing land degradation in the highlands of Kabale. For a summary of studies see Tukahirwa (1997) and Raussen et al. (2002) for inventory of technologies. The status of agricultural-based NRM in the highlands of Kabale cannot be better summarized than with this explanation by an elderly farmer, Zaburooni, now in his late 70s, who came to the village in 1944 when he was about 18 years old.

This area was not occupied before the 1940s. The first people settled on the hilltop, as there were forests and jungles lower down. There were about seven families present at that time. They built houses on the top and cultivated around the houses....When more people came to the area, the clan leaders would allocate enough land that could support a family, depending on the family size. They did not think about the future or acquire huge chunks of land ready for expansion....In the past you could stand on a hilltop and only see another hilltop because of the dense and tall bushes in the valley.

Everything was just trees; all the valleys and slopes were also covered with forest. (...) Cultivation started at the mid slopes, moving down to the lower slopes, in order to scare away predators (wild pigs, leopards and lions). (...). The east-facing slope was the first to be cultivated, starting from the mid slope to the valley, then expanding south on the eastern slope. (...) We used to plant plots in alternate years (3 to 5 yr, even more) to regain its fertility. When you leave a plot to rest, grasses grow up and later rot and the soil gains its fertility (...). The hills top and valley bottoms were used as grazing lands for everybody. Now because many people came into the village and with constant tilling without resting the land, people are now forced to cultivate both the valley bottoms and the hilltops.

Some rich and powerful people have also bought the fertile parts of the valley bottoms for their exotic dairy cows. Some used their power to grab communal grazing land, like the whole of that hill...The Government also is stopping people from using the wetlands and swamps, where we used to fish and collect papyrus and building material.

Now people are arrested for collecting papyrus from the swamps, or firewood from a village woodlot...This is very difficult for the poor and old people like me who don't have money. When we came to this village, money was not the issue, and there were plenty of resources for the village. Now we have so many disputes over the use and property of land, even for grazing land and other communal properties. People are now competing for everything (...)

Historically, NRM regimes were often regulated through customary and traditional institutions and dispute resolution mechanisms. These institutions still operate through clans and other farmer's local associations. Clans play an important role as an important feature of social organization that facilitates coordination, cooperation, and for managing the social structures and institutions for NRM.

Though local communities have long been known to manage their NRM effectively over a long period, many common- pool resources have now come under the jurisdiction of the state, turning some into protected areas, and restricting the use of many others with strict policies. Even in the case of private property regimes, individual farmers are not entirely free to decide for themselves how to make use of natural resources, but participate in a process of collective choice that sets rules and regulations, or bylaws for individual and collective use.

The penetration of the State was accompanied by the breakdown of traditional practices and the emergence of strict regulations or policies based on the traditional cônception that common-pool resources (CPR) need protection from the destructive actions of people and local communities. The authority for resource use has been invested in government institutions by the colonial legacy. Most of the initial laws in Uganda, as in most parts of Africa, were not drafted in the interests of the communities that lived near these resources. After the independence in 1962, government policies have concentrated on their conservation mandate for the protected areas, paying little attention to the legitimacy of the needs and rights of local communities, but implementing policies imposed by international conservation treaties and conventions. For decades there has been systematic failure to recognize that traditional institutions and local knowledge has been the basis of the survival of most rural communities. However, over the last decade, the decentralization of government and environmental management, various government policies, and institutions recognize the right of communities to participate in environmental management, and recognize that local communities can manage common pool resources in an effective and sustainable manner.

The mechanisms of decentralization are established and functioning, with the structure of a five-tier system of local councils and local government structures, a bottom-up planning process, and powers to collect and disburse local revenue, develop and implement bylaws and local policies for land use, environmental management, and agricultural production. At the base of the local government structure, the local council or LC1, A village of about 50–100 households, consists of all adults residing in a particular village who elect a nine-member village local council executive committee. Beyond the village or LC1, in ascending geographical size, there are parishes (LC2), subcounty or *gombolola* (LC3), county (LC4), and district (LC5) councils. The sub-county level (LC3) is the basic unit of local government, both political and administrative. The district (LC5) is the highest level of local government and links with central government. The provision of local government elections guarantee widespread representation at the various councils and include quotas by gender, people with disabilities, and youths. For example, at least one-third of the council members must be women, an affirmative action to empower women and promote gender equity.

In this chapter, we use the term policy in its broad sense to refer to laws, rules, and regulations and their implementation resulting from public, state, or collective decision making. Policies can be generated and operate at different levels: international, national, regional, district, and local levels. In this study, we are particularly concerned with those local-level policies and community regulations usually referred to as bylaws. Bylaws are rules made by lower local government councils (LC1 and LC3) and provide the local policy guidelines to be followed in sectoral developments, such as agriculture and natural resource management. These bylaws or local arrangements for natural resource management are now receiving greater attention as a viable alternative for enforcing government policies and rectifying their inefficiencies in agriculture and NRM.

In a social capital framework, these local policies or bylaws can be defined as negotiated rules, social norms, and agreed behaviours that exist within communities to prevent and manage conflicts. Colleman (1988) identified different forms of social capital: obligations and expectations, informal channels, and social norms. Fukuyama (1999) and Bowles and Gintis (2002) regard social capital as an instantiated set of informal values or norms shared among members of a group that permits to cooperate with one another. It is the willingness to live by the norms of one's community and to punish those who do not. In the context of this study, bylaws are rules made by lower local decentralized councils and local communities and provide viable alternative for enforcing government policies and rectifying their inefficiencies in agriculture and NRM.

Use and Management of Common-pool Resources

We define conflicts as situations involving people or social groups with different interests, and mutually antagonist tendencies and opposing influences competing for the use of limited resources to ensure or enhance their livelihoods. Their manifestations, dimensions, and level of intensity vary greatly. They can be implicit or explicit, proximate, local, regional, national, or international, latent or violent. Following Ramirez (1999) and Means et al. (2002), the analysis of conflicts began with identifying and describing the conflict, its boundaries and interrelationships, the origins, levels, issues, and stakeholders. To encourage people to speak about and see conflicts as part of human interactions, we asked:

"From working in other areas, we have seen that problems and disputes over the use of natural resources, e.g., land, crops, trees, livestock, wetlands, forests, can be common among people in the same area. Would you give use some examples of such problems and disputes in your areas? Please tell us what was the problem, who was involved? What were the reasons? How have the people tried to address the conflict? How were problems resolved? What was accomplished? What were the consequences or damages caused?"

We interviewed 203 farmers in 16 villages and found that almost all the farmers have been involved in conflict over the use and management of natural resources in one way or another. About 43% of farmers have experienced at least one to three conflicts, whereas the majority (55.6%) has experienced more than three conflicts. One out of each five households has experienced more than seven conflicts. There was however no significant difference in the number of conflicts reported by men and women (t value = -0.327). The survey inventoried 701 conflict cases. These conflicts are multifaceted, multidimensional, and multi scale, involving a variety of stakeholders and resource users ranging from intra-household and supra-household gender relations, property rights disputes to antagonist, distrustful relationships, and violent clashes amongst and between farmers, local communities, government, and external institutions.

These conflicts can however be grouped into three broad categories: community-level conflicts opposing farmers within same communities; intercommunity conflicts opposing different communities or farmers from neighboring villages, and supra-community conflicts opposing farmers and communities with higher-level formal institutions or individuals. The most common type of intra-community-level conflicts concerned hillside management, causing destruction of terrace bunds and boundary disputes, which affect over 70% of households. This type of conflict is fuelled by the excessive fragmentation of very small agricultural land, and the high competition over the use of farmland. This increasing competition has also created different types of conflicts related to property rights (43.9%), from competing inheritance claims, illegal sale of land, land grabbing, and other issues of resource ownership and access, destruction of terraces, cutting of trees and theft of resources. More than 74% of households were affected by conflicts arising from animals grazing on field crops.

This type of conflict is more pronounced shortly after the planting season when livestock graze on young plants and trees. Most communal grazing lands have been turned into individual properties and farmland, leaving people with livestock with limited resources for grazing their animals. Other forms of conflicts included bush burning (40%), cutting of trees (43%), and theft of crops, livestock, and farm implements (45%). Competing rights and claims often caused intercommunity conflicts over common pool resources, e.g., wetlands, grazing lands, woodlots, and paths, theft of resources, as well as bush burning. Bush burning often started by herd boys or by farmers as a land preparation practice has caused several conflicts within and among communities, especially during the dry season. In many cases, such fires have been difficult to control and have destroyed property, sometimes even burning houses. In some cases, the competing claims over common-pool resources (CPR) have resulted in violent clashes among farmers and among communities as illustrated in this case:

Farmers from these three neighbouring villages used to graze their animals communally on one hill and valley bottom in this village. However, these grazing lands deteriorated quickly and could not sustain all the animals that kept on increasing in numbers. The village council met and decided to restrict grazing lands to residents of this village. Farmers from the other two villages did not comply, and this has always resulted in violent clashes and endless disputes. Efforts to resolve this conflict have involved community leaders, local council (LC1) members of the three villages, and even the sub-county authorities, but these clashes continue every dry season, and people have lost animals and property.

There has also been escalation of different types of supra-community conflicts. These are grouped into four main types: Conflicts over protected areas and parks oppose local community concerns for livelihoods and national and international concerns for environment and biodiversity conservation- Most of these conflicts were confined to areas around the Bwindi Impenetrable National Park, and opposed park authorities to communities living around the park. These were of two particular forms: crops that destroy wildlife and property, and people's encroachment on park resources. Crop raiding by wildlife was reported as a major form of conflict contributing to the hostility between local communities and the park authority. These animals, especially baboons and bush pigs, usually leave the park and destroy crops planted by farmers surrounding the park. These types of conflicts affect over 70% of farm households with farmland bordering the park in Ikumba, causing considerable crop losses.

Encroachment on wetlands, forests, and protected areas- Although government agencies involving international actors restrict the use of such resources, e.g., wetlands, woodlots, forests, and associated resources, local communities consider them as common-pool resources with many opportunities for their livelihoods. Conflicts between different government policies and agencies over authority to regulate natural resource management, e.g., district agricultural office, environment, forest, and health departments. These conflicts are often caused by uncoordinated sectoral policies and regulations. Conflicts among local communities and elites, e.g., government authorities, NGOs, rich farmers, over grabbing and eviction from lands, privatization and expropriation of CPRs and trespassing on private property.

The most common type of conflict opposed local communities to the Bwindi Impenetrable National Park (BINP) in Ikumba sub-county. Previously designed as a forest reserve with relatively liberal and rarely reinforced regulations regarding access rights, Bwindi was accorded high protection status in 1991 as a national park and designated a World heritage site since 1994, and was renamed Bwindi Impenetrable National Park. This had immediate effect of closing all access to the forest products by adjacent communities, resulting in huge amounts of conflicts and resentment. The park is surrounded by sloping terrain supporting one of the highest population densities in Uganda.

Role of Social Capital

Over the last decade, the concept of social capital has risen dramatically to become one of the most fertile concepts in social science literature. Some of pioneering scholars of social capital such as Bourdieu, Colleman (1988) and Putman (1993) considered social capital as a resource for action, which is developed and accessed through membership in formal organizations, Putman defined social capital as the features of social organizations such as social networks, social interactions, norms, social trust, and reciprocity, cooperation that facilitate coordination and cooperation and that enable people to act collectively for mutual benefits.

More recent formulations and studies using the concept of social capital build on these principles. Uphoff and Mijayaratna (2000) distinguish between structural and cognitive forms of social capital, refining the notions of shared norms and trust at individual and household levels, and the horizontal and vertical social networks constituting social capital. They define structural social capital as referring to the networks, linkages and practices within and between communities, including membership in formal and informal associations, participation in decision making and the forms of social organization within which networks of relationships are located. In contrast, cognitive social capital refers to the attitudes, values, beliefs, social norms, and behaviours that exist within a community.

The two dimensions relate to a further refinement of the concept of social capital into "bonding," "bridging," and "linking" social capital. Pretty describes bonding social capital as the social cohesion within groups or communities resulting from relationships between people of similar ethnicity, social status and location, based on local ties, trust and shared moral values, reinforced by working together. Bridging social capital refers to the structural relationships and networks which cross social groupings, involving coordination or collaboration with other groups, external associations, mechanisms of social support or information sharing across communities and groups. Linking social capital crosses describes the ability of groups to engage with external agencies, either to draw on useful resources or to influence policies. Linking social capital crosses status, linking poor people and those in positions of influence.

The different aspects and dimensions of social capital determine whether a community can act as a cohesive unit, i.e., bonding, whether people comply with the norms and bylaws, i.e., structural; whether they have links with other community organizations, i.e., bridging, or whether they can access and influence institutions with more power and resources, i.e., linking, for managing natural resources, including conflicts. Results of this study show that farmers use several social capital mechanisms for managing conflicts. Although the specific mechanisms for managing conflicts vary with the conflict type, nature, levels, and stakeholders or actors involved, we found that people generally rely on five general mechanisms to manage conflicts: avoidance, negotiation, and mediation, arbitration, adjudication, and coercion. In many situations however, there is a combination of different resolution mechanisms, some time in synergy or sequence, but sometimes in contradiction and conflicts. These mechanisms correspond to and are activated by different types of social capital.

One of the traditional institutions for managing conflicts is the clan. Traditionally, the basic social organization of the *Bakiga* people of Kabale uses the agnatic lineage structure based on principle of patrilineal descent, which forms the core of social structures and permeates practically every aspect of life. There are several clans in each village, although two or three may be dominant. For example, in Karambo village, there are two dominant clans: *Abagyeri* and *Abarihira*, and four minor clans, *Abaheesi*, *Abanyangabo*, *Abasigi* and *Abakongoro*. In Kagyera, clans in order of size are the *Abayondo*, *Abagunga*, *Abakongwe*, *Abaheesi*, and *Abasigi*. Relationships between clansmen cut across neighbourhoods. We found that 34% of conflict cases between farmers are handled by clan elders and community members who facilitated negotiation between conflicting parties to reach a mutually agreed decision. From the interviews, it was often reported that:

... There have not been serious (violent) conflicts in the village in the last 15 yr. Simple cases of disagreement with neighbors are solved locally by the elders. Misunderstandings between two people are taken to clan leaders who call four to six people as witnesses, to mediate the case and reach a decision. Usually what is decided is respected. If not, the cases are referred to the local councils (LCs) for arbitration. Avoidance was often used when the conflict is trivial or of passing importance. The desire to avoid confrontation outweighs the need to bring conflicts into public domain. Interviews with a male farmer better capture such cases:

This woman... has been planting her sorghum in my farm without my permission for two seasons. The first time I allowed her to harvest her sorghum. The following season she went back and planted beans and now she is planting sorghum again. I have asked her to find another place to farm but she has refused. She is a widow and has no one to help her. If I take the case to the LC1, they will decide against her. I am just being patient hoping the woman may reform but she is not reforming. Maybe I will now take the case to the LC1 if she continues for six months. But I will see...

However, in a considerable number of cases (30%), bonding social capital mechanisms, e.g., clan leaders, neighbors, relatives, village members, are perceived as having lower capacity for resolving conflicts, as most cases taken to them are often unresolved and often require intervention of other institutions for arbitration. The main factor of this distrust is lack of power to improve sanctions. There is nothing clan elders and relatives can do to ensure that those who break the rules are punished. A combination of social, economic, and political factors has undermined the ability of local mechanisms, clan elders and community organizations to manage conflicts.

Also the more educated and wealthier farmers are not willing to accept decisions by local communities and clan elders and prefer to take their cases to government institutions at higher levels for arbitration rather than mediation and negotiation within the village. Other problems included biases, corruption and laxity of clan leaders. Although there are no financial costs associated with local mechanisms for resolving conflicts, a considerable number of farmers perceived local mechanisms as being biased.

This perception was particularly significant for women compared to men, corroborating women's perceptions that local mechanisms are biased against them. Indeed most conflict cases involving women, or opposing women to their husbands' relatives are seldom resolved in women's favor, as illustrated by this woman's case:

When my husband died, my brothers-in-law wanted to take our land and cows because I had five daughters and only one small boy. I pleaded with them that I needed the property to raise the children. They were only interested in the land, but not the welfare of their brothers' children. I appealed to the clan elders, but they were in favor of their relatives (my brothers-in-law). My own relatives, neighbors and friends also tried to mediate, but the clan elders still decided to give the land to my brothers-in-law. Then I had no choice but take the case to the village local council (LC1). The LC1 leaders knew the background of the case as many of them were already involved in mediation and reconciliation attempts. They ruled in my favor, allowing me to continue using the land until my son becomes an adult to decide. But they also decided that I couldn't dispose of this land, or rent it, or exchange it with a more fertile land near the house. My brothers-in-law are not happy and they don't talk to or visit us.

In some other cases, conflicts between clan members or with other farmers emerged and become increasingly public, developing gradually and or rapidly because of a few significant events. In such cases, the capacities of clan leaders to resolve conflict become inappropriate, and conflicting parties take their cases to other social structures within the community. We also found that farmers' groups, and particularly women's groups have relatively high capacity to resolve conflicts and most cases are resolved through mediation and negotiation. Farmers' groups usually have high levels of structural social capital, e.g., trust and cooperation, norms and rules within groups, as well as bridging social capital, i.e., capacity of groups making links with other groups, and linking with the LC system.

Since a considerable proportion of farmers belong to several groups, such groups have the advantage of facilitating mediation and negotiation, a voluntary process in which conflict parties meet to reach mutually acceptable decisions, and seek to create a win-win outcome. However, this is most effective when conflicts oppose people belonging to the same group. For example, in Habugarama village, i.e., about 55 households, we identified about 10 local groups and organizations ranging from labor parties, credit and savings groups, pig rearing, farming groups, swamp association, to "Determined women," a drumming and singing group, mothers' unions, church-based groups, etc. This high density of local organizations suggests a relatively high level of social capital with a stronger capacity for managing conflicts.

However, although some communities have long been known to manage their natural resources conflicts effectively, recent years have seen the emergence of strict regulations or policies for sustainable management of natural resources. The decentralization process has established the local councils at village levels who concentrate both political and administrative powers to manage community life, including arbitrating disputes, making byelaws and enforcing government policies. A considerable number of farmers believed that a strong enforcement mechanism is the only way to prevent and resolve conflicts: "A Bakiga nibategyekwa kifuba" The Bakiga people are stubborn. Many conflicts were resolved through arbitration, taking the case to lower levels of local government, LC1, who facilitate negotiation between parties and renders a decision. The LC1 has power to impose decisions and sanctions on the people.

Results show that many of the NRM bylaws were perceived as being effective in preventing and resolving conflicts. About 40% of conflict cases were resolved through arbitration by local government village council members who are empowered by the Local Government Act to resolve disputes and conflicts. There are also some cases of conflicts, which were resolved through adjudication. We inventoried about 79 land related conflicts involving a variety of stakeholders. These involved conflicting and overlapping claims over land, including inheritance rights, land grabbing, and criminal trespass.

The main outcomes of adjudication have been imposing fines (67.8%) to the offenders, and imprisonment of offenders, i.e., 10 cases. Results concur with the observations of Means et al. (2002) that the court mechanisms are intimidating and inaccessible to the majority of farmers, especially women and the poor, who are often uneducated and live far from the magistrate courts at the sub-county and district headquarters. The judicial language and administrative procedures used in these courts are also alien to farmers. The time to resolve conflicts, administrative procedures, and other socioeconomic and political barriers also prevent farmers from resolving their conflicts using this channel.

Limits of Social Capital

One important finding from this study is that social capital mechanisms were not effective for managing conflicts between local communities and external powerful stakeholders. There are some disadvantages and limitations of different conflict management mechanisms. In most conflict cases opposing local communities to park authorities and to government structures, the use of force and coercion including harassment, physical assault, intimidation, fines and imprisonment, was most common. Several cases and narratives confirm that the park authorities impose heavy fines for any encroachment on the park resources. On the other hand, although farmers have reported such conflicts to local councils (LCs), they are often left unresolved. In many cases the park authorities used coercion as a mechanism to resolve conflicts, imposing their will through the use of force, exerting unequal power relation. The conflict is exacerbated by the lack of clear mechanisms of compensation and conflict resolution.

There are unclear provisions in the Wildlife Statue and Local Government Act and uncertainties over who should deal with such conflicts as well as reluctance from Park authorities to consider the option of culling the animals. As a result of their frustrations and anger, farmers have also resorted to some forms of violence like setting fires to the park. Interviews with key informants confirmed Bloomley's report that about sixteen fires were started in and around the park by local residents with deliberate intent of destroying the park. The closure of the park to surrounding communities immediately resulted in violent escalation of conflicts between local communities and park staff. In such supra-community conflict situations, the extent of linking social capital, that is the vertical relations between organizations, institutions, and communities and links with external and formal organizations, should become important in resolving conflicts. Kabale is arguably one of the districts where there is a high concentration of research and development organizations working on various dimensions of common-pool resources (CPR) and natural resource management (NRM) issues.

For example, villages in Ikumba appeared to be well covered by external organizations (94%) followed by Rubaya (81%) and Bubare (57%). The high concentration of development organizations in Kabale is mainly related to increasing concerns of environment conservation and protection of natural parks and forest reserves. Some of the international organizations have been facilitating community conservation initiatives, including conflict management. Bloomley (2003) provides an account of CARE-Development through Conservation (DTC) project attempts to manage park conflicts through mediation and negotiation between local development interests of resource poor households and the national and international interests of environment and biodiversity conservation. Although there have been some cases of successful arbitration and negotiation, the unequal power relation between the local communities and national and international stakeholders has often meant that conflicts are resolved through coercion.

He found that there is an inequitable sharing of conservation costs and benefits between different stakeholders. Conservation costs are borne by marginalized poor households adjacent to the park, whereas the benefits are enjoyed by wealthier tourists in the global community and national and international level stakeholders. Revenue sharing scheme between the park and local communities remains an issue of conflict, in particular contested by local government. We also found that in many cases, the adjudication process combined different mechanisms of conflict resolution in a complex fashion, and involved different actors at different levels. Some conflicts taken to the higher levels are referred back to the LC1 for more effective resolution mechanisms. In a significant number of cases, we found a positive synergy between social capital and local policy institutions or administrative procedures for resolving conflicts, as illustrated by James' case, a male farmer in Rubaya:

James had a problem with his brother who was trying to use force to grab land from him on the basis that he was the eldest son and had worked on the land with their father. They went to the elders who found the brother guilty, but the brother did not accept the verdict and decided to go to the Grade two magistrates. The magistrate referred the case back to the LC1 and village leaders. The LC1 and village leaders still ruled in favor of James. The brother was not satisfied and decided to take the case to the district court in Kabale where he could use money to win the case. He then sold that land. Subsequently he suffered some misfortunes and suspected his brother had bewitched him. He finally came back to the clan elders and village leaders to ask for reconciliation with James. He was fined and forced to give another piece of land to James...

The results of the study showed that a range of conflict minimizing strategies flow from different types and combinations of social capital and local polices. There is evidence that farmers and communities use a plurality of strategies, processes and avenues to resolve conflicts, and create checks and balances that a single conflict management system cannot generate. Social capital mechanisms have certainly a number of strengths and have been effective in a number of cases. For example, bridging and structural social capital as expressed in the density of farmers' groups, and particularly women's groups, have a relatively higher capacity to resolve conflicts as most cases are resolved through mediation and negotiation within these groups.

The study also shows that social capital mechanisms have some limits, and were not always effective in resolving certain types of conflicts. This is not surprising with respect to bonding social capital, given the characteristics of this capital. In fact, bonding social capital can be coercive and often leads to homophily. Thus, there is a need for bridging and linking social capital as well as policy interventions. Many conflicts were resolved through arbitration and adjudication at different levels of local government. The village local council (LC1), which is the lower level of decentralization, was perceived as the most effective in resolving conflicts. Conflicts taken to the LC1 are usually resolved through arbitration and mediation, involving other community leaders. However, this confidence decreased significantly as one moves higher up the ladder to the LC2 and LC3, which are more remote and distant to community social relations. At these levels, adjudication and coercion are generally used, and many farmers perceived the process as being biased and not equitable.

There is substitution and exclusion of social capital mechanisms by policy structures. Many of these formal conflict resolution mechanisms often have a high social cost for local communities, especially to women and other vulnerable groups, who end up taking the burden of paying fines and other forms of social exclusion and coercion. Often, low levels of linking social capital and dysfunctional policies led to rampant conflicts. In many cases, there was substitution and exclusion of social capital mechanisms by formal administrative and political structures. Results show that policies or social capital alone do not possess the resources needed to promote broad-based and sustainable conflict resolution strategies. Rather, when local policies and social capital were combined in a positive sum way, as in the case of LC system, conflicts were likely to be minimized.

We therefore suggest the "synergy approach" of social capital and local policy for managing conflicts. The synergy between local policies and social capital is based on complementarities and embededness. Complementarity refers to mutually supportive relations between public and private actors, local government, and local communities and is exemplified in the decentralization framework that links state institutions to local communities in Uganda. Embededness refers to the nature and extent of the ties connecting people and communities and public institutions. With recent decentralization efforts in Uganda, the village local council is embedded in social relations and hence may be under pressure by the community to perform and be responsive to them. The LC is also seen as complementary to traditional mechanisms for resolving conflicts. In the same vein, farmers groups and clan elders have been assisting the LC1 in arbitration and mediation of conflicts.

However, this synergy may only work where there are high levels of social capital and well functioning government policies that are coherent and credible. Where there are high levels of social capital, communities have the ability to develop coping mechanisms to deal with conflicts. Conversely, as shown in the cases of supra-community conflicts, where there are low levels of linking social capital and dysfunctional policies, conflicts tend to become of high intensity and violent. Exclusion, coercion and violence are the mechanisms used to manage such conflicts. Better understanding of how synergy between social capital and local policy can be strengthened is crucial to promote alternative conflict management mechanisms. Formal policy and informal social capital mechanisms work best when, through redistributive, integrative and capacity building measures, they strengthen the capabilities of stakeholders to enter into voluntary negotiation and mutually beneficial collective action to resolve conflicts.

The tasks of research should therefore be to determine how the positive manifestations of social capital, e.g., cooperation, trust, norms, and institutional efficiency, can enhance the formulation and implementation of bylaws and rectify dysfunctional policies, and how local policies can strengthen community mechanisms for conflict prevention and resolution. Promoting a positive synergy between social capital and policy requires participatory social learning processes and more integrative policy processes that strengthen and build social and human capital to transform NRM conflicts into opportunities for mutually beneficial collective action for sustainable livelihoods. As noted by Evans 1996 and Tendler 1997, successfully participatory projects have frequently depended upon a creative synergy between state policy and civil society.

3

The Role of Pre-existing and Evolving Social Institutions

This chapter, focusing on the Sungusungu justice system of Tanzania as an example, describes an informal institution of social control that emerged in response to weak law enforcement by the state. Using ethnographic data and secondary sources, the author highlights the importance of considering both the cultural histories of different ethnic groups, as well as more recent changes that continue to modify social institutions among various groups and communities. In this case, particular ethnic groups were differentially prepared to generate and sustain Sungusungu organizations. However, variable social forces continue to change ethnic-specific social institutions, and in some regions, certain communities are more prepared than others to sustain prosocial organizational behaviour.

Theoretically, the article challenges the assumption that individual agency (self-interest and power) commonly dominates the sometimes conservative nature of institutions. From an applied perspective, this case study, along with comparative data, illustrates that organizations require cultural rules to define goals and sustain effective actions. One must recognize that these sets of cultural rules are often found among particular populations, and efforts to spread them can be a slow process.

An understanding of these conservative cultural processes are important to policy makers and applied scholars attempting to understand, control, or harness the public goods produced by grass-roots social movements and organizations. Anthropologists have described numerous ways that people organize informal institutions of social control. Some groups rely more on personal and family honor to protect their property and interests, whereas others act collectively across a wider social scale to provide the publicly beneficial good of law-and-order. Such informal institutions are especially important when state provisioning of law and order is weak or corrupt; to protect themselves, individuals and groups provide their own mechanisms of order. In this chapter, I discuss a particularly strong non-state system of justice in Tanzania, East Africa that originally emerged among the Sukuma and Nyamwezi ethnic groups. The organizations were called Sungusungu (possibly because of their similarity to biting black ants found in Tanzania), but are known by the Sukuma as basalama, or "people of peace." Like extra-legal organizations found in other parts of the world, the Sukuma were unable to rely on the state to protect property and resolve disputes.

With state corruption, as well as weak resources to provide adequate services to the vast rural areas of Tanzania, informal organizations of social control emerged as an institutional or cultural adaptation to provide protection and resolve disputes. In contrast to many other non-state justice organizations, Sungusungu organizations with institutionalized rules provide order not only within small communities, but also to a number of different ethnic groups across vast regions of Tanzania. It is a testimony to the success of Sungusungu that the state legitimized the informal system, and made the organizations part of the national justice system (albeit with some reservations) following favorable support by many of Tanzania's socialist leaders. Thus, although the Sungusungu have been compared to vigilante organizations from the 19th century American West, the system may be more adequately categorized as a quasi-national justice system. With attention to institutional rules, and dynamic patterns of Sungusungu emergence, I illustrate below how cultural evolutionary processes have shaped, and continue to shape, the organizational behaviour of Sungusungu.

Substantial evidence from my field research and from other published studies illustrates that the dynamic nature of Sungusungu is partly explained by the ongoing cultural evolution of ethnic-specific social institutions. With pre-existing institutions similar to Sungusungu, the Sukuma quickly created and spread the justice organizations to even distant migrant populations. However, variation in local custom and "tradition" among communities influences variable behaviour among different Sungusungu organizations. From a theoretical perspective, this chapter posits that although culture and social institutions often change quickly, and individuals with variable amounts of resources and power can ignore or change institutional rules, institutions are often conservative social forces that constrain human action. From an applied perspective, this study highlights the importance of institutional "matches" between pre-existing and future institutional arrangements; self-help and other types of organizations function best when groups can build off preexisting institutional resources. In addition, the erosion of "traditional" institutions may lead to variation in the effectiveness of organizational behaviour.

The Sukuma implemented Sungusungu as a hierarchical justice system to protect cattle and other property. The combination of a weak state with an influx of newly armed and unemployed men following the war with Uganda in 1979 led to intolerable cattle rustling rates. Starting in the early 1980s, and using charismatic leadership, one or two villages in the Kahama district of northern Tanzania organized villagers into a rank-and-file hierarchy to locate and punish cattle rustlers.

The organizations soon began to monitor and punish other types of social violations such as adultery, debt disputes, and theft. As discussed below, the Sukuma had pre- existing social institutions that provided the foundation for the structure of Sungusungu. Thus, with pre-existing social capital, the organizations spread rapidly from village to village as members indoctrinated and socialized villagers into the new system. Within a year, the Sungusungu had spread to migrant Sukuma populations living in distant regions such as Rukwa where this research was conducted.

Modeled after the Modern

Tanzanian political system introduced by the British, and possibly the national army, Sungusungu subordinate and leadership positions were created at the village, ward, division, district, and regional political levels. At the village level, the Sungusungu are organized by an elected central leadership controlling subordinate lower ranks, with overarching influence from both a secret council and all the organizational members.

The highest-ranking leadership positions include a chief (ntemi), followed by a chairman (mwenyekiti). The chief is expected to use his knowledge of divination to protect those under his command and to identify suspected deviants. The chairman is usually a charismatic public speaker able to effectively lead public meetings, as well as control members when heated disputes occur. Although ranked below the chief and chairman, a secretary (katibu) holds a highly respected position.

The secretary is responsible for documenting in writing the names of people who attend meetings, the details of civil and criminal complaints, and the outcomes of cases and punishments.

The secretary plays a vital role in documenting all organizational business to ensure that members abide by the rules and those transgressors pay their fines. Younger males who are expected to track down cattle thieves and other deviants hold the subordinate ranks of the Sungusungu. In addition they have the duty of finding witnesses for ongoing cases, and delivering organizational information to often distant chapters.

These young Sungusungu "soldiers" or "guards" (askari) are led by higher ranked commanders. In each village, local commanders, under the guidance of one grand commander, are in charge of the young males in approximately ten nearby households. Although the leadership has central power in the village organizations, a dozen or more council members (wajumbe) secretly work with the leaders to hear cases involving thievery and other deviations. Each member is expected to attend meetings involving case arbitration, elections, and discussion of Sungusungu activities.

In addition, every Sungusungu member has voice in the organization, and cases that cannot be resolved in the secret committees are opened up for discussion in a public forum among all the organizational members. Elsewhere I discuss the democratic structure of Sungusungu, and how even the lowest ranking members are constantly monitoring and evaluating organizational leaders. The Sungusungu positions governing higher political units (ward, division, district, region) include chiefs, chairmen, and secretaries, as well as secret councils. These political bodies are responsible for oversight of village-level chapters, as well as dealing with larger political and social problems.

With oversight and coordination of various political units, the Sungusungu have effectively replicated a state-like justice system. I conducted ethnographic research in the villages of Mirumba and Kibaoni in the Rukwa region of southwestern Tanzania. The area sits in the western Rift Valley adjacent to the escarpment of the Fipa plateau. The region has a wet season running from early December through April, and receives an average of 600-900 mm of annual rainfall. The area is potentially an important food-producing region for Tanzania, but some ethnic groups in the region experience food shortages. The Pimbwe, the native ethnic group in the area, are small-scale maize horticulturalists. However, their traditional part-time subsistence strategy of hunting large and small game has been substantially curtailed following the implementation of Katavi National Game Reserve in the 1950s and by decline of wildlife populations outside of the reserve.

Historically, the Pimbwe governed themselves with loosely linked clans controlled by a chief in a central village. Overall, there was little need for extensive large-scale cooperation, and their institutions remained strongest within village and clan polities.

A substantial number of Fipa (an ethnic group from the nearby Fipa plateau) also live among the Pimbwe, but often in secluded settlements on the outskirts of the densely settled Pimbwe villages. The Fipa are linguistically and culturally similar to the Pimbwe in many aspects, and for purposes here, are considered together, and contrasted with the Sukuma. Today the Pimbwe are faced with food shortages, especially during the season before harvest, and many individuals have turned to heavy drinking of locally brewed beer and distilled spirits. Pimbwe are often employed as cultivation laborers by migrant Sukuma who arrived in their area in the early 1970s, and many individuals express envy and anger towards the Sukuma migrants. Witchcraft remains an important concern for Pimbwe, and in combination with food insecurity, envy of wealthier immigrant groups, and disease, there is general mistrust within Pimbwe villages. Sukuma agro-pastoralists have migrated from Shinyanga and Mwanza in large numbers to many regions in Tanzania, including the Rukwa region.

The Sukuma live outside of the Pimbwe villages in large extended households, and often cultivate large amounts of maize, sweet potatoes, millet, and rice. In addition, many Sukuma households have a few dozen cattle, and some have large herds numbering in the thousands. In comparison to the Pimbwe and Fipa, the Sukuma have social institutions that operate on much larger scales. Historically, the Sukuma lived in a multiple chiefdom system in which local chiefs controlled large areas but also cooperated with distant chiefs. The Sukuma also had powerful organizations and clubs at the village level, which may have facilitated the adoption of State-sponsored agricultural cooperatives. The Sukuma are easy to identify in the study area with their distinctive jewelry, black capes, and sometimes gaudy dress patterns. Finally, the Sukuma are renowned by Tanzanian citizens for their generosity, and anthropologists have written about how Sukuma mothers socialize generosity in their young children. Sukuma generosity, and propensity to share money with ethnic members, was substantiated in a study using methods developed by experimental economists. Given the choice to divide real money with another ethnic member, Sukuma on average gave away more than half of the money, even to an anonymous individual in a neighboring village. Pimbwe choose to take more of the money for themselves, and substantially smaller portions of money were given to anonymous Pimbwe living in a distant as compared to a local village.

Early ethnographic accounts of Pimbwe and Sukuma provide insights about past institutions of the two groups. However, the processes that have brought the Sukuma and Pimbwe to live in the same environment have also brought changes to the groups. In general, reports from informants support the notion of cultural "decay," or loss of local custom among the Pimbwe. In contrast, the migrant Sukuma may be some of the more "traditional" Sukuma in the county, and such a pattern may influence how their Sungusungu organizations operate. A number of ethnographic observations support the notion of culture change among the Pimbwe. A good example comes from a case in which a pregnant woman died in one of the study villages. Past custom dictated that the fetus be physically removed from the body and that it be buried beside the woman (Craig Hadley, personal communication). However, when it came time to perform the ritual, there was a daylong village debate about if and how such a procedure should be done. In part, the conflict may have resulted from conflict with the rules of the local churches.

However, only a few elders had any knowledge of this custom at all. In another case, my colleague Craig Hadley used Willis's (1966) ethnography to probe people's knowledge of Pimbwe religion and rituals. Most people could name only a few of the Pimbwe Gods. Finally, in day-to-day interviews many Pimbwe complained about their ethnic group's inability to deal with their problems because of the loss of many of their past customs. Concerning Sukuma cultural variation, a national politician explained to me that in his inter-regional travels he was astounded by the differences he observed between the Sukuma in Rukwa region and the Sukuma in northern regions. His comments reflected in general what I observed when traveling within different Tanzanian regions and talking to local Sukuma. The first observation is that Sukuma in Rukwa are more likely to wear gaudy combinations of Western clothes, traditional bracelets, and distinct black capes that symbolize and display their ethnicity and spiritual beliefs.

Next, even the wealthiest Sukuma with large herds of cattle, live in customary mud and thatched houses without modern amenities. Ethnographic observations from the cultural practice of chagulaga—a system of choosing romantic partners—strengthens the hypothesis that Sukuma are more traditional in the study area. Chagulaga occurs after dance competitions and other large gatherings; a number of young males surround a young woman and chase her until she chooses one of the young men for a romantic meeting. Traditionally, this has been a formal marriage market for parents to find husbands for their daughters. Hangaya (1989) discusses chagulaga in Sukumaland, the traditional Sukuma region in northwest Tanzania, where young males now break the rules of the institution by acting extremely aggressively in the ritual and sometimes raping the women. As a result, the Sungusungu in his study area have banned chagulaga due to the decay of the institutional rules preventing violence and rape. In contrast, the institution remains legitimate in my study area, and informants suggest that young males generally abide by the rules or face strong punishments by the Sungusungu.

There are a number of reasons why the Rukwa Sukuma may adhere to past customs in the study area. First, because many Sukuma invest their wealth in cattle, Sukumaland has become environmentally degraded, thus pushing Sukuma to migrate in search of new pastures. The Sukuma that are unwilling to give up their cattle by trading them for other investment opportunities are forced to move. As a result, the migrant Sukuma in Rukwa may be a selective sample of Sukuma holding on to their cattle traditions, and possibly other traditional institutions. Further, similar to Moore's (1977) findings among the Chagga from northern Tanzania, it could be that the wealthy Sukuma have greater opportunity to follow traditional lifestyles. Second, Rukwa is a frontier region with few state or non-government organizational activities bringing development schemes or education programs that might erode Sukuma traditions. Finally, theoretical models suggest that immigrant ethnic groups moving into new areas are likely to generate exaggerated symbolic markers as a consequence of the costs of imitating maladaptive behaviour. Such processes could result in the enhancement and strengthening of Sukuma customs.

Theoretical Perspectives

Experiencing similar problems under a weak state, different Tanzanian ethnic groups and urban populations have not been equally successful in creating and sustaining institutions of social control such as Sungusungu. Thus, I consider why the Sungusungu among the Sukuma have been more successful as compared to attempts by other ethnic groups to generate similar self-help organizations. Further, because Sungusungu is a model for effective provisioning of law-and-order, it is interesting that other groups have been slow to adopt such a system. To explain these patterns, it is first important to conceptualize social institutions as sets of cultural rules that inform individuals about expected behaviour, and what will happen to them if they violate or heroically uphold such rules. With definitions of organizational roles and expectations of behaviour, social institutions are the cultural foundation of various types of organizations.

Similar to other organizations of social control, Sungusungu organizations are guided by sets of primary rules that specify the types of substantive behaviours to be controlled (e.g., theft, debt, and adultery). Further, secondary rules are important in sustaining the organizations by encouraging cooperation. Such rules also specify the procedures for administering punishments and codes of conduct organizational participants must follow. Finally, rules also inform individuals requiring aid from third parties which social controllers (e.g., police or Sungusungu) should be selected. Because cultural rules of social institutions sustain and guide organizations, it is important to consider the forces that generate and change cultural variation. Cultural evolutionary theory elucidates possible mechanisms of cultural change, and generally predicts that culture is sometimes a conservative force that changes on intermediate time scales such as decades or centuries. Generally, because obtaining information is costly, reliance on custom and one's ethnic members is often an adaptive strategy. Such forces generate two important outcomes with respect to institutional change. First, the trajectory of institutional evolution is often path-dependent, and thus, institutions are often modifications from pre-existing institutional arrangements.

Different societies find different ways (with variable effectiveness) to resolve adaptive problems, and such processes lead to variable institutional histories among groups. However, an important finding is that institutions often lag behind ecological or societal changes, and there are abundant examples of new institutions emerging and functioning more effectively among populations that had similar historic institutions. Second, because institutions are comprised of rule sets in which the meaning and benefits may not be clear to others, institutional diffusion between groups may often occur slowly. Sometimes even technological innovations with clear benefits do not readily diffuse among culturally similar individuals. In addition, ethnic boundaries may inhibit individuals from understanding the value of institutions among other ethnic groups because such behaviour may or may not be adaptive in different environments.

Ingroup loyalties can exaggerate ethnic markers, limit social learning between groups, and subsequently inhibit diffusion of institutions between groups. Ultimately, an important goal of social theory is to connect micro and macro forces, and cultural evolutionary theory provides a link between the forces of group-level institutions and individual decision-making. Thus, although I stress in this chapter the importance of cultural lags, I recognize the important force of agency, or individual decision-making and power.

For example, in many cases individuals rely on individual decision-making over social learning, or choose to ignore culturally specific rules and values; institutional systems are ideal types, leaving individuals with varying degrees of power and resources to violate rules or create new rules. However, in other cases (such as making decisions about whom to marry) individuals conform to the behaviour of others, or follow the rules of their group's "traditions" or customs. Although such processes may lead to cultural continuity to some extent, this by no means implies that culture often does not continually evolve. For example, as discussed below, some Sungusungu organizations may be evolving from prosocial civic organizations into profit-seeking protection rackets.

Traditionalism and Sungusungu Behaviour

Sungusungu enthusiasm is very high in the study area, and one possible explanation for the high effort of Sungusungu in Rukwa—despite lower direct payoffs received from punishing cattle raiders and thieves—is that the traditional Sukuma maintain Sungusungu for cultural as well as for utilitarian reasons. In other words, the institution is important to Sukuma because they believe Sungusungu is an important part of their lifestyle, regardless of the direct need to punish deviants.

It is worth considering the degree to which Sukuma traditionalism in Rukwa helps explain differences in Sungusungu behaviour in areas that may be less traditional. First, a greater degree of reliance on traditional customs may reduce interpersonal and intergenerational conflict, and possibly increase the degree to which young males respect elders. One important source of conflict between generations is how Sungusungu's organizational procedures function to collect and retain fines. The organizations often obtain numerous cattle and money from fines, and an important part of the institution is how to use this wealth. Bukurura (1994) discusses tense conflict between young and older males in northern Tanzania, an area with more modernization and possibly less traditionalism.

The conflict occurs because older members prefer to use fines to buy beer and food, instead of saving the money in the organizational bank, as is preferred by younger members. The Sungusungu in Rukwals conflict over how to use the fines, but compromise by allocating one cow to a feast, and one to the bank. They would tease the elders about why they were so addicted to eating beef and drinking beer, but generally did not push the issue very far. When asked about this topic, many of my informants explained that little intergenerational conflict occurs. A second influence of traditional customs is the degree to which the Sungusungu organizations uphold the interests of their members (and non-members) as a whole, or use their powers to extort citizens and privately sell their services of protection. Gambetta (1993) describes how mafia organizations provide the service of protection and dispute resolution, but actively seeks business by creating distrust between potential clients.

Further, they actively extort payments and use violence against those not under their "protection." In contrast to Mafias, the Sungusungu generally provide public goods across a wide social scope because of ethnic and interethnic cooperation and trust. However, the decay of institutional rules may result in the emergence of less pro-social Sungusungu organizations seeking only profit for their services. Such a change could alter how public goods are distributed, and the modern Sungusungu that generally produce effective public policing could evolve into Mafia-style organizations seeking private payment. For example, in the study area, informants stress that soldiers are not allowed to resolve disputes themselves—disputants must bring their cases to Sungusungu. In addition, the council determines

Sungusungu fines, with the decisions monitored by the community as a whole, thus reducing the likelihood that a few individuals can exploit the power of Sungusungu for their own interests.

Many Tanzanian ethnic have experienced crime problems, but have not yet been successful in adopting Sungusungu. Groups such as the Kuria quickly reverted to their clan systems to protect their cattle after a brief attempt to adopt Sungusungu. Various Tanzanian societies use different types of institutions to control social deviants, and adopting the institutional rules of Sungusungu is problematic for them. However, over time, individuals from non-Sukuma ethnic groups have joined the Sungusungu, and their gradual participation may reflect the slow process associated with learning institutional rules, especially when ethnic conflict exists. Theorists highlighting the importance of human agency are troubled by the idea of cultural "traditions" and cultural continuity. '

However, cultural evolutionary theory incorporates the power of individual decision-making and agency as well as the notion that individuals rely somewhat on shared cultural patterns when solving individual and collective problems. In sum, social institutions involve flexibility and change, but they also lead to conservative outcomes; various ethnic groups will be guided in part by their institutional history and will often be slow to adopt institutional innovations invented by other groups.

Finally, this essay is applicable for applied anthropologists who often work in formal bureaucratic settings. First, non-governmental self-help organizations will be difficult to generate unless institutional precursors are in place. Attention to a group's cultural history will provide some insights into the types of institutions that will emerge among different groups. Further, because of cultural evolutionary processes, an organization may continue to function and evolve even when its original goals have been secured. Second, the institutions that support organizations are likely to diffuse slowly across cultural boundaries, especially when "outgroup" prejudice and conflict inhibit the transmission of information.

Lastly, because cultural rules influence the behaviour of organizations, and such rules continually evolve and change, organizations will vary with respect to prosocial outcomes. In the case at hand, the Sungusungu of Rukwa function as an effective and legitimate social control institution that can benefit most individuals in the region. However, with changes in customs, these organizations could become more predatory, similar to Mafia-style organizations that seem to be emerging among some northern Tanzania groups. Ultimately, it is important for individuals from both theoretical and applied backgrounds to pay attention to the cultural evolutionary processes associated with the dynamics of organizations; culture, sometimes changing rapidly, and sometimes slowly, alters the degree to which people are able to solve their own problems.

Non-linear Dynamics of Meaning-Processing in Social Systems

The social phenomenon of meaning can be modeled. Meaning can be understood as holding current value as well as an *anticipation* of possible futures. Rosen (1985) defined anticipatory systems as systems that contain a model of themselves. The modeling part advances on the modeled one and provides meaning to the latter from the perspective of hindsight. The time axis of the historical process can thus locally be inverted within a system. The modeling system can also be considered as a semantic domain in which historical developments can be appreciated and provided with value. From a biological perspective, Maturana (1978) distinguished between a first-order "consensual" domain in which organisms interact recursively, and a second-order one "within the confines of a consensual domain" in which organisms are additionally able to observe one another and provide one another's actions with interpretations. Such a domain would be "indistinguishable from a semantic domain".

From this (biological) perspective, "language" would make it possible to recombine components of historically generated consensual behaviour into the generation of new consensual behaviour. Meaning would in this case be constituted by the exchange, and a next-order *social* system with its own dynamics would be shaped. Luhmann (1984) built his sociological theory on this next step by considering the *communication* of meaning as the operator of social systems: meaning is the medium of social systems and communication the operator.

Meaning is selectively used and reproduced by communication. Thus, meaning is not merely generated and positioned as in a semantic domain, but can again be communicated using a dynamics which is proper to the social system and potentially different from those of individuals. The social system not only contains a model of itself, but the model can also be entertained within the system, for example, in a discourse. In biological systems, meaning is processed as wear and tear along the time axis in accordance with the "natural" (life) cycle of the system. In social systems, specific meanings can be stabilized, for example in social institutions, but all meaning generated in inter-human communication arises with reference to a global horizon of possible meanings.

These cultural horizons of meaning can also change historically, as Weber noted in 1904:

At one moment or another, the colour will change: the meaning of the perspective which was used without reflection will become uncertain; the road seems now to lead into zones of twilight. The light of the important problems of culture has gone beyond. (...) Science follows the constellations which make it a meaningful enterprise. Whereas this selection between the system and its environment is determined and therefore fixed in biological systems (e.g., by assuming natural selection), a non-linear dynamics of meaning-processing can be generated when this selection mechanism is considered as another degree of freedom in the communications between the system and its environment.

When three sub dynamics operate upon one another, all kinds of chaotic behaviour can be generated. Thus, the emergence of social order can no longer be taken for granted, but needs always to be explained. In other words, the social system can be expected to evolve as a non-trivial machine *because* it contains a non-linear dynamics of meaning.

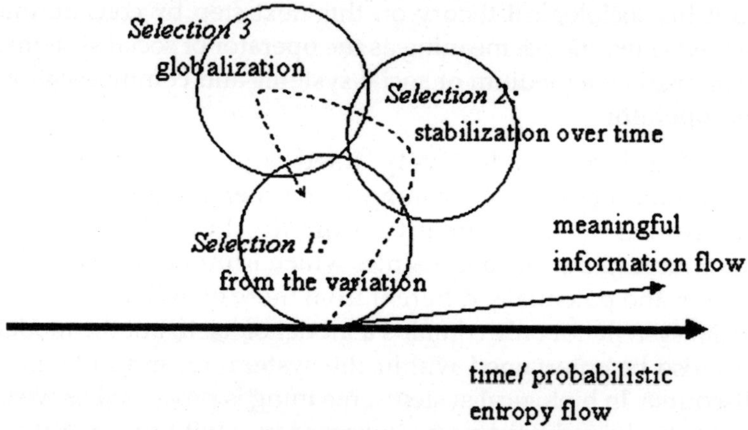

Figure 3.1: Three Selections Cycle in the Case of Processing Meaning on Top of the Information Flow.

The dashed arrow in Figure given above indicates the resulting dynamics. The cycle may have a direction feeding backward or forward on the time axis, since the three selections can be expected to operate without *a priori* coordination. For example, selections in the present on the variation operate at the same time as selections from global horizons of meaning. However, one can expect that the results of the three sub dynamics will be different, since selections operate asymmetrically.

Furthermore, the selections can operate upon each other: some selections can be mad for stabilization, while other are selected for globalization. Selection mechanisms may thus co-evolve in a process of "mutual shaping." A third selection mechanism can be expected to disturb such mutual shaping by adding another source of uncertainty. In the case of biological systems, this third selection mechanism is determined as "natural" selection, and thus would drive the aging of the system. In Luhmann's social systems theory, the globalizing horizons of meaning tend to remain unspecified otherwise than with reference to Husserl's transcendental phenomenology.

The three selection mechanisms have in common that meaning is provided from the perspective of hindsight and can therefore be modeled using incursive equations. Incursive equations—to be explained below—invert the time axis by appreciating the past from the perspective of the present. Leydesdorff & Dubois (2004) have shown that the incursive formulation of the logistic equation can be used to model interaction and aggregation in inter-human communication. Interaction and aggregation can be considered as the building blocks of social systems of communication because:

- Interaction is recursive (that is, interactions can operate on previous interactions),
- Interactive processes can be aggregated, and
- Aggregations can interact.

In this chapter, I attempt to formulate how these building blocks can be organized into the architecture of a social system. How can the cycle of meaning processing be closed as a feedback loop upon the linear movement of the entropy flux? First, I generalize the model—that is, the incursive formulation of the logistic equation—for the case of differentiated structures of meaning-processing at the supra-individual level.

Secondly, I specify a hyper-incursive mechanism of anticipation as yet another possibility in a system which contains more than a single mechanism for anticipation. The hyper-incursive mechanism interacts with the incursive anticipations and makes historical decisions unavoidable. One can expect the resulting system to be *strongly* anticipatory. Unlike weakly anticipatory systems—which entertain a model of themselves—strongly anticipatory ones cannot provide predictions because these systems use expectations for the construction of their future states.

Incursion

A self-referential system can be considered as a function of itself and its environment. Baecker (2002, at p. 86) proposed modeling such a system using the following equation:

$$S = f(S, E)$$

However, the environment is only relevant for a self-referential system as its carrying capacity; the environment sets limits to growth. This specific relation between the development of a system and its environment can be modeled using the logistic equation as follows:

$$x_{t+1} = ax_t(1 - x_t)$$

The carrying capacity of the selection environment (1 – *xt*) inhibits further growth of the system as a feedback term. For relatively small values of the parameter *a* (1 < *a* < 3), this generates the well-known sigmoid curves of systems which grow and undergo transitions. For larger values of *a*, the model bifurcates into an oscillation (at *a* e" 3) or increasingly generates chaos (3.57 < *a* < 4).

Unlike this biological (e.g., population-dynamic) model which operates with the arrow of time pointing forward, meaning is provided in the present with hindsight. This can be modeled using the same equation, but with different time parameters as follows:

$$x_{t+1} = ax_t(1 - x_{t+1})$$

In this case, the system builds on its previous state, but the current state provides the selection environment. Without any addition, Equation 3 can analytically be reorganized into Equation 4 as follows:

$$x_{l+1} = ax_t(1 - x_t)$$

This system cannot generate chaotic phenomena because it converges into a stable state for all values of the parameter (*a*). Because incursion provides us with a model of a historically developing system, one is able to generate an observer in the simulation who reflexively follows the development of the observed system. The challenge, however, remains the construction of an observing system which is able to predict developments in the complex system under observation.

Longitudinal and Transversal Incursion

All systems which entertain a model of themselves can provide meaning to the modeled system with hindsight, that is, by inverting the time axis locally. I shall call this the "longitudinal" generation of meaning, which will be distinguished below from the "transversal" generation of meaning. Transversal meaning can only be generated by systems which stabilize different codes for providing meaning. Thus, these systems can be expected to contain more than a single meaning. Furthermore, transversally generated meaning can again be provided with longitudinally generated meaning: the time axis stands perpendicular to the differentiation. In other words, the system spans a multidimensional space that develops over time.

Meanings may vary at each moment of time, but differently codified meanings can be stabilized only in systems that are *functionally* differentiated in terms of the codes of communication. The functionality of the differentiation means that the system is able to use the differentiation among the codes for its reproduction. By using the codes, events can then be appreciated differently within the system. Here, Luhmann's (1984) contribution becomes particularly valuable because he argued—following Parsons (1951)—that functional differentiation is prevalent in *modern* societies. He added that the differentiation should be considered as a differentiation of the symbolically generalized media of communication, that is, of next-order codification structures.

Parsons (1967a and b) introduced "symbolic generalization" to explain the sometimes binding character of collective action. His concept remained close to Weber's concept of values, except that the values are not given; symbolic generalization would function as a mechanism to integrate the social system despite the structural differences within it (caused by functional differentiation). Using money as the model of an exchange medium, Parsons (1967a and b) extended this concept to include power and influence as other exchange media that can be generalized symbolically. Luhmann (1975) elaborated on Parsons's concept by considering power, etc., as codes of communication, each of which can be generalized under the condition of functional differentiation. In a previous, hierarchical, order the different media were subsumed under each other: for example, the Holy Roman Emperor had to go to Canossa because the Pope had eventually the power to "excommunicate" him.

Under the condition of modernity, exchange systems can develop according to their own logic, and thus science, politics, the economy, affection, etc., can further develop their specific codes of communication along (nearly) orthogonal axes. Symbolic generalization implies that every event can be assessed from the specific perspective of each code of communication. For example, everything can be assessed in terms of its economic value or its esthetic beauty, and these assessments do not have to correspond because they are coded differently. Assessments using codes can be considered as events that can be assessed using different perspectives. How do the assessments assess one another using different codes? For example, technologies which develop in generations over time have to compete for markets in the present. The markets code the technologies in terms of prices or price/performance relations, while engineers code the technologies according to professional standards. Thus, two codes of communication are operating simultaneously: the prices on markets and the professional coding expressed in engineering textbooks. The markets select in the present among the technologies which are developing over time.

This can again be modeled using the incursive formulation of the logistic equation (Equation 3 above) because the development of the technology contains both a reference to a previous state of this technology (*i*) and a reference to a current state, but in a different subsystem of society (e.g., the market *j*). The corresponding equation can be formulated as follows:

$$x_{t+1} = ax_t^i(1 - x^j_{t+1})$$

These transversal selections among subsystems are

additional to the longitudinal development of meaning at all levels within self-referential systems. Note that the longitudinal selection is hierarchical, while the transversal one changes with the nature of the differentiation. The two axes stand orthogonally under the condition of functional differentiation. In other words, the longitudinal generation of meaning was already available as an incursive mechanism in premodern societies, while the transversal updates provide modern societies with an analytically independent mechanism for organizing communications.

Functional Differentiation

Let us return to Equation 1 to understand what functional differentiation means for a system that can operate both incursively (that is, against the axis of time) and recursively (that is, historically). Adding the time subscripts, one can first reformulate Equation 1 for the (more general) recursive case:

$$x_{t+1} = f(S_t, E_t)$$

When functionality of the differentiation prevails, the external environment *E* is decomposed for each subsystem in other subsystems (with a remaining term å as a representation of the residual environment). This can modeled at the subsystems level—let me use the lower-case *s* for this level—as follows:

$$s^i_{l+1} = f(s^i_t, s^i_t, s^t_t, s^l_t \rightarrow \varepsilon_l)$$

In a functionally differentiated system, the windowing of the subsystems upon each other becomes horizontal. A biological system, however, would remain also integrated for the sake of survival. A communication system can also develop in terms of differentiated fluxes that are integrated by being organized historically.

How might functional differentiation in the communication take control over development away from the historical organization of a social system? Luhmann distinguished between the self-organization of the differentiated fluxes of communication and their integration into organizations. The organization of interfaces is historical, while the self-organization of the differentiated communication operates evolutionarily, that is, by providing meaning to the events with hindsight and by using potentially different codes. The social system would thus be able to entertain a set of models of itself. In other words, an additional equation can be formulated for each subsystem given selections by the others from the perspective of hindsight:

$$s_{t+1}^{i} = f(s_{t}^{i}, s_{t+1}^{i}, s_{t+1}^{t}, s_{t+1}^{l} \rightarrow \varepsilon_{t})$$

Note that all systems and subsystems continue to operate historically, and thus provide meaning to their own development along the longitudinal axis at the same time as they provide meanings to one another. The relations between subsystems can be expected to function to variable degrees both incursively and recursively because Equation 6 and Equation 7 are both operational. However, the functionally differentiated system contains an additional Δt at each interface within the system. This Ät can be used for a local reversal of the time axis and thus generate a transversal incursion which stands orthogonally to the longitudinal incursions.

The two types of incursion—the transversal and the longitudinal ones—stand orthogonally, but they can interact in systems that are able to *process* meaning. This interaction can perhaps be considered as the crucial difference between biological and social systems. Differentiated biological systems can hold different meanings, but are not supposed to vary them over time for reasons other than natural one (that is, survival purposes). The integrity of these systems would be endangered if the codes were varied, that is, by entertaining them playfully. Social systems, however, allow for this type of (potentially innovative!) processing and recombination of meanings. Interactions among differently codified meanings over time provide us with other combinations in a horizon of possible meanings.

Using the logistic equation, one can formulate Equation 7 for the case where other subsystems provide relevant environments for the development of subsystem *i*, as follows:

$$x_{t+1}^{i} = ax_t^i(1-x_{t+1}^{j})(1-x_{x+1}^{i})(1-x_{t+1}^{l})-\varepsilon$$

Each subsystem (*i*) develops with reference to its own previous state, but one can expect that all other subsystems feedback upon this development by entertaining a model of the reference system in the present using their respective codes. Since each meaning-providing subsystem (*i*) also provides meaning to its own development longitudinally, and the two types of meaning-providing can interact, one can generalize Equation 8 as follows:

$$x_{t+1}^{i} = ax_t^i\prod_{1}^{t}(1-x_{t+1}^{i})-\varepsilon$$

In this formula *n* represents the number of subsystems of the functionally differentiated system. While this number was analytically restricted in Parsons's structural-functionalism—using his so-called four-function paradigm—the number of subsystems can vary in Luhmann's (1997) theory with the historical development of the media of communication and their symbolic generalization into codes.

When the subsystems use different frequencies for their updates, parameters have to be added to the corresponding selection mechanisms.

Stabilization, Meta-stabilization and Globalization

Let us now turn to the question of what one can expect when one type of meaning operates upon a differently codified meaning at one or more interfaces. I mentioned above that the operation of two differently codified incursions upon each other may lead to "mutual shaping" and the consequent stabilization of a co-evolution along a trajectory. The formalization will enable us to distinguish between stabilization in a co-evolution between two sub dynamics and the possibility of globalization in the case of three sub dynamics.

When selection is represented by the feedback term of the logistic equation, that is, by $(1 - x)$, two selections of the same system operating on a variation *a* would result at the systems level in a quadratic expression of the following form:

$$f(x) = a\,(1 - x)\,(1 - x) = a\,(x^2 - 2x + 1)$$

This function is represented by the solid line in Figure (a) given below (on the left side): a system with two selections can be stabilized at the minimum of a quadratic curve. When this minimum is extended along the time dimension, a valley is shaped in which the system can follow a trajectory.

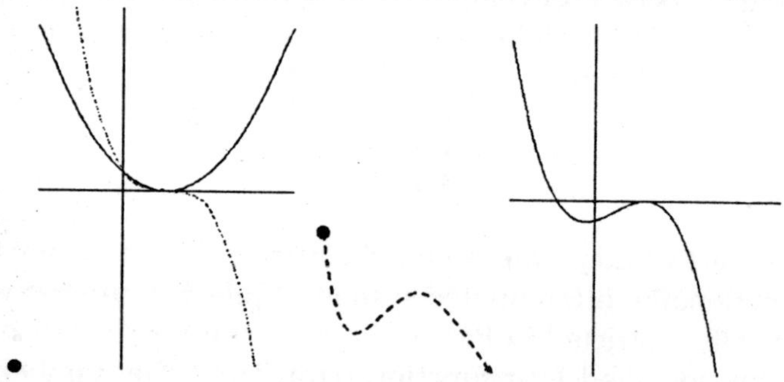

Figure 3.2: (a) $f(x) = x^2 - 2x + 1$ (stabilized) $f(x) = x^3 - 3x^2 + 3x - 1$ (globalized) (b): Globalization and stabilization are no longer harmonized; a local optimum can be sustained temporarily.

Adding one more selection term leads analogously to the following equation:

$$f(x) = a\,(1 - x)\,(1 - x)\,(1 - x) = -\,a\,(x^3 - 3x^2 + 3x - 1)$$

This latter function is represented. As long as the selections operate with the same parameters, the global and the stable points of inflection coincide (in a so-called "saddle point"). The historically stabilized system can then be identical with the global one.

Perhaps such a harmonized system can be said to have an identity, since the global optimum coincides with the localized one.

In this (more general) case, one would expect the curve to show both a maximum and a minimum. At the minimum the system is stabilized, but at the maximum it can be considered as meta-stable. A bifurcation is thus induced because the system can go backward (to the stabilization of an identity) or forward (to globalization into a next-order regime). As long as the system remains stable (that is, at the minimum), it can develop along a trajectory. However, the flux tends to move the system towards the other basin of attraction. This attraction is caused by the possibility to communicate in an additional dimension, and thus to process more complexity in the newly emerging configuration.

The sign of the equations merits further attention. Equation 10 has a positive sign if one assumes the logistic equation as the basic format for the selection. If this sign is reversed, another sub dynamic has to play a role because this inversion cannot be endogenous to the mutual selections that co-evolutionarily stabilized the system. The third (sub) dynamic may either reinforce the prevailing equilibrium and make the system hyper-stable, or invert the sign and make the system meta-stable. Thus, both meta-stability and hyper-stability indicate that a third sub dynamic is operating (but not yet necessarily manifest).

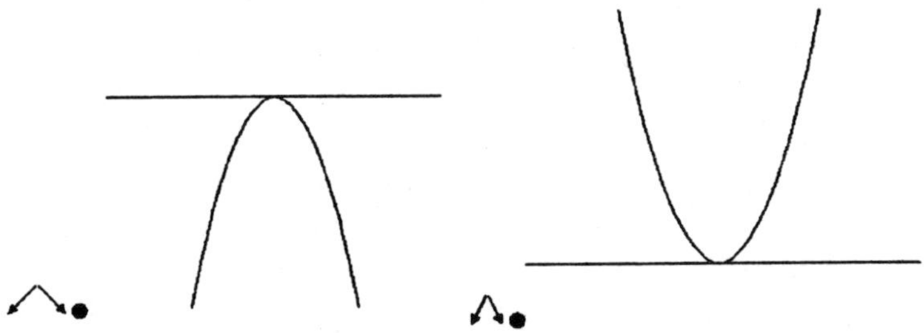

Figure 3.3: (a) Meta-stabiliziation **Figure:** (b) Hyper-stabilization

For example, the change in the sign can be appreciated as a market with decreasing marginal returns versus one with increasing marginal returns, as in the case of information and communication technologies. Increasing marginal returns can lead to a bifurcation at the meta-stable vertex of the hyperbole and a consequential lock-in on either side. In the case of a lock-in, the previously meta-stable system is hyper-stabilized by using the third term as a feedback which reinforces the co-evolution between the two other sub dynamics.

Stabilization can be considered as a result of integration (e.g., by organization), while differentiation among the self-organizing fluxes can be expected to prevail when the system is less organized. However, the distinction between these two sub dynamics—integration and differentiation—remains analytical; in the social system they can be expected to concur, since the global system cannot be historically manifest without some form of stabilization occurring at the same time. The interactions between the various sub dynamics make the system complex and result in the expectation of continuous transitions between provisional (that is, local) stabilizations versus globalizations at the systems level. How would these sub dynamics of stabilization and globalization operate in the case of a meaning-processing system?

Hyper-incursion

The historical realization of meaningful information by the first incursion at each moment remains a necessary condition for the development of the social system, but this operation does not have to be attended by the other two selection mechanisms continuously.

The other two selection mechanisms can also be expected to interact. A third incursive mechanism can interact with the interaction term between two incursive selections, and this can generate a next-order selection or hyper-incursivity. A hyper-incursive equation no longer refers necessarily to a historical realization because it can interact with the interaction term between the two anticipatory mechanisms which refer to the new state.

The most radical of the hyper-incursive equations reflects this orientation to the future as follows:

$$xt = ax_{t+1}\,(1 - x_{t\,+\,1})$$

This system no longer contains any reference to its previous state x_{t-1} or its current state xt (at t = t), but the emerging state is considered as a function of different expectations about the future. Note that both expectations interfaced in this equation can only be based on previous incursions. When incursions are interfaced *recursively*, only a historical variation can be produced (Leydesdorff, in print). However, when the two incursions are interfaced *incursively*, hyper-incursion can also be expected.

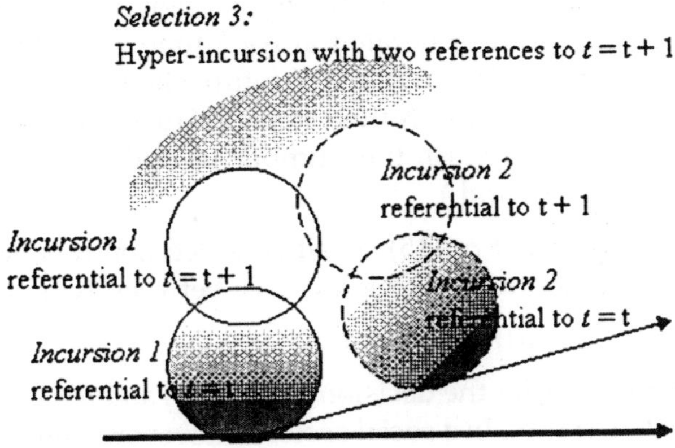

Figure 3.4: Hyper-incursivity at the Interface between two Incursive Selections: *Incursion 1* as Selection on the Variation at each Moment of time, and *Incursion* 2 as Stabilization with Reference to Change over time.

While each incursion generates meaningful information and thus becomes organized both historically (with reference to t = t) and reflexively (with reference to t = (t + 1)), hyper-incursion is by itself not yet organized at t = t because it contains only a reference to t = (t + 1). An additional sub dynamic, therefore, would be needed in order to make the results of this hyper-incursion again organized in historical time. Luhmann (2000) hypothesized that self-organization among the (differently coded) fluxes of communication—which generate only expectations—is brought under organizational control by making decisions. Let us first see how this works in terms of the equations.

Equation 12 can be rewritten as follows:

$$x_t = ax_{t+1}\,(1 - x_{t+1})$$

$$x_t = ax_{t+1} - ax_{t+12}$$

$$ax_{t+12} - ax_{t+1} + x_t = 0$$

$$x_{t+12} - x_{t+1} + (xt/a) = 0$$

For $a = 4$, xt+1 is defined as a function of xt as follows:

$$x_{t+1} = ½ ± ½ \sqrt{(1 - xt)}$$

Depending on the plus or the minus sign in the equation, two future states are generated at each time step. Since this formula is iterative, the number of future states doubles with each next time step. After N time steps, $2N$ future states would be possible. (For $N = 10$, the number of options is already more than a thousand.)

Dubois (2003, at p. 115) specified a decision function u(t) that can be added for making a choice between two options:

$$u(t) = 2\ d(t) - 1$$

Where $u = +1$ for the decision $d = 1$ (true) and $u = -1$ for the decision $d = 0$ (false). In a social system, however, more choices than these two extremes are possible. Social systems operate in a distributed mode, and therefore one would expect a probability distribution of preferences. This distribution contains an uncertainty.

In distributed systems, decisions can be organized and codified into decision rules.

Note that the decisions or decision rules do not determine the hyper-incursive dynamics of the system, but only guide these dynamics historically. (A codified decision rule could function as yet another incursive mechanism.) However, hyper-incursion continues to create possible futures as interactions among expectations on the basis of incursive subdynamics. Decisions change the *historical* conditions by organizing the system, that is, by closing the circle. However, decisions don't have to be taken at each step. Without historicity, the interfacing of expectations would remain in the virtual realm of fantasy and speculation.

The horizon of possible meanings itself could not be further developed historically without any social realizations.

The relevant decisions, however, are no longer taken about historical facts, but about expectations. Thanks to this orientation towards the future, the social system can become increasingly knowledge-based because anticipations are continuously being fed into its historical development. The historical realizations *result* increasingly from the interfacing of expectations as a base other than—but in interaction with—the historical organization of "reality" (Equation 6). The cycling among the selections adds meaningful information to the information flux which develops with the time axis. By bending the time-axis, the meaning-generating system increasingly reconstructs its own history.

In other words, decisions specify instantiations among the available options when anticipations are interfaced. The organization of decisions along a historical axis potentially stabilizes a trajectory within the phase space of expectations. Social order is made contingent on coupling expectations about other possible realities with the historical reality of observable actions and institutions. The latter are increasingly reconstructed as the results of interactions among expectations. Historically, one may be inclined to consider actions and institutions as the causes of expectations because the former precede the latter. However, anticipations are based on the perspective of hindsight, while the latter becomes analytically prior to the historical sequence of events if the time axis is locally inverted.

When the feedback is codified and the codification reinforced by global horizons of meaning, the reconstructive arrow (from the perspective of hindsight) can in the longer term become more important than the forward arrow of historical development. While the historical construction continues to feed into the cycle bottom-up, control in communication systems thus tends to become top-down when the cycle can be closed and reinforced as a next-order dynamics. Unlike "natural" preferences grounded in the historical direction of the time axis, informed decisions guide development into an increasingly knowledge-based order given the contingencies of historical situations as relevant contexts.

Mutual anticipation in social systems

Two other hyper-incursive models follow from the logistic equation:

$$x_t = ax_t(1 - x_{t+1})$$
$$x_t = ax_{t+1}(1 - x_t)$$

Equation 16 evolves into $x = (a - 1)/a$ = Constant. I submit that this evolution towards a constant through anticipation can be considered as modeling the self-reference or the expectation of an (individual) identity. Identity is based on the expectation of continuity of the "self" in the next stage. At the level of the social system a group can also be expected to have an identity;

Equation 17 evolves into $x_{t+1} = (1/a)\ \{xt/\ (1 - xt)\}$. Since the latter term approaches –1 as its limit value and the former term is a constant $(1/a)$, this representation can alternate between itself and a mirror image. This sub dynamic thus formalizes the reflexive operation.

In other words, the three hyper-incursive equations specify the fundamental processes of meaning-processing: identity formation (Eq. 16), reflexivity (Eq. 17), and the mutual expectation of expectations (Eq. 13). While identity and reflexivity are more commonly defined in social theory, the expectation of expectations among systems may require additional explanation. Let me develop this as an analog on of the concept of "double contingency," but at the level of differently coded subsystems of society.

"Double contingency" was theorized in sociology as an interaction between *Ego* and *Alter*. *Ego* and *Alter* are used in order to emphasize that in the relation between two human beings, the *Ego* knows the *Alter* to be a reflexive *Cogito* who entertains expectations. Thus, a social reality is constructed in which a symbolic order is invoked. For the *Ego* this means that one's own reflexivity is reinforced in the encounter. The *Ego* in the present (*xt*) no longer has a reference to itself other than in a future state (x_{t+1}), that is, as an *Alter Ego*. The orientation of providing meaning with reference to other possible meanings thus constitutes the social world as an order different from psychological ones.

Habermas (1987) criticized Luhmann's social systems theory for having replaced the traditional subject of transcendental philosophy (that is, the *Ego*) with the concept of a social system. Let me use this critique as a heuristics for understanding meaning-processing in a social system. Unlike the multitude of subjects—who can entertain relations and experience double contingency in these relations—there is only a single social system. This system can contain Luhmann-type subsystems at each moment and Rosen-type models of itself over time. One can expect differently codified *sub*systems of communication only under the condition of functional differentiation.

These different subsystems interact in historical organizations, but additionally they entertain and develop expectations which contain references to other possible expectations. Given this feedback, the reference of an organization to the time horizon may evolve from developing within history to developing in terms of expectations about the future, and thus to being increasingly knowledge-based. Note that the phenotypical organizations remain a mixture of the two principles of organization, since both Equations 6 and 7 can be expected to operate, albeit with variable weights. Unlike the self-organizing fluxes of communication in social systems, organized systems contain a reference to themselves as an identity (Equation 16). (Individuals can then be considered as the smallest units which organize the fluxes.)

The social order of expectations remains structurally coupled to historical formats of organization because the systems dynamics cannot otherwise become historical. The self-organization of fluxes in terms of functional differentiations is not itself historically observable, but only perceptible after a reflexive turn. The coupling between the social system of communications and the agents carrying it is provided by the reflexivity formalized in Equation 17. Because of this reflexivity, the social system can be entertained by individuals as a notional order, that is, an order with the epistemological status of a hypothesis. *Vice versa,* the individuals and institutional agents are reflected in the social system as addresses or nodes. Since both systems can be expected to contain the reflexive operation expressed in Equation 17, a co-evolution ("mutual shaping") can also take place between the social system and individuals. However, this co-evolution can be interrupted when expectations are further codified (e.g., stabilized) on either side beyond the control of the other side.

On the side of social systems, an eigendynamics of codifications may lead to "alienation". On the side of individuals, the recursive application of the reflexive operation provides discretionary room for private thinking and tacit knowledge. In summary, functional differentiation changes the social system so that a double contingency between functionally differentiated (that is, differently coded) subsystems of communication becomes possible. Each of the subsystems can be expected to generate its own set of expectations. As these sets of expectations are made relevant to one another, their identity is no longer given, but has to be organized. Organization means in this case limiting the range of options by making decisions about the relevant expectations. For example, in the case of innovation one combines market perspectives with technological options.

From this perspective, the individual (e.g., the entrepreneur) can be considered as the minimal carrier of decisions because decision-making itself can also be a social process. As was shown, this process guides the self-organizing dynamics by organizing it, since the complexity would otherwise explode. In technical terms, development would rapidly become non-computable because it would be non-polynomial (NP) complete (Equation 14).

Like all self-referential systems, social systems can generate meaning in an incursive mode and thus be anticipatory, that is, by entertaining expectations along the axis of time. The functional differentiation of society in terms of different codes of communication provides the social system with an additional mechanism of anticipation because of asynchronicity in the updates among the different subsystems. In organized systems and hierarchies, these transversal updates at sub systemic levels are synchronized at the top with reference to an external environment, but a functionally differentiated system has replaced this option for survival by considering the subsystems as relevant environments for one another. The transversal generation of meaning among the subsystems can be recombined with the longitudinal generation of meaning and thus provide a field of possible meanings.

This second-order incursion upon the anticipatory terms of the first-order incursions provided us with the hyper-incursive equation which models a third selection mechanism. The uncertainty generated by this model, however, forces the system to be organized periodically like an update mechanism. I submitted that the minimum unit for this historicity is the individual. At the level of individual interactions, hyper-incursivity is also available as a "double contingency": the meeting of the other as entertaining a similar, but potentially different set of expectations. "Double contingency" can thus be considered as a transversal encounter between different sets of meanings, but in the case of individuals whole systems (agents) meet and update, and not subsystems. Subsystems of communication operate at a different level, and they can only reproduce a double contingency towards one another if the functional differentiation between them is warranted in terms of codes developing along different axes.

The social system shares with psychological systems the other two hyper-incursive operations (identity formation and reflexivity). Unlike individuals, the social system is able to generate within the system a non-linear dynamic among *three* selection mechanisms:

- Selections from a *variety* of global horizons of meaning,
- Historical realizations in organizations at each moment, and

- The transformation of the latter by the need to recombine expectations based on previous realizations over time. Individuals can meet and experience a double contingency in the relation between *Alter* and *Ego*, but by doing so they already constitute a social system. Thus, a hyper cycle between three selection mechanisms of meaning can be shaped at the level of the social system.

The three selections operate as in a triple helix: when the configuration allows for interaction of a third selection mechanism with the interaction between two other selections, hyper-incursion becomes a possibility, and when this occurs the systems can be expected to avalanche towards the strongly anticipatory regime of a knowledge-based society. In a knowledge-based order, decisions can increasingly be informed by expectations. Let me finally note that the argument in this chapter would indicate that the social system as a strongly anticipatory one would *not* be able to construct its own next stage in the longer run without historical decision-making by an external agency. Thus, social systems can be considered as semi-autonomous. While Dubois (2002) showed that a strongly anticipatory system is able to predict the development of a complex system given a fixed relation between the modeling and the modeled system, this relation can be expected to remain variable in social systems because the modeling system provides meaning to the modeled system using a non-linear dynamics. Decision-making structures (e.g., individuals) are a necessary condition for the historical development of the non-linear dynamics of meaning in social systems.

4

The Dynamics of Social Transformation

Social change is an elusive concept. It is inevitable and yet, paradoxically, it depends on the will and the actions of ordinary individuals. We embrace change, yet something in our nature fiercely resists it. We structure social movements, political campaigns and business strategies around the need for change, yet we hardly understand how it works. These apparent contradictions may partly explain the increased attention to change today in a number of disciplines, from anthropology to quantum physics to management theory to social science. How do cultures evolve? Can orderly patterns be found in the midst of apparent chaos? Is it possible for organizations to maintain stability under conditions of constant change? How do groups and individuals consciously bring about change?

These questions, which preoccupy researchers in numerous fields, all revolve around the crucial function of change in the maintenance of dynamic systems. This chapter takes a broad look at the literature on the subject in order to better understand why change occurs, how it unfolds, and what strategies might be developed for consciously bringing it about. While a great deal has been written about social change in the fields of history, sociology, organizational theory, and even psychology, much of it focuses on the recalcitrance of social systems — how and why they resist change — rather than the change process itself. This may have something to do with the ambiguous nature of the concept. First, there seems to be little consensus about what constitutes change. The causes, the processes, and the effects of change are often spoken of as if they are one and the same thing. Second, it is notoriously difficult to measure change — how do you know when a change has taken place?

And third, change occurs on many levels — cultural, social, institutional, and individual — and it is often hard to draw clear distinctions between them. Sometimes change occurs spontaneously on several levels at once. This problem is especially troublesome given the specialization of academic research today. Psychologists, physicists, and anthropologists rarely exchange notes and so the connections between, say, complexity theory and cultural change are easily missed. As a result, the academic literature is brimming with definitions of change and yet the confusion is as great as ever.

Philosophies of Change

The cyclical process of birth, growth, breakdown, and disintegration has been a perennial theme in philosophy dating back to the ancient Greeks, and perhaps further. Heraclitus, who is remembered for his maxims "there is nothing permanent except change" and "you can never step into the same river twice," compared the world order to an ever living fire, "kindling in measures and going out in measures." His compatriot Empedocles attributed the changes in the universe to the ebb and flow of two complementary forces which he called "love" and "hate." Correspondingly, the ancient Chinese philosophers viewed reality as the dynamic interplay of two opposites — the yin and the yang. Their keen understanding of change is reflected in the term they use for "crisis" — *wei-ji* — which is composed of the characters for "danger" and "opportunity."

While the function of change preoccupied many of the great Western philosophers, it was not until the late-nineteenth and early twentieth centuries that the first comprehensive change theories were articulated. During this time social philosophers sought to make a science out of history and began more systematic analyses of social change. Among the foremost, if more conjectural, of these was Arnold Toynbee's *A Study of History*.

Based on exhaustive studies of some thirty civilizations, Toynbee postulated that the genesis of a civilization consists of a transition from a static condition to one of dynamic activity. This transition may occur spontaneously, through the influence of some civilization that is already in existence, or through the disintegration of one or more civilizations of an older generation.

Toynbee saw the birth of civilizations as the result of a dynamic interplay which he called "challenge-and-response." A challenge from the natural or social environment provokes a creative response in a society, or a social group, which induces that society to enter the process of civilization. The civilization continues to grow when its successful response to the initial challenge generates cultural momentum that carries the society beyond a state of equilibrium into an overbalance that presents itself as a fresh challenge. In this way, the initial pattern of challenge-and-response is repeated in successive phases of growth, each successful response producing a disequilibrium that requires new creative adjustments.

After civilizations have reached a peak of vitality, they tend to lose their cultural momentum and decline. An essential element in this cultural breakdown, Toynbee suggested, is a loss of flexibility. When social structures and behaviour patterns have become so rigid that the society can no longer adapt to changing conditions, it will be unable to carry on the creative process of cultural evolution. It will then break down and eventually disintegrate. Whereas growing civilizations display endless variety and versatility, those in the process of disintegration show uniformity and lack of inventiveness. The loss of flexibility in a disintegrating society is accompanied by a general loss of harmony among its elements which inevitably leads to the outbreak of social discord and disruption.

Toynbee noted, however, that during the painful process of disintegration, the society's creativity — its ability to respond to changes — is not completely lost. Though the cultural mainstream has become ossified by clinging to fixed ideas and rigid patterns of behaviour, creative minorities will appear on the scene and carry on the process of challenge-and-response. The dominant social institutions will refuse to hand over their leading roles to these new cultural forces, but they will inevitably go on to decline and disintegrate, and the creative minorities may be able to transform some of the old elements into a new configuration. The process of cultural evolution will then continue, but under new circumstances and with new protagonists.

Toynbee's ideas echo those of Oswald Spengler, Pitirim Sorokin, and other social thinkers who viewed change as fundamentally cyclical in nature. The major alternative to this model is the linear or evolutionary view of change perhaps best articulated by Herbert Spencer, Karl Marx, and August Comte. This interpretation recalls the faith in science and the inevitability of progress which swept through the social sciences in the nineteenth century. Spencer, who coined the phrase "survival of the fittest" (often misattributed to Charles Darwin); saw all social change as the manifestation of a natural law of progress. The dynamic force in progress was, like that in biological evolution, the competitive struggle for existence in which the fit survive and the unfit perish. This interpretation of social change was especially popular among the so-called Social Darwinists (even though Darwin himself was no Social Darwinist and Spencer's theory of social evolution preceded Darwin's theories of biological evolution by several years.)

If Spencer's evolutionary philosophy provided a philosophical justification for individualism, Karl Marx's theories did the same for collectivism. Marx's theories were based in large part on Hegel's view of history as a dialectical progression. Hegel postulated that one concept (thesis) inevitably generates its opposite (antithesis), and that their interaction leads to a new concept (synthesis), which in turn becomes the thesis of a new triad. Marx adapted this model to his analysis of social change, asserting that all changes in society arise from the development of its internal contradictions. He saw the contradictory principles of social organization as being embodied in society's classes, and class struggle as a consequence of their dialectic interaction. Class struggle was the driving force of history for Marx. He held that all important historical progress was born in conflict, struggle, and violent revolution. Human suffering and sacrifice was a necessary price that had to be paid for social change.

Paradigm Shifts

A more recent perspective on change comes from historian of science Thomas Kuhn. In *The Structure of Scientific Revolutions,* which has been called the most important book of the twentieth century, he introduced the concept of a *paradigm* — a conceptual model or set of assumptions about reality that allows researchers to isolate data, elaborate theories, and solves problems. A scientific paradigm, as Kuhn defined it, can be as all-encompassing as Newtonian physics or as specific as the notion that life exists only on earth. The chief characteristic of a paradigm is that it has its own set of rules and illuminates its own set of facts. In this way it becomes self- validating and therefore resistant to change. Kuhn observed that as long as a paradigm explains most observed phenomena and solves the problems most people want solved, it remains dominant. But as new phenomena begin to contradict it, the paradigm succumbs to increasing doubt. As these anomalies multiply, it is thrown into crisis.

When a new paradigm is articulated — such as Einstein's theory of quantum mechanics — a broad paradigmatic shift occurs. In this way, long periods of "normal" science are followed by brief "revolutions" that involve fundamental changes in basic theoretical assumptions. In Kuhn's view, the history of science is not one of linear, rational progress moving toward ever more accurate and complete knowledge of an objective truth. Instead, it is one of radical shifts of vision in which a multitude of non-rational and non-empirical factors come into play. While Kuhn was dealing with paradigms in the history of science and has repeatedly cautioned against over generalizing in applying the concept to the process of social transition, it nevertheless provides a very useful metaphor for understanding the nature of change. This is reflected in the near-universal usage of the word *paradigm* today.

A good example of how the word has been applied in a more general sense is offered by physicist and philosopher Fritjof Capra. A paradigm, he says, "is a constellation of concepts, values, perceptions and practices, shared by a community that forms a particular vision of reality that is the basis of the way the community organizes itself. It's necessary for a paradigm to be shared by a community. A single person can have a worldview, but a paradigm is shared by a community."

The paradigm concept illustrates the extent to which social change can hinge on the state of mind of individuals. In *Global Mind Change,* Willis Harman observes that "throughout history, the really fundamental changes in societies have come about not from the dictates of governments and the results of battles but through vast numbers of people changing their minds — sometimes only a little bit." Because of the way these changes of mind occur, the effects can appear sudden and spontaneous. We tend to think of cultural innovation as the work of small elites, or what Toynbee called "creative minorities" — leading philosophers, religious thinkers, scientists, and artists — who infuse society with new ideas. But, as Daniel Yankelovich points out in *New Rules,* "every now and then a new way of conceiving life and its meaning arises spontaneously from the great mass of the population."

Kuhn's model also sheds light on how change operates in the natural world. For example, biologist Elisabet Sahtouris describes how the metamorphosis of a caterpillar into a butterfly follows a similar change pattern. In metamorphosis, small cells known as imaginal discs begin to appear in the body of the caterpillar. Since they are not recognized by the caterpillar's immune system, they are immediately wiped out. But as they grow in number and begin to link up, they ultimately overwhelm the caterpillar's immune system. Its body then goes into meltdown and the imaginal discs build the butterfly from the spent materials of the caterpillar. These imaginal discs can be likened to the anomalies in Kuhn's model of paradigmatic change.

The caterpillar's immune system does not recognize them, just as the dominant paradigm in Kuhn's model fails to account for anomalies. Finally they overwhelm the system and usher in a new phase. Interesting parallels can also be drawn between imaginal discs and the "creative minorities" in Toynbee's theory of the rise and fall of civilizations. As Toynbee showed, the seeds of the new civilization are contained within the old one just like the blueprint of the butterfly is contained in the cells of the caterpillar.

Cultural Renewal

Another model of social change has been described by anthropologist Anthony F.C. Wallace based on his studies of both indigenous and modern societies. In his 1961 book *Culture and Personality,* he observed that the change process begins with a shift away from cultural harmony, a change that shows up first in the form of increased individual stress. A growing number of individuals find that they are unable to meet certain cultural expectations. At first this is perceived by both the individual and the society at large as an individual problem. But as the number of these individual deviations grows, it begins to weaken the social fabric, eventually to the point where the society must acknowledge that the problem is more than personal. At this stage, it is difficult for the society to return to a state of equilibrium without undergoing a process of revitalization. According to Wallace, this process depends on a number of variables: The formulation of a code-

An individual or small group — typically people who have been directly affected by the stresses in question — builds a new idealized image of a "goal culture" that stands in attractive contrast to the existing situation.

Communication- The formulators then communicate their vision to others, beginning with those most affected by the stresses at the root of the problem.

Organization.-Once the vision begins to attract converts, some form of organization is required to manage the group and implement a plan.

Adaptation- As the new vision gets broader exposure, it generally grows and changes. This happens for various reasons: the initial vision is usually incomplete, especially in its practical details; certain accommodations may be made to broaden the appeal of the vision; and the original vision may include such things as predictions that fail to materialize, thus requiring re-explanation.

Cultural Transformation- If the movement is able to gain enough support within the society, the thrust shifts from communications to implementation. If the "goal culture" cannot be immediately established, then a "transfer culture" is adopted as the route to get to the full vision and if this cultural shift is successful, then the stress experienced by individuals declines dramatically.

Routinization- Once the initial shift of cultural transformation has taken place, the next stage is to establish the new vision as the new steady state, which generally means institutionalizing it in various ways. Those in the vanguard of the transformation process may find this last stage difficult and disappointing, but the majority of the population is glad for a return to normalcy so that they can get on with their lives.

Wallace observes that this kind of revitalization can be either reactionary or innovative in its basic thrust. The reactionary mode is characterized by a belief that present problems can be resolved by "doing the old way harder," and generally tries to undo or suppress recent changes that are seen as the cause of the problem. The innovative mode, on the other hand, attempts to get "lagging" parts of the culture to catch up to recent changes that are seen by the innovators as either positive or unchangeable. In complex societies under stress, there are usually many revitalization movements competing for attention and converts as the culture begins to disintegrate. Wallace notes that the inherent conservatism in most social systems favors reactionary movements.

It is common for a culture to attempt a "let's do the old way harder" revitalization as the first response to realizing that something must be done to get society back in track. It is only after the failure of a reactionary revitalization attempt that a culture is willing to risk fundamental change. This shift from innovation to reaction and back again is often described in common parlance in terms of a swinging pendulum. The metaphor suggests that social change follows predictable laws of motion and that movement is static in one direction or another. But, as Daniel Yankelovich points out, social change is better described as a process of "lurch and learn."

In his forty years of monitoring social trends in the United States, Yankelovich had found that society tends to lurch, often mindlessly, in a new direction and it is only after a period of reaction that integration takes place. For instance, in the 1960s young people lurched away from the prevailing notion of duty to the search for pleasure. Similarly, there was a lurch away from work to leisure. "The reaction of young people to their father's nose-to-the-grindstone way of life was to see in leisure the possibilities of genuine self-fulfillment. After that lurch, they gradually found that the kind of self-fulfillment they were seeking often could be fulfilled better through a certain kind of work than through leisure."

Scientific Perspectives on Change

Some of the most fascinating contributions to the theory of change in recent decades come not from sociology or anthropology but from an eclectic, multidisciplinary group of researchers at the frontiers of quantum physics, general systems theory, and the emerging theories of chaos and complexity.

Nobel laureates such as chemist Ilya Prigogine, physicist Murray Gell-Mann, and economist Kenneth Arrow, along with of host of others engaged in the study of complex systems have pioneered a new approach to understanding the instability and fluctuations that characterize seemingly random events, be it at the level of molecules, of biological systems, or even of social systems. The science of complexity can be loosely divided into two disciplines. The first is non equilibrium physics which is based on the discovery of fundamental new properties of matter under far-from-equilibrium conditions.

The second discipline is the modern theory of dynamical systems, which is especially relevant for our purposes here since dynamical systems include a wide range of processes including chemical reactions, individual organisms, ecosystems, economies, and social systems. The central discovery here is the prevalence of instability. In essence, instability means that small changes in initial conditions may lead to large amplifications of the effects of the changes. Ilya Prigogine, who won the Nobel Prize in chemistry in 1977, has been at the center of the emerging science of complexity. In his book *Order Out of Chaos* he explores the nature of change in what he calls "dissipative structures." Dissipative structures are best described as open systems in the sense that they interact with the larger world around them by constantly trading energy and maintaining themselves through an endless dynamic flow. One of the chief characteristics of these systems is that they are subject to constant fluctuations or perturbations, sudden shifts that allow for novelty and unpredictable change.

A river can be taken as an example of a dissipative structure: while it acts in consort with the larger environment of which it is a part, it can be seen as an independent system; like all living systems it is subject to constant, erratic and apparently random fluctuations. According to Prigogine, a single fluctuation adding its strength to other fluctuations may become powerful enough to reorganize the whole system into a new pattern. The points at which this happens are "bifurcation points," at which deterministic description breaks down and the system follows one of several possible forks in the road. These "stochastic" (i.e., not predictable) processes demonstrate that open systems are not mechanistic but random. Prigogine uses the term randomness to denote not blind chance, but rather non-determinism, spontaneity, and novelty. Open systems can thus be thought of as dynamic and "creative."

Prigogine likens the universe to a living organism because it has room for random behaviour, allowing dissipative structures to recreate themselves into unforeseeable patterns. These novel patterns are often triggered by small variables or perturbations whose presence can pull the entire system away from one kind of behaviour toward a new and unexpected one. In this way, matter is not something static — inert molecules that are governed by pushes and pulls — but as something active and alive. Except for systems at equilibrium in which no further exchanges take place, open systems are constantly attuned to their environments.

In these open systems, matter is not isolated and solitary, as scientists once assumed, but instead it is responsive, relational, and self-modifying in response to the activities of other matter. In these systems, the smallest change may "destabilize" the system and bring about an outcome not predicted by the logic of linear equations.

Prigogine's theory of dissipative structures and order by fluctuation echoes emerging theories in other fields, such as quantum physics and biology, which are challenging our traditional understanding of change on several fronts. There is growing evidence that systemic change is not a mechanistic, progressive, and linear phenomenon whose causes and effects can be clearly isolated.

While Newtonian science has long sought to isolate the

basic building-blocks of nature, recent theories suggest that nature appears more like a complicated web of relations between various parts of a unified whole. As the German quantum physicist Werner Heisenberg put it, "the world thus appears as a complicated tissue of events, in which connections of different kinds alternate or overlap or combine and thereby determine the texture of the whole."

Theories of Social Change

The science of complex systems offers some intriguing parallels between the natural and the social world. Just as the notion of direct causation has been found to be faulty in dynamical systems, it is now widely recognized that so-called "prime movers" such as strong leadership or economic dislocation, once largely unquestioned in sociology, are impossible to isolate from the other causal factors that prompt social change. Social philosopher Alvin Toffler has expressed the emergent view this way: "I think more in terms of process, interrelationships, rhythms, non-equilibrium, and fields than individual causal vectors; more in terms of mutually interactive systems, than of one-way causality."

As sociology has adopted a less deterministic approach, one that acknowledges the inherent interdependence and reciprocity at work in social systems, the emphasis has shifted from the *causes* of change to the *conditions* that are most conducive to change. As sociologist Bruce F. Ryan put it, "if cause is to be sought for change, it is to be found through the analysis of the conditions and processes giving rise to the particular sequence of events." Conditions that tend to precipitate change include:

- A lack of cohesion among the various constituents of a social system.
- The inability of groups or individuals to adjust to their larger social or physical environment.
- Rigid and centralized social structures.
- High population densities.

- Social diversity.
- Creativity and innovation.

Each of these conditions leads to the kinds of social tensions which ultimately manifest in change. By way of comparison, it's interesting to review the characteristics of social systems which are relatively stable over time. Typically these societies have been 1) small in size, 2) isolated from contact with other cultures, 3) technologically unsophisticated, 4) unable to store or transmit knowledge through writing, 5) highly respectful of tradition, and 6) bound to a shared and consistent value system.

Another condition at the root of social change is the oftcited theory of cultural lag developed by William Fielding Ogburn in the 1920s. He explained that when different systems within a society are out of sync with one another, different rates of change affect different social sectors in varied ways. The result is that institutions struggle to adapt to the time-pacing of other institutions. For example, in the business world innovation and renewal tend to occur very rapidly, whereas public schools and government bureaucracies typically change very slowly. These lags in adaptation create powerful tensions in society. Alvin Toffler, who has been much influenced by Ogburn's theory, attributed the condition of "future shock" in part to this phenomenon of cultural lag.

The literature on social change focuses to a large extent on the dynamics of social interaction — how groups are formed, how minorities deviate from established norms, how conflict is born and resolved, and the fluctuations in collective behaviour. A growing body of research also looks at the process of "diffusion" — the process by which innovative ideas are spread and ultimately take root in society. The trouble with much of the academic research on change is that, on its own, it's not very useful. In the words of one observer, "sociologists put primary emphasis on attempting to build a body of verified theory about social behaviour, including social change, rather than themselves trying to induce change. The practitioner, on the other hand, although likewise interested in understanding, is principally concerned with inducing change, rather than merely accounting for it."

This shortcoming has not been entirely lost on social scientists. In fact, a subfield of sociology has emerged in the past few decades devoted to "planned change." This development is a reaction in part to the shift from the *study* of change to the *methods* of controlling and directing it. One especially useful, if perhaps excessively academic, roundup of "General Strategies for Effecting Changes in Human Systems" is provided by Robert Chin and Kenneth Benne in their classic textbook *The Planning of Change*. In their analysis, change strategies fall into three categories: 1) rational-empirical, 2) normative- reductive, and 3) power-coercive.

The *rational-empirical* approach assumes that men and women are rational and practical and will change on their own given the appropriate conditions. These strategies include:

- Provide the right information, education or training to allow individuals to change of their own volition.
- Ensure that the "right" people are in the right "place" to bring about needed changes.
- Invite the perspectives or expertise of outsiders.
- Engage in research and development.
- Promote utopian thinking to stimulate creativity and "best-case" scenarios.

Clarify the issues and/or reconceptualize the situation in order to bring about greater overall understanding among members of the group. The second category of strategies — the *normative- reductive* — is predicated on the view that change begins from the bottom up, not the top down. That is to say, it focuses on changing the individuals that make up a social system. It is the preferred method of counselors, trainers, and therapists. Two strategies characteristic of this approach are to:

- Improve the problem-solving capacities of a system by encouraging individuals to be self-diagnosing.
- Release and foster growth in the persons who make up the system.

The *power-coercive* approach to effecting change is the one most commonly associated with political movements and social activism. In the words of Chin and Benne, "these strategies are oriented against coercive and nonreciprocal influence, both on moral and on pragmatic grounds." Strategies in this category include:

- Using political institutions to achieve change.
- Shifting the balance of power between social groups, especially ruling elites.
- Weakening or dividing the opposition through moral coercion or strategies of nonviolence.

Taxonomy of change strategies is offered by Roland Warren, a sociologist who has devoted much attention to social change at the community level. His list of community-based change strategies include: consensus planning, bargaining, protest movements, research- demonstrations, social action, non-violence, organizations of client populations, community development, conflict, elite planning, organization of indigenous groups, and civil disobedience. He classifies these under four headings: 1) collaborative strategies, 2) campaign strategies, 3) contest strategies, and 4) a combination of strategies.

What this literature shows is that there are at bottom two modes of viewing change: the reactive and the proactive. From one perspective, individuals and groups are the objects of change. They are at the receiving end, in the sense that change happens to them. From the other perspective, individuals and groups are the initiators of change and change follows from human volition. Both perspectives have their validity, of course, and they are closely interrelated. For instance, when one social group actively tries to bring about change, there are invariably other groups who feel put upon and try to resist the change.

Management Theory

One field of inquiry that has taken a particularly proactive approach to the subject of change is management theory. This is not surprising, perhaps, given the competitive pressures confronting many organizations today. In a world buffeted by change, many organizations have learned that the only way to survive is by innovating, that the only stability possible is stability in motion. In the opening lines of *Managing the Future: Ten Driving Forces of Change for the 90s*, Robert Tucker writes:

> Two years after *In Search of Excellence* reported on forty-three of the "best run" companies in America, fourteen of the forty-three firms were in financial trouble. The reason, according to a *Business Week* study: "failure to react and respond to change."That "change" and "innovation" have become the bywords of organizational management in the 1990s is reflected in a myriad of business books with titles like *Mastering Change: The Key to Business Success, Knowledge for Action: A Guide to Overcoming Barriers to Organizational Change* and *The Change Masters*. As Common Cause founder John Gardner has said, "Perhaps the most distinctive thing about innovation today is that we are beginning to pursue it systematically. The large corporation does not set up a research laboratory to solve a specific problem but to engage in continuous innovation."

One of the more influential management books to emerge in recent years is *The Fifth Discipline* by Peter Senge, director of the Systems Thinking and Organizational Learning Program at MIT's Sloan School of Management. Senge believes that the greatest challenges confronting organizations today involve fundamental cultural changes. Addressing these challenges requires what he calls collective learning. Organizations must be able to learn in order to survive. The traditional approach to dealing with complex problems is to break them down into smaller, more easily managed problems. But this approach could be fatal to organizations, according to Senge. When we reduce complex problems and try to isolate their various parts we "can no longer see the consequences of our actions; we lose our intrinsic sense of connection to a larger whole," he writes. "As daunting as it may seem, we must destroy the illusion that the world is created of separate, unrelated forces. When we give up this illusion, we can then build learning organizations."

The learning organization is one in which five learning disciplines are continually pursued:

Personal Mastery- "the discipline of continually clarifying and deepening our personal vision, focusing our energies, developing patience, and seeing reality objectively."

Analyzing one's mental models and envisioning alternative ways of thinking about the world. Working with mental models means exposing our own ways of thinking, as well as making that thinking more open to the influence of others.

Building a shared vision- "unearthing shared pictures of the future that foster genuine commitment and enrollment rather than compliance."

Learning as a team, which starts with dialogue and the skill of overcoming defensiveness and other patterns of interaction that keep members from learning — individually and as a team? Thinking systemically, seeing patterns and the "invisible fabrics of interrelated actions, which often take years to fully play out their effects on each other." According to Senge, the fifth discipline — systems thinking — ties all the other disciplines together. This kind of thinking involves "a shift of mind from seeing parts to seeing wholes, from seeing people as helpless reactors to seeing them as active participants in shaping their reality." If one were to explain systems thinking in terms of an equation, he says, it would not be "A causes B," but rather "A causes B while B causes A, and both continually interrelate with C and D."

Senge notes that the really significant and enduring innovations he has observed have grown out of people from multiple constituencies working together. In education, for instance, "it's been a few committed teachers with some bright ideas, in concert with a principal who has a particular view of his or her job, in concert with a superintendent who is in line with that principal, and in concert with people in the community who are very much part of the innovation process." Many of Senge's ideas are echoed by Rosabeth Moss

Kanter and her colleagues in *The Challenge of Organizational Change*. They focus on how organizations learn to change, emphasizing "the sad fact... that, almost universally organizations change as little as they must, rather than as much as they should." They characterize learning organizations as "self-designing," "self-renewing," and "post-entrepreneurial."

They are flexible and open, and all levels of development — individual, team, work group and organizational — occur simultaneously and synergistically. The importance of systems thinking and creating a common vision also figures prominently in the organizational approach of Gary Frank, David Angus, and Bob Rehm. In what they call "future search conferences" or "visioning meetings," they bring together a diverse group of people to create a shared vision, innovation, and joint planning. The rationale here is that meaningful, deliberate, consensual, and preferred change must involve as many people with a stake in the issue as possible. It also recognizes that any organization is a part of a larger environment. "The relationship of the organization to its external environment, how that environment is changing, what the change either means to us or how we can influence the change are the key ingredients of the search."

Individual Change

The emphasis on systems thinking is a recent development in organizational thinking and has yet to be embraced in the mainstream management literature. The same might be said about the role of individual change, or what Senge calls "personal mastery." While much has been written about the processes which help people achieve change, a more fundamental question involves whether they are willing to change in the first place. Is a person prepared to open up to new inputs, insights, and understandings? Is he or she prepared to be changed in the process of effecting change? From this perspective, social change has a great deal to do with individual motivation. Effective strategies for change must build on the caring and personal commitment of all the players involved.

Social philosopher Philip Slater makes this point in his book *A Dream Deferred*. "People are reluctant to change because change is uncomfortable and demands a great deal of energy," he says. "Therefore when people ask where to start working [for change], the answer is that since change makes heavy demands on motivation and energy, you should start where you *care* the most and do what you like to *do* the most — that will be where you contribute the most energy and be most effective." Robert Theobald has spent the better part of three decades organizing communities for change. In his book *The Rapids of Change*, he notes that people often ask him whether a particular change is possible. "I respond by saying that this is the wrong question," he writes. "Instead, each of us needs to ask where our commitment is and where we shall act. Once we are committed, we will find ways to be effective."

Developing Strategies for Change

As this brief survey of the literature suggests, a considerable amount of research has been done on how and why change occurs and the methods people use to consciously bring it about. But much of the literature consists of post hoc explanations and tentative theories which have a limited usefulness unless they can be translated into effective action. The question, therefore, is what practical wisdom can be culled from the ever-expanding body of research on change. By way of conclusion, I would like to outline a number of practical strategies that may be taken to consciously effect change as well as successfully negotiate conditions of flux and uncertainty — be it in communities, organizations, or groups. This is not intended as a comprehensive step-by-step approach — after all, there can never be such a thing as a blueprint for change. Instead, what I have tried to do here is bring together a number of key insights from the literature on change and extrapolate some of their practical applications.

Build new relationships. A crucial first step in any process of effecting change is what David Mathews calls "banding together." It means forming relationships, organizing, and claiming collective responsibility for a given issue or situation.

This can range from highly organized community town meetings to a few neighbors getting together in someone's living room to discuss their concerns. In some cases, building new relationships may only be possible by fundamentally changing relationships that are already in place. The key is to develop a sense of group identity as well as a sense of agency. Banding together generates "a sense of the possibility for change," Mathews writes. "Being associated with, and committed to, others gives people a feeling that they are equal to their problems." It is therefore an essential prerequisite to bringing about desired changes.

Discuss and deliberate. All effective change strategies hinge on discussion and deliberation. At a minimum, discussion allows the issues to be named and framed. It also helps individuals develop a shared perspective. As Robert Theobald points out, "most fundamental change activities break down because those involved in them do not take the time to gain a shared model of reality." At a more fundamental level, dialogue allows for what physicist David Bohm calls a "higher social intelligence." One of the chief obstacles to change, he says, is that "we've organized our societies by algorithms — that is, by sets of rules by which we try to affect each other like parts of a machine. The result is that we can't talk with each other about things that are really important." Dialogue helps to eliminate false divisions among people, builds common ground, and allows for the emergence of a more systemic perspective.

Develop shared visions and goals. Setting new directions for the future is one of the most powerful ways of effecting change. When people come together "in such a way that their individual visions can start to interact," as Peter Senge puts it, a creative tension is established that gives focus, direction, and context to changes as they occur. Some techniques for developing common visions include futures commissions, search conferences, and visioning meetings in which participants develop "best case" scenarios and articulate common goals. As Senge says, "we communicate our individual visions to one another and eventually start to create a field of shared meaning where there really is a deep level of trust and understanding — and we gradually begin to build a shared vision." This process is very different from such perfunctory strategies as writing "vision" statements. It often involves a great deal of reflection, listening, and mutual understanding.

Foster social capital. Robert Putnam and others have used the term "social capital" to denote the networks and norms of trust and reciprocity that characterize healthy social orders. The term suggests that capital can be measured in social as well as economic terms, that relationships have an inherent value. Scott Fosler, author of *The Public/Private Partnership*, has studied the nature of community collaboration in cities across the United States. "If you look back at what it was that was really the key in the development of civic and political institutions," he says, "it was trust that was based on personal relationships." Building networks and relationships within and between individuals and groups is not something that can be done overnight, but it is no doubt one of the most effective change strategies available to communities and civic organizations.

Ensure broad participation and diversity. Fundamental change is impossible without the participation of everybody with a stake in the problem or issue. Without the full participation of all concerned, perspectives will be missing and there is a good chance that some of the issues involved will go unaddressed. Another aspect of this is the inherent value of diversity. Research in anthropology, sociology, and biology shows that homogeneity fosters stability, while diversity invariably produces change. It follows that planned change is best achieved by promoting diversity.

Determine leadership roles. There are many types of leaders, from presidents and mayors to teachers, neighborhood activists, and even parents. But no matter what form they take they lend cohesion to a group and act as spark-plugs for change. Their vision, drive and personal commitment can be keys to galvanizing a group into action. Leaders are also able to champion and protect those within groups who are most willing to risk change.

Identify outside resources. Fundamental change tends to be difficult and painful and always involves uncertainty and risk. Since most communities and organizations that embark on the journey need outside help — from foundations, consultants, civic organizations, trade associations, government departments, etc. — they need to develop linkages to outside sources of capital and information. These linkages not only facilitate the process of change they often provide opportunities for lateral learning and growth. Set clear boundaries. When planning for specific kinds of change, it is important to operate within clearly defined boundaries - - for both psychological and practical reasons. Boundaries provide frameworks for measuring change and give focus and direction to one's efforts. They also provide a sense of what is feasible. On a practical level, clearly defined goals allow one to make realistic plans.

Draw on the examples of others. Change takes place in an infinite variety of ways and there is no single strategy that will work for every individual or group. Still, those seeking to effect change may take comfort and inspiration from the examples of others. Not only does this provide mentors from whom they can learn, it offers them conviction that their goal is attainable.

Adopt a change mindset. Nothing precipitates change like a crisis. Necessity, after all, is the mother of invention. The question is whether it is possible to adopt a crisis-perspective without a crisis, or at least a mindset that is constantly attuned to change. Many innovators and change agents insist that it is possible. What is required, they say, is a shift of perception from seeing change as disequilibrium to seeing it as a constant. Strategizing for change ultimately comes down to whether individuals are motivated to change, learn, and grow. As John Gardner says, "unless we foster versatile, innovative and self-renewing men and women, all the ingenious social arrangements in the world will not help us."

5

Social Dynamics in Operation

Likening women to nature is a practice of ancient origin. Practice of exploiting women like nature is also as old. Moreover, both are global features of human behaviour down the centuries. As Yugoslavian feminist Rada Ivekovic says, the globalization of patriarchy is the first of all globalizations. It can be argued that all primitive virtues and vices can be traced to a common ancestry. As Samuel Bowles reminds us, 'commonality of different traits of humans spread across different cultures may be explained by the predominance of the influence of the common ancestral social institution which lasted for ninety percent of the span of the biological modern human existence.'

Primitive women were physically weak and biologically constrained, which seems to explain their subjugation of a primitive nature. They were mostly confined inside the house, engaged in household chores and rearing children. In modern days, however, importance of brawn has been replaced by the importance of brain. Advances in medical science, like measures of birth control and family planning, have also considerably lessened the biological dependence of women. Availability of modern household gadgets has considerably eased the work of housekeeping and has thereby given women more time of their own.

Television, films and other forms of popular mass media have given them an exposure to the outside world and they have started perceiving a different type of well-being, a different type of life. Women have proved their abilities in diverse fields as successful professionals. Their profession is no longer restricted to nursing, and they have become successful doctors, architects, pilots and so on. Many have even joined the army and some have led nations. Still, male dominance refuses to give way. We may call it the inertia of patriarchy.

But this inertia is long, much longer than the Newtonian physical one. Incidental power relations that put the male in the driver's seat thousands of years ago took firm roots in social institutions, which resist newer power relations even in the face of gender equating changes in objective situations. Despite the proven abilities of women, in most LDCs a male child is still preferred to a female child, the female members of the family get to eat what is left for them by the male members and among the poorer section of the population, expenditure on a male child is thought to be a better investment than on a female child.

Even though she may have to forgo formal school education, she is 'educated' in the art of good house keeping, sacrificing everything for her husband and sons, in short, in making herself a glorious domestic. Thus the culture of patriarchy prepares the female mind to calmly accept discrimination and injustice. But as the objective situation tries to pull away from the social institution, a tension develops between the two. On the one hand, technological advances create an enabling condition for women in a technical sense and development of democratic ethos fuel women's aspirations, and on the other, the patriarchal social order, because of its very nature, has all the mechanisms to suppress such aspirations. Feminist struggle is an outcome of this tension. Our effort in this chapter is to investigate the possibility of such an outcome in terms of the contributing factors. Analysis is conducted in a simple game theoretic framework. The focus will be on LDCs, not only because conditions of women are worse there, but also because these countries need more of women's agency as an instrument of development. Examples are drawn from India. Since we do not claim that India is a good representative case for the LDCs, inferences that we have drawn from the examples should be contextualized.

At the outset let us clarify a few issues. This will help conceptualize the gender game and the related discussion that will ensue. Firstly, we share the view that women's empowerment is the acquisition by an average woman of the capability to actively participate in decision making activities of her family and community. Her empowerment is complete when she participates on equal terms with her male counterpart. Clearly, empowerment is a positive concept, and should not be confused with a rise in women's happiness, which is a normative concept. Women's happiness is a state of mind, conditioned as it is by historically determined social and cultural norms. Thus, a woman, subjugated and exploited in every possible way, may still remain happy.

Not only that, she may even profess her brand of happiness to her daughter or daughter-in-law. Our proposition is that human action is shaped not by the objective condition of life, but by subjective evaluation of that condition. Our emphasis on awareness as the prime mover of social change is grounded on this premise. Secondly, empowerment is a process, namely acquisition of capability. Hence, lack of empowerment does not imply a state of absolute powerlessness. It merely implies that the process of acquisition of power is not at work. In every society women do have certain capabilities. Such capabilities might not have been won by women. They might have simply resulted from the need of self-perpetuation of the patriarchal order. It is found in most societies that routine household decisions are mostly taken by women though the strategic decisions are taken care of by male members.

Thirdly, patriarchy by its very nature is an antithesis of women's empowerment. Family is a seat of cooperative conflict, but the institution of patriarchy ensures that the breakdown position weighs so heavily against women in intra-family distribution that they have to cooperate more and get less. Dominance is bolstered by marriage and property norms and manifests itself through division of labor into paid and unpaid work.

Unpaid work assigned to women underestimates their contribution and in the process makes them diffident to demand their fair share. In the end, they find themselves overworked but undernourished. Even when marriage and property laws are matrilineal, decision-making process is largely patriarchal. No wonder, economic and political discrimination against women is prevalent even in these matrilineal societies. As a large body of literature on the impact of women's empowerment on social, economic and political development has evidenced, society can gain immensely by way of better ecosystem, better nourished children, more effective human capital, and a world largely devoid of bloodshed and torture of war if women have a say in the society. According to the Eco-Feminist school there is an apparent "closeness" between nature and women.

Moreover, since women are directly dependent on the forests for their own survival and that of their children it is only natural that they would make more judicious use of the forest resources. Since deforestation makes women travel a longer distance to collect fuel-wood and water, it is no wonder that there are several instances when women resistance groups have stood up against private contractors and saved forests from the latter's onslaught. The Adwani forest in the Garhwal Himalayas was auctioned in October 1977, and the trees were to be felled in the first week of December that year. Bachhni Devi, wife of the local village headman, led a large group of women to the forest and persuaded the forest laborers to refrain from tree felling and demonstrated against it. They tied sacred threads around each tree and vowed to protect them. The contractors, who arrived with a strong contingent of police force, were forced to make a hasty retreat. Surely, these benefits cut across genders. But these benefits lying as they are in distant future are often not well perceived.

On the other hand, the loss of power and privilege to

dominate is immediate and acutely felt by men. This seems to account for the indifference of patriarchy, if not cruelty, to women. This patriarchal indifference, however, is not the only stumbling block to women. Patriarchy has within it a mechanism of self-sustenance. If girls are least valuable and resources are scarce in the family (which they are in LDCs), then parents would invest in boys and neglect girls. This will in turn make girls less valuable.

In a society where a girl is meant only to be married off and dowry is the essence of marital engagement, educating girls only adds to the cost of marriage. The reason is that an educated bride can only be married off to an even more educated bridegroom, and the dowry rate is directly proportionate to the level of education of the bridegroom. Given this social matrix, the rational decision of parents is not to educate the female child. Women's empowerment, under such circumstances, has to be a result of adversarial public action.

It is true that some enabling conditions are created as byproducts of social, economic and technological changes. But these conditions by themselves do not change the lot of women. They, however, contribute by way of making the environment more congenial for adversarial public action by women. To take an example, disintegration of joint family system in many developing countries has created a pressure on the male member of the family to share the burden of household chores and to allow his wife to seek outside job for reason of economic security.

While there are some evidences to show that the workforce participation rate for women has been rising over the years, outside work does not by itself indicate empowerment for women. If women take up employment to support their families and continue to suffer the same unequal distribution of household activities and consumption then their employment can hardly be considered empowerment. It may instead be taken to reflect their increasing distress. However, women's employment raises their bargaining position in the intra-family distribution of decision making. This in turn makes conditions conducive for women to take move for emancipation. Our contention is that the act of emancipation must come from women themselves. It is not uncommon to come across instances where domestic violence is perpetrated on women who are educated and earning for the family, precisely because of that. As is revealed by a multisectoral survey done by the International Clinical Epidemiology Network, over ninety percent of Indian women who had reported experiencing domestic violence were involved in paid work. The survey also found out that this phenomenon cuts across social and educational status. This result reflects a conflict arising out of intra-family balance of power getting disturbed by the fact of women's employment. Intensity of opposition to women's adversarial public action, however, depends on the nature of women's project.

As long as their demands are confined to practical gender needs, and do not extend to strategic ones, opposition can be expected to be of a lower intensity and of a more localized nature. Fourthly, social institution of gender, with all the political, economic and cultural gender norms that it embodies, is constantly in a process of change. In this process there exists a part, which is evolutionary. This works very slowly through time, mainly through the economy and culture. There is another part, which may build on the first, but is essentially engineered, and hence works much faster. The impetus comes from a catalytic agent of change. This catalytic agent can be thought of as of two kinds. Firstly, it might have already established its supremacy, and is merely forcing the speed of its entrenchment, like the Talibans in Afghanistan some five years back. We may call it pro-establishment catalytic agent. If in a world of unequal gender relation, there exists a pro-establishment catalytic agent of change, it spells doom for women, and makes recovery that much dangerous project, as experiences of Afghan women indicated. Fortunately, a second kind of catalytic agent can be thought of.

We can christen it anti-establishment catalytic agent of change, whose role is to engineer an adversarial public action to bring in gender justice. The anti-establishment catalytic agent may be indigenous, or it may come from outside the system. Its essential function is to create among women a demand for change. It will of course give them leadership in the collective action that will ensue. Its continued presence is also sometimes necessary to sustain the project. Fifthly, there are many sub-societies in a country. Each of them has its very own domain of gender norms. Yet, it is not an island. It has its outside world in its own country as well as abroad. Changes in one such sub-society have external effects on others. The combined strength of these external effects and internal dynamics of each sub-society constitutes the matrix of domestic effects on a society. To this we have to add the effects from abroad.

Caged Women are in Equilibrium

Let us begin with a truism. The process of empowerment of women must start from a point of relative powerlessness. The fact of women's subordination to men for a long period of time lends some justification to the view that their relative powerlessness is a state of equilibrium. We can view this equilibrium as the outcome of a game.

Gender Game

We start by assuming a closed society with patriarchal norms. Since the social order is patriarchal, the movement for women's empowerment must come from women themselves. It is, therefore, a question of collective action by them, determinants of which form the object of enquiry of this chapter. Women's collective action materializes only when the average woman, say Ms. R, finds it to her advantage to join the project of empowerment. It is far from obvious that she will always and everywhere find it advantageous to join the project. Firstly, she may live in a social space steeped in patriarchal values, and she may have internalized those values so much so that she is unable to see advantage in empowerment, and is happy to live with whatever capability the patriarchy allows her to have. She may even frown on them who are sympathetic to feminist cause, so high is her sympathy with the establishment. Since she is a representative woman of the society, the majority of women in that society will think in a like manner, and the collective action will not materialize. This situation can be termed 'siege of patriarchy'.

Secondly, even if the situation is not as prohibitive as in the above case, and allows the average woman to believe that empowerment is not only desirable but also has a chance to result from women's collective action; she may not in the end join the project. Going one step further it may be claimed that she may not join even if she thinks that collective action will result and the mission will be successful, in spite of being in favor of empowerment. Her decision to join or abstain from joining a project of empowerment in such situations is predicated on a number of factors, and we have decided to use a game theoretic framework to capture these factors. This theoretical structure can also incorporate the case termed above as siege of patriarchy, where the outcome follows trivially.

The reason why game theory can be useful to capture the determinants of collective action is as follows. As has been already mentioned, collective action materializes only when a representative woman decides to act in favor of collective action. Her decision, however, depends on her perceived advantage of joining vis-à-vis that of not joining a project of empowerment.

However, the outcome of her decision is not a certainty to her. If she joins, but is not joined by other women, she cannot expect empowerment to result. If, on the other hand, others join, she can expect with some probability that empowerment will result and therefore, the perceived relative advantage of joining hinges on action by other women.

But she is far from sure that she will be joined by others in her action of revolt in the event of her choosing that. This uncertainty is generated by a communication failure, which results not primarily because women do not have a forum where they can meet and exchange ideas, but mainly because they are born into the dominant discourse of patriarchy, which keeps them unsure of the very legitimacy of their demands.

Since there exists this absence of communication between Ms. R and other women, but Ms. R's decision to join a project of empowerment depends on what other women do, it becomes a matter of strategic choice for Ms. R.

This strategic aspect of her choice makes the theory of game a useful tool of analysis. A more formal presentation of the game can be found in the Appendix. Let us now describe the game structure. The question of Ms. R joining a project of empowerment pits her against other women whose action is a matter of conjecture to her. This means that Ms. R is playing a game against 'all other women', say O. Though Ms. R is a representative woman in the context of this analysis, she does not, however, consider herself to be a representative, because of communication gap among women mentioned in the previous paragraph. This, in fact, is the very basis of her playing the game. Had she known that the every other woman would do exactly what she would under a given situation, the structure would not have been one of game.

The second point to note about this game structure is the totally mysterious nature of the other player O. This amorphous body of other women cannot make any strategy choice in reality, yet its existence as a player is real and potent in the mind of Ms. R. Whenever Ms. R contemplates an action, she has to consider the possible 'action' of this ubiquitous O. In this game, Ms. R can either join the mission of empowerment (in which case she is playing the strategy 'cooperate' or 'C'), or defect from this mission (in which case she is playing D).

She knows that O also has the same options of strategies. She, however, does not know, as is wont in game theory, the strategy O will actually choose. Instead, she assigns subjective probabilities to O's choosing C and D. She chooses C or D depending on which one gives her a higher expected Pay-off. Since she is representative of the collective, her choice turns out to be the choice of every woman. If Ms. R chooses C, everyone else also chooses C by symmetry, and collective action materializes. Similar logic implies that Ms. R's choosing D presages that collective action will not be launched. It is, therefore, necessary to explore the Pay-offs of Ms. R under different situations. In doing so, the first step is to conceptualize the outcomes of the gender game. The second step is to conceptualize the Pay-offs from these outcomes. Once the Pay-offs under different outcomes are clearly delineated, the prediction about Ms. R's decision becomes possible, given her conjecture about O's choice of strategy. The matrix of Pay-offs together with Ms. R's conjecture about O's action defines the game environment for Ms. R.

Outcomes of the Gender Game

The different strategy pairs for Ms. R and O are: (i) both Ms. R and O defect, i.e., (D, D) (ii) Ms. R cooperates, but O defects, i.e., (C, D), (iii) Ms. R defects, but O cooperates, i.e., (D, C), and (iv) Ms. R cooperates, O cooperates, i.e., (C, C). For each combination of strategies, there is an outcome of the game, which is defined from the perspective of Ms. R's problem of choice. Hence, an outcome is as is perceived by Ms. R at the point of choice, and not what will actually obtain in the end. The outcomes of different strategy combinations can be enumerated as follows.

i. *Outcome of (D, D):* Since everyone defects, the outcome is 'no empowerment with (D, D)'.
ii. *Outcome of (C, D):* Since O defects, Ms. R being only an average and insignificant woman in the milieu, cannot expect to single handedly salvage empowerment. The outcome, therefore, can be legitimately called 'no empowerment with (C, D)'.
iii. *Outcome of (D, C):* If Ms. R thinks that O is a potent force; this strategy combination yields the outcome 'empowerment with (D, C)'. However, if she is not certain that O is powerful enough to overcome the coercive force of patriarchy, then the outcome of the strategy pair is not 'empowerment with (D, C)', but a randomized outcome lying somewhere between 'empowerment with (D, C)' and 'no empowerment with (D, C)'.

A higher degree of optimism about O's ability takes the

randomized outcome closer to 'empowerment with (D, C)'. On the other hand, a higher degree of pessimism takes the outcome closer to 'no empowerment with (D, C)'. We can, therefore, think of two pure outcomes, namely, 'empowerment with (D, C)' and 'no empowerment with (D, C)', and innumerable mixed outcomes corresponding to different degrees of optimism attached to O's power to cooperatively bring about empowerment. Outcome of (D, C) should, therefore, be viewed as a mixed outcome, which is a randomization between the two pure outcomes, 'empowerment with (D, C)' and 'no empowerment with (D, C)'

(iv) Outcome of (C, C): By the same logic as in (iii) above, the outcome of (C, C) should be viewed as a mixed outcome, which is a randomization between the two pure outcomes, 'empowerment with (C, C)' and 'no empowerment with (C, C)'.

Two points in the above description of outcomes need special mention. Firstly, Ms. R finds herself too insignificant to have any perceptible contribution to the common cause of empowerment. Accordingly, she perceives that her effort is neither necessary nor sufficient for empowerment. Secondly, empowerment is a public good characterized by non-rivalry and non-excludability of consumption. As a result, Ms. R's non-participation cannot be a cause of her being denied the fruits of empowerment. These two factors have far-reaching implications for the possibility of collective action.

Pay-offs from Outcomes

Each outcome has a different implication for Ms. R. Evaluation of an outcome is a subjective process, and hence depends on the mindset of Ms. R. Given a certain mindset, Ms. R evaluates different outcomes in a determinate way. The value that Ms. R assigns to each outcome is her Pay-off from that outcome. Pay-offs from the six pure outcomes mentioned in the previous subsection can be analytically decomposed as follows.

Pay-offs from Pure Outcomes

i. *'Empowerment with (C, C)'*: This is one of the two pure outcomes of the strategy combination (C, C). It obtains when Ms. R believes in the potency of O. Now, it can be legitimately argued that when Ms. R cooperates in a project of empowerment, the very fact of participation manifests a commitment value, say 'c', she derives from participating in the project, irrespective of what this project yields. In another part of her mind there may be a place for patriarchal values she was born into and inculcated with in course of her upbringing. When she cooperates in a project of empowerment, she severs her association with patriarchal values, and that constitutes a psychological cost to her, say 'v'. Therefore, whenever Ms. R cooperates, (c-v) is a component of her Pay-off, irrespective of whether empowerment is won or not. If on top of this, empowerment is won, some value flows from that to Ms. R. This is the value, say 'b' that Ms. R assigns to empowerment per se. The Pay-off from the outcome (a) can thus be expressed as (b+c-v).

ii. *'Empowerment with (D, C)'*: This is one of the two pure outcomes of the strategy combination (D, C). It obtains when Ms. R believes in the potency of O. Here, since Ms. R does not cooperate, she not only saves the loss of 'v', but also enjoys 'v', and hence the latter forms a positive component of her Pay-off. She, however, gets alienated from O, which constitutes a psychological cost, say 'h', to her. Since empowerment is a public good characterized by non-exclusion, she cannot be denied the fruits of empowerment even if she does not cooperate. Hence, she will enjoy 'b'. The Pay-off from the outcome (b) is thus (b+v-h).

iii. *'No empowerment with (C, D)'*: This is the only pure outcome corresponding to the strategy combination (C, D). As explained in (i) above in this subsection, (c-v) constitutes a part of the Pay-off. However, since the project of empowerment is unsuccessful, an explicit penalty imposed by the patriarchy is to be borne, and let Ms. R deems it as 'x'. Moreover, since Ms. R is a lone crusader, there is a psychological cost of alienation from O, say 'm', which may be called the implicit cost of a lone crusade. There is, however, some utility, say 'e', to be derived from whatever capability is granted by unaffected patriarchy. The Pay-off from the outcome (c) is thus (e+c-v-x-m).

iv. *'No empowerment with (D, D)':* This is the only pure outcome corresponding to the strategy combination (D, D). Since nobody cooperates, there is no empowerment to be won, and no penalty to be suffered as well. Nor can there be any cost of alienation since in this case strategy of Ms. R matches with that of O. Pay-off in this situation is the perceived benefit from whatever capability is available under patriarchal bondage, and the sense of security from blindly following the dominant discourse of patriarchy. In terms of our variables, it is (e+v).

v. *'No empowerment with (C, C)':* This is another pure outcome associated with (C, C). While this outcome yields a value (c-v), which is always associated with the fact of Ms. R's cooperation, it fails to deliver 'b' since Ms. R does not believe that O is potent enough to overcome patriarchal resistance. Moreover, since the project of empowerment is expected to fall through and Ms. R has joined it, explicit cost of patriarchal sanction (x) must be borne by Ms. R. To this must be added the usual benefits from unaffected patriarchy, 'e'. Pay-off, therefore, comes to (e+c-v-x).

vi. *'No empowerment with (D, C):* This is another pure outcome associated with (D, C). This obtains when Ms. R is certain that O will not be able to wrest any benefit from the patriarchy. Here Ms. R does not get 'b'. Instead, she gets 'e'. Since Ms. R has not joined other women in the struggle for empowerment she avoids the explicit patriarchal sanction, 'x', but in the bargain incurs the psychological cost of alienation from other women, 'h'. She, however, enjoys upholding patriarchal values, 'v'. The Pay-off is, therefore, (e+v-h).

Pay-offs from Randomized Outcomes

As has been pointed out, outcome of a strategy pair

involving O's cooperation is a mixed outcome, as empowerment is not a certainty in face of patriarchal resistance. Therefore, the corresponding Pay-off is also a randomized value of Pay-offs from corresponding pure outcomes. When Ms. R joins other women in a project of empowerment she has to take into account not only the benefits of empowerment that may accrue to her, but also the possible persecutions she may have to suffer as well as continuation of bondage in case the project fails. Similarly, when she defects from other women who are waging a struggle, she does not know which world she will live in after the struggle is over.

Ms. R weighs her two options – cooperation and defection – in terms of expected Pay-off. While section 3.1.2 has built the Pay-offs associated with different strategy pairs, Ms. R does not know which strategy pair will actually materialize, because she is never certain about the strategy O will end up choosing. Therefore, it is vital for her to form an idea about what O is likely to do. If she knows the likelihood of O's cooperation in addition to the Pay-offs associated with different strategy pairs, she can be said to be in a position to weigh her two options and come to a decision about her choice. If she believes that other women are bent on cooperating, we should expect her to focus on Pay-offs corresponding to outcomes attached to others' united struggle. The corresponding prediction about her choice of strategy is much brighter than if she is pessimistic about others' cooperation, in which case she cannot harbor much expectation about empowerment, and hence her decision to defect is almost imminent.

It is now possible to make some observations about the factors that influence Ms. R's choice of strategy. We can conceive of a society with patriarchal norms well entrenched in the psyche of the victims. If we take note of the fact that patriarchy is not merely a system of gender relation, but a well-entrenched culture, exploitative gender relation may not, after all, look that despicable to the victims. The culture with its preference changing norms may take such a heavy toll on them that they may even see their empowerment as a sin. Since to such an indoctrinated mind, patriarchy is the omnipotent system, any attempt to disturb it is only to be met with a heavy hand, and the isolation resulting from a lonely battle is extremely painful not only because of the fact of isolation, but also because of an extremely low level of commitment which is expected to characterize the battle.

In comparison, psychological cost of isolation for not having cooperated with other women in the event of their revolting is not very high presumably because the idea of revolt is not at all attractive to an indoctrinated mind. Under such a scenario the Pay-offs are so heavily tilted towards defection that Ms. R is sure to defect no matter what other women do. This is a trivial result when patriarchy holds the female mind in a state of siege. The 'siege of patriarchy game' is of course an extreme example of patriarchy, where brainwashing is complete. Women here are so thoroughly steeped in the dominant discourse that they are unable to see merit in freedom. While such an extreme view on women's self-assessment is too harsh, this does bring into sharp relief the fact that traditional norms and customs, deeply rooted in people's mind, are among the hardest obstacles to development and change, even harder than the obstacles created by formal laws. The first step towards women's empowerment thus seems to be coming into existence awareness among women of their own bondage. This will create a desire for change, a demand for a new institution.

Awareness about her bondage is, however, not sufficient to drive Ms. R onto action of revolt. This is because Ms. R perceives that if other women cooperate and the mission is accomplished, then no one can be excluded from its benefits, empowerment being a public good. Similarly, if empowerment does not materialize, everybody has to share the resultant predicament. Moreover, she is also given to the perception that success or failure of others' cooperative move does not depend on her cooperation, because she is insignificant in the milieu. These two factors together constitute the basis of what is known in the parlance of economics as the problem of free riding. There are a number of factors, which make defection attractive to Ms. R. First, at the level of ethics there is a sense of security in siding with the dominant discourse of patriarchy. This sense of security is lost once she deviates from the beaten track. Secondly, there is the fear of persecution by patriarchy in case of an unsuccessful revolt, which can be avoided through defection. Thirdly, there is a psychological cost of isolation associated with struggle in case other women do not cooperate. However, the latter two incentives to defect are lower if other women are more likely to wage the battle, and the possibility of that battle being successful is also higher. There are two other factors that work to counteract the incentive to defect. First, Ms. R may be committed to the cause of emancipation.

Secondly, sense of guilt associated with lone defection weighs on the mind of the defector. If these countervailing forces are strong enough Ms. R may end up choosing to fight. Anyone having some knowledge of the gruesome repression during the now disintegrated Taliban regime in Afghanistan will understand that the women involved with the Revolutionary Association of Women of Afghanistan (RAWA) were led to action by an extremely high commitment value. But RAWA was a case of desperation. The abject debasement of the self made the game environment explosive. In most cases situations are less turbulent, and incentive to free ride dominates the mind. Since almost every woman tries to free ride like Ms. R, collective action does not materialize despite every woman wanting empowerment. Thus, like in the case of 'prisoners' dilemma', rational choice by each individual leads to collective irrationality. Ironically, collective action fails to materialize and women settle for a sub-optimal equilibrium by their own choice. This is not to claim that collective action would have ensured empowerment. This is just to claim that having not gone in for collective action, women have forgone any possibility of empowerment.

Catalytic Agent of Change

The equilibrium of bondage cannot be disturbed unless the Pay-offs and belief about other women (i.e., the game environment) change for Ms. R. However repugnant the game environment may seem to her, she is incapable of changing it. The game environment is set to her by the patriarchal social order. Discontinuous changes in that social order has the potential to make the game environment explosive, thereby disturbing the equilibrium of bondage within a short span of time. Obviously, the agent of such change cannot be found, unless accidentally and inadvertently as in the case of Taliban-controlled Afghanistan, in the patriarchal order.

The agent must come from an extra patriarchal space. The primary task of such an external agent is to elevate the game environment from a condition where free riding is lucrative to one where it is not. Let us call this agent of change a catalytic agent. The work of a catalytic agent is to undertake an awareness campaign among women so that they become aware of their bondage. As our analysis suggests, the campaign cannot stop there. It must instill in every woman a sense of commitment and responsibility.

Presence of a catalytic agent can also considerably reduce the communication gap among women. As a result a situation can be created where Ms. R can expect that other women will come forward, and the project of empowerment will succeed. What will then be the identity of a catalytic agent? Seen from the perspective of this game, any extra patriarchal agent Ms. R does not represent can be a catalytic agent. A catalytic agent does not play the game, but influences the game environment hence the name. There are quite a few who would like to see the State in the role of a catalytic agent. Our contention is if the society is patriarchal, the State is no different. By its very construction the political institution of a country cannot be at odds with its social counterpart. Those who have innocent faith in democracy should be reminded that the Law under democracy reflects rather than changes the society. There may, however, be a disjuncture of the government with the State at times. We have seen in history instances of proactive government trying to bring in sea change in social institution. But we must not delude ourselves into believing that the government is a benevolent despot or a neutral umpire. It is rather a self-interested player with a mission of its own, and there is no reason to believe that its mission is the mission of the underprivileged.

As a matter of fact, those at the helm of affairs do quite frequently represent the dominant discourse, and are interested in maneuvering the system further in their favor. The gender-regressive Brahminical regime into which the Indian civilization relapsed during the Gupta era, or the more dramatic and cruel repression the Afghan women went through in recent times are reminders of atrocities a pro-establishment catalytic agent can unleash on women from a position of institutional power. The above appears to give us a picture of closure. Since State is internal to the patriarchal social structure, the impetus of any positive change cannot come from it in any direct way. There are, however, three considerations that help dispel this specter of closure.

Firstly, since in our framework catalytic agent is an analytical category, it can be argued that education and economic development can act as potent catalytic agents by changing consciousness of women. One may at this point argue that educational and economic progress too cannot escape the long arms of patriarchy. A districtwise analysis of 2001 census of India reveals that while decline in child sex ratio is all-pervading in India, it is higher for 'front-ranking' states like Punjab, Haryana, Gujarat and part of Himachal Pradesh and the decline is also higher for the urban areas than it is for the rural ones. Those familiar with the field situation in these advanced provinces and cities have found that increased access to pre-natal sex detection techniques and abortion facilities has helped affluent, urban and 'educated' people to do away with female births.

Economic and educational progress has evidently failed to make people more humane to unborn daughters. This is not to suggest that education and economic progress are of no consequence. This is just to highlight the difficulty of the task at hand when it comes to strategic gender needs. In this particular example, the culture of patriarchy is so firmly entrenched in the mind of even formally educated women that they fail to realize that saving a female fetus is a strategic gender need. However, as has been evidenced later on in this section, women's awareness about their practical gender needs is greatly facilitated by educational progress.

Secondly, a nation is not a closed entity. Changes in the outside world impact on it through transmission of information and through the channel of diplomacy. These impacts have historically changed the game environment and have made it more congenial to women's collective action. Thirdly, a nation is not also a monolith. A society has within it a number of sub-societies, each having its very own gender norms. While at the macro level the sway of patriarchy may be overarching, there can be considerable leeway within a sub-society. Moreover, since the sphere of outside with respect to a smaller (sub) society is correspondingly larger, it is now easier to conceive of an outside agent of change.

A voluntary organization, which is a strong outside force with respect to a given sub-society, may turn out to be not only weak, but also internal with respect to a larger social sphere. However, the impact it creates on the game environment of a sub-society, may generate a force of its own, and snowball into other contiguous sub-societies through a chain of external effects.

Women in each sub-society play their own game defined by the specific game environment of that sub-society. Sub-societies vary in their patriarchal intensities. For example, matrilineal sub-societies can be expected to have a lower intensity of patriarchy than patrilineal sub-societies. Lower the intensity of patriarchy easier is the task of external anti-establishment catalytic agents to make inroads into the game environment. Sometimes, the degree of patriarchy may be so low that no catalytic agent is needed. This may explain why women in Kerala have been important participants in trade union movements, peasant and agricultural labor movements, movements for land reform and movements for food.

The same factor explains why Naga Mothers' Association could rise against insurgency, albeit in the informal space of politics, in the troubled North-eastern India. These are instances of adversarial collective action of women to empower themselves. As a matter of fact, actively participating in the public space is itself a constituent of empowerment (section 2, para 2). However, most sub-societies are not as fortunate. For them, a catalytic agent of change is essential.

It should be quite clear by now that the identity of catalytic agent can take on many forms, from an abstract one of education to concrete organizations or lone mavericks. Persons involved may even be men. The only requirement is that in order to be a catalytic agent, the latter must be delinked from patriarchal values, and reasonably powerful to affect the Pay-off matrix and the belief system of women. Let us now take note of a few cases of women's adversarial public action in India to highlight the key role played by anti-establishment catalytic agents. Lalita Pulavarti has this to say about the role of Sumangali Seva Ashram, a voluntary organization working for women's empowerment in the Bangalore district in South India:

> Many of the member Mahila Mandals had originally been set up by the government under the non-institutional welfare schemes. However, most of them were inactive when SSA entered the scene... By setting up the federation, SSA revived the Mahila Mandals, increased their membership, and re-energized them by providing the necessary leadership.

Evidently SSA was an outside force in each single Mahila Mandal area where local male resistance was not potent enough. The frustration betrayed by the sarcastic question put to a Mahila Mandal member by a local self-appointed leader "What has your Mahila Mandal done for our neighbourhood?" reflects this impotence before an autonomous outside force. Vanangana, a women's group working in Banda district of Uttar Pradesh, not only organized women in effective self-help groups and broke their silence on the issue of chilling incidences of domestic violence, they were also successful beyond their own expectation in impressing upon many of the men, many of whom were themselves wife beaters, to do away with domestic violence.

The relentless campaign through street plays followed by discussions in 30 villages generated a public debate and, as Vanangana organizers say, "The police and the bureaucracy will have to take notice".

Another interesting example can be found in the work of Disha, a voluntary organization, in Pather village of Saharanpur district of Uttar Pradesh. It has been working in the village for several years particularly to mobilize women and it had set up a Mahila Jagriti Sangh or women's awakening committee in the village. This had a remarkable effect on the women who spearheaded a brave, uncompromising anti-liquor movement against heavy odds from the administration. Here also they could rally the male villagers around them, such was the moral force created by the movement. In Andhra Pradesh a series of struggles against government-backed sales of arrack took place during 1980s and early 1990s. While in Telengana region and in a few other districts the catalytic agent could be found in CPI (M-L) groups, in the coastal districts the spurt came mainly from the adult literacy program. It is interesting to note that the adult literacy program was not devised as a catalytic agent, but it had this unintended consequence. History, fortunately, cannot be entirely designed. Moreover, adult literacy programs are themselves results of catalytic agents of change on a broader social plane, and the source can be located, inter alia, in the relentless campaign by international development agencies and globalized communication.

Apart from the triggering and nurturing role of a catalytic agent, there is another feature common to almost all the above movements. It is their tendency to spread. The anti-arrack movement spread like wildfire and forced the Andhra government to ban arrack in the entire state from 1October, 1993. After the success in Pather, Disha started getting request from neighbouring villages to help them get rid of their liquor shops. Similarly, activities of Sumangali Seva Ashram picked up rapidly later on as the success stories came pouring into adjoining Mahila Mandals. SAWERA, acronym for Sustainable Agriculture and Women's Empowerment through Rural Approach, a new UNDP supported ongoing sub-programme in UP, is premised precisely on this external effect of women's movement in one region on another. Needless to say, this has far-reaching consequences. This is the route, the march to gender equality may successfully take even in a country of overarching patriarchy, a case of sub-nations overwhelming the nation.

In the present era of Information Technology, pace of this development can only be expected to speed up. There is, however, one caveat regarding the fruitfulness of a catalytic agent. The most vital factor behind the success of an empowerment project is sustained effort. The consonance of the interests of a catalytic agent and that of its target group of women is a crucial determinant of sustained effort. Husain has shown in the context of common property resources that a catalytic agent may have some covert agenda which may benefit from its leading role in the community action, but once that benefit is exhausted, it will lose interest in the project, which will then have to fend for itself, most of the time unsuccessfully. It is pretty much the same thing in a project of women's empowerment. NGOs, funded and encouraged by the government and foreign agencies, are not all equally motivated. People having first-hand knowledge of ground realities have related to the authors that many of the so-called success stories of self-help women's groups have their disheartening inner stories.

Often, helpless women are used by some NGOs to get access to institutional finance, which are then spent on hidden business. But this downright dishonesty is not the only caveat. It is not very uncommon to come across bored housewives of affluent husbands forming women's organizations of social work, interested more in socialite meetings and press conferences than actually helping the cause of women of another social and economic class. In the success stories that we have considered in this section, women in the voluntary organizations were dedicated to the cause of women's empowerment, coming as they did from backgrounds of similar victimization.

As argued in the last section, there is no reason why a government, or for that matter, the opposition on their own should be particularly sympathetic to women. The way the Indian legislators are dragging their feet on the bill on Women's Reservation in Indian Parliament is just one of many instances of patriarchy structured in administration and politics. Still, the Constitution (73th Amendment) Act, 1992 provides for reservation for women of no less than one-third of total number of posts of members and chairpersons at all three tiers of Panchayati Raj institutions. The National Nutritional Policy, National Policy on Education, National Health Policy, and National Population Policy – all have components for women aimed at their empowerment. The Ministry of Rural Development has components for women in all poverty alleviation programs. All these are pointers to the constant pressure on the government, past or present, to sensitize itself to gender issues.

One source of pressure is in the cumulative external effects of women's empowerment in various sub-societies of the nation, as discussed in the previous section. We have noted there that Andhra government had to bow to the statewide anti-arrack movement. This kind of victory changes the game environment dramatically for further movements in future. There is a second source of pressure on the government – the pressure from the international community. It should be borne in mind that India is a signatory to the UN "Convention on Elimination of all forms of discriminations Against Women" (CEDAW) adopted on 18 December, 1979. International community can be a very strong catalytic agent, not only through its pressure on national governments, but also through its impact on the milieu through the media and other lightning forms of communication devices in an IT-enabled age.

In this chapter we tried to evolve an analytical framework to analyze the emergence or otherwise of women's struggle. We do acknowledge that struggle for practical gender needs invites less resistance from the patriarchy than would a struggle for strategic gender needs. As a matter of fact, all the women's movements described here dealt with only practical gender needs – more family income, less domestic violence, family peace and better health for everyone in the family. None of these threatens to destabilize status quo of power relation within a family. Radical left feminists consider this an unacceptable compromise that only help prolong the patriarchy. We beg to differ. We believe that small gains accumulate and prepare the ground for the final war.

Revolution, so dear to the radicals, is not easily comprehensible to ordinary women. Radical thoughts involve abstract categories and distant foes. Women in the common walks of life are more concerned with drinking habit of their husbands, domestic violence, dowry related ignominy and torture, and other directly visible kinds of problems they have to put up with. They can grapple with radical concepts only after attaining some degree of empowerment and awareness. Our difference with the radical feminists is not with respect to the goal, but in sequencing the project to reach that goal.

Secondly, this chapter does not have any policy prescription, precisely because it is our contention that there does not exist any policy-maker, which on its own is willing to follow that prescription. A government can only become gender-sensitive under public pressure. While situating government in such an unenviable position we do not, however, suggest that it has no positive role to play in the project of women's emancipation. When a government makes a policy choice or legislators promulgate a law in favor of women, that by itself makes the game environment better for feminist struggle, firstly by changing the Pay-offs, and secondly, by raising the subjective probability of others' cooperation.

But, certainly, the government does not hold the key. The key is in the hands of catalytic agents committed to the cause of women, working in scattered pockets where they can be reckoned as powerful enough to influence the local level game environment for women. Their stance must be proactive rather than bureaucratic. They must reach out to the local community through informal interactions and participatory practices. The time is now as conducive to them as it has never been before.

6

Origins of Group Dynamics

While focusing attention on the central role of groups in human society, Dorwin Cartwright and Alvin Zander defined group dynamics as a "field of inquiry dedicated to advancing knowledge about the nature of groups, the laws of their development, and their interrelations with individuals, other groups, and larger institutions." They emphasized the role of empirical research, dynamics and interdependence, the social sciences, and practical application as hallmarks of the field. By presenting the historical background that enabled the emergence of group dynamics in the late 1930s, they help us understand and appreciate this major intellectual stream which buoys the practice of group facilitation.

Dorwin Cartwright was recruited to the faculty of the Research Center for Group Dynamics at MIT when it was founded in 1945 by Kurt Lewin. Upon Lewin's death in 1947, he succeeded as its Director and oversaw the Center's move in 1948 to the newly founded Institute for Social Research at the University of Michigan. At this time, Alvin Zander joined the Center faculty, later to succeed Cartwright as its Director from 1959-78. The two collaborated to produce Group Dynamics: Research and Theory, first published in 1953. Dorwin Cartwright was honored in 1977 by the Society for the Psychological Study of Social Issues with its Kurt Lewin Award. He retired from the University of Michigan in 1978, having authored some 50 articles, chapters, or books related to social psychological research or practice. He lives in Santa Barbara, California. Alvin Zander, among whose books are Making Groups Effective, Making Boards Effective, and Motives & Goals in Groups, retired from the University of Michigan in 1980. He died in 1998 in Walnut Creek, California.

If it were possible for the overworked hypothetical man from Mars to take a fresh view of the people of Earth, he would probably be impressed by the amount of time they spend doing things together in groups. He would note that most people cluster into relatively small groups, with the members residing together in the same dwelling, satisfying their basic biological needs within the group, depending upon the same source for economic support, rearing children, and mutually caring for the health of one another. He would observe that the education and socialization of children tend to occur in other, usually larger, groups in churches, schools, or other social institutions. He would see that much of the work of the world is carried out by people who perform their activities in close interdependence within relatively enduring associations. He would perhaps be saddened to find groups of men engaged in warfare, gaining courage and morale from pride in their unit and a knowledge that they can depend upon their buddies. He might be gladdened to see groups of people enjoying themselves in recreations and sports of various kinds. Finally, he might be puzzled why so many people spend so much time in little groups talking, planning, and being "in conference".

Surely he would conclude that if he wanted to understand much about what is happening on Earth, he would have to examine rather carefully the ways in which groups form, function, and dissolve. Now if we turn to a more customary perspective and view our society through the eyes of Earth's inhabitants, we discover that the functioning or malfunctioning of groups is recognized increasingly as one of society's major problems. In business, government, and the military, there is great interest in improving the productivity of groups. Many thoughtful people are alarmed by the apparent weakening and disintegration of the family.

Educators are coming to believe that they cannot carry out their responsibilities fully unless they understand better how the classroom functions as a social group. Those concerned with social welfare are diligently seeking ways to reduce intergroup conflicts between labor and management. The operation of juvenile gangs is a most troublesome obstacle in attempts to prevent crime.

It is becoming clear that much mental illness derives in some way from the individual's relations with groups and that groups may be used effectively in mental therapy. Whether one wishes to understand or to improve human behaviour, it is necessary to know a great deal about the nature of groups. Neither a coherent view of man nor an advanced social technology is possible without dependable answers to a host of questions concerning the operation of groups, how individuals relate to groups, and how groups relate to larger society.

When, and under what conditions, do groups form? What conditions are necessary for their growth and effective functioning? What factors foster the decline and disintegration of groups? How do groups affect the behaviour, thinking, motivation, and adjustment of individuals? What makes some groups have powerful influence over members, while other groups exert little or none? What characteristics of individuals are important determinants of the properties of groups? What determines the nature of relations between groups? When groups are part of a larger social system, what circumstances make them strengthen or weaken the more inclusive organization? How does the social environment of a group affect its properties? Questions like these must be answered before we will have a real understanding of human nature and human behaviour.

They must be answered, too, before we can hope to design an optimal society and bring it into being. The student of group dynamics is interested in acquiring knowledge about the nature of groups and especially about the psychological and social forces associated with groups. Such an interest has, of course, motivated intellectual activities of thoughtful people for centuries. The earliest recorded philosophical literature contains a great deal of wisdom about the nature of groups and the relations between individuals and groups. It also contains a variety of specifications concerning the "best" ways of managing group life. During the period from the sixteenth through the nineteenth centuries, there was created in Europe an impressive literature dealing with the nature of man and his place in society.

In this literature one can find most of the major orientations, or "basic assumptions," which guide current research and thinking about groups. It is evident that the modern student of group dynamics is not essentially different in his interests from scholars writing at various times over the centuries. And yet, it is equally clear that the approach to the study of groups known as "group dynamics" is strictly a twentieth century development; it is significantly different from that of preceding centuries. What, then, is group dynamics? The phrase has gained popular familiarity since World War II but, unfortunately, with its increasing circulation, its meaning has become imprecise.

According to one rather frequent usage, group dynamics refers to a sort of political ideology concerning the ways in which groups should be organized and managed. This ideology emphasizes the importance of democratic leadership, the participation of members in decisions, and the gains both to society and to individuals to be obtained through cooperative activities in groups.

The critics of this view have sometimes caricatured it as making "togetherness" the supreme virtue, advocating that everything be done jointly in groups that have and need no leader because everyone participates fully and equally. A second popular usage of the term group dynamics has it refer to a set of techniques, such as role playing, buzz-sessions, observation and feedback of group process, and group decision, which have been employed widely during the past decade or two in training programs designed to improve skill in human relations and in the management of conferences and committees. These techniques have been identified most closely with the National Training Laboratories whose annual training programs at Bethel, Maine, have become widely known.

According to the third usage of the term group dynamics, it refers to a field of inquiry dedicated to achieving knowledge about the nature of groups, the laws of their development, and their interrelations with individuals, other groups, and larger institutions. It is not possible, of course, to legislate how terms are to be used in a language. Nevertheless, it is important for clarity of thinking and communication to distinguish among these three quite distinct things which have been given the same label in popular discussions.

Everyone has an ideology, even though he may not be able to state it very explicitly, concerning the ways in which group life should be organized. Those responsible for the management of groups and the training of people for participation in groups can fulfill their responsibilities only by the use of techniques of one sort or another. But there is no rigidly fixed correspondence between a particular ideology about the "ideal" nature of groups and the use of particular techniques of management and training. And it should be obvious that the search for a better understanding of the nature of group life need not be linked to a particular ideology or adherence to certain techniques of management.

In this, we shall limit our usage of the term group dynamics to refer to the field of inquiry dedicated to advancing knowledge about the nature of group life. Group dynamics, in this sense, is a branch of knowledge or an intellectual specialization. Being concerned with human behaviour and social relationships, it can be located within the social sciences. And yet it cannot be identified readily as a subpart of any of the traditional academic disciplines. In order to gain a better understanding of how group dynamics differs from other familiar fields, let us consider briefly some of its distinguishing characteristics.

Significant Empirical Research

We noted above that an interest in groups can be found throughout history and that such an interest cannot, therefore, distinguish group dynamics from its predecessors. The difference lies, rather, in the way this interest is exploited. Until the beginning of the present century, those who were curious about the nature of groups relied primarily upon personal experience and historical records to provide answers to their questions. Not being burdened by the necessity of accounting for an accumulation of carefully gathered empirical data, writers in this speculative era devoted their energies to the creation of comprehensive theoretical treatments of groups.

These theoretical systems, especially the ones produced during the nineteenth century, were elaborate and widely inclusive, having been created by men of outstanding intellectual ability. The list of names from this era contains such impressive thinkers as Cooley, Durkheim, Freud, Giddings, LeBon, McDougall, Ross, Tarde, Tonnies, and Wundt. Their ideas can still be seen in contemporary discussions of group life.

By the second decade of this century, an empiricist rebellion had begun in social science, principally in the United States and especially in psychology and sociology. Instead of being content with speculation about the nature of groups, a few people began to seek out facts and to attempt to distinguish between objective data and subjective impression. Although rather simple empirical questions initially guided this research, a fundamentally new criterion for evaluating knowledge about groups was established.

Instead of asking merely whether some proposition about the nature of groups is plausible and logically consistent, those interested in groups began to demand that the proposition be supported by reliable data that can be reproduced by an independent investigator. Major effort went into the devising and improving of techniques of empirical research that would provide reliability of measurement, standardization of observation, effective experimental design, and the statistical analysis of data.

When, in the late 1930s, group dynamics began to emerge as an identifiable field, the empiricist rebellion was well along in social psychology and sociology, and, from the outset, group dynamics could employ the research methods characteristic of an empirical science. In fact, group dynamics is to be distinguished from its intellectual predecessors primarily by its basic reliance on careful observation, quantification, measurement, and experimentation. But one should not identify group dynamics too closely with extreme empiricism. Even in its earliest days, work in group dynamics displayed an interest in the construction of theory and the derivation of testable hypotheses from theory, and it has come progressively to maintain a close interplay between data collection and the advancement of theory.

Interdependence of Phenomena

Although the phrase group dynamics specifies groups as the object of study, it also focuses attention more sharply on questions about the dynamics of group life. The student of group dynamics is not satisfied with just a description of the properties of groups or of events associated with groups. Nor is he content with a classification of types of groups or of forms of group behaviour. He wants to know how the phenomena he observes depend on one another and what new phenomena might result from the creation of conditions never before observed. In short, he seeks to discover general principles concerning what conditions produce what effects.

This search requires the asking of many detailed questions about the interdependence among specific phenomena. If a change of membership occurs in a group, which other features of the group will change and which will remain stable? Under what conditions does a group tend to undergo a change of leadership? What are the pressures in a group which bring about uniformity of thinking among its members? What conditions inhibit creativity among group members? What changes in a group will heighten productivity, lower it, or not affect it at all? If the cohesiveness of a group is raised, which other of its features will change? Answers to questions like these reveal how certain properties and processes depend on others.

Theories of group dynamics attempt to formulate lawful relations among phenomena such as these. As these theories have been elaborated, they have guided work in group dynamics toward the intensive investigation of such things as change, resistance to change, social pressures, influence, coercion, power, cohesion, attraction, rejection, interdependence, equilibrium, and instability. Terms like these, by suggesting the operation of psychological and social forces, refer to the dynamic aspects of groups and play an important role in theories of group dynamics.

Interdisciplinary Relevance

It is important to recognize that research on the dynamics of groups has not been associated exclusively with any one of the social science disciplines. Sociologists have, of course, devoted great energy to the study of groups, as illustrated by investigations of the family, gangs, work groups, military units, and voluntary associations. Psychologists have directed their attention to many of the same kinds of groups, concentrating for the most part on the ways groups influence the behaviour, attitudes, and personalities of individuals and the effects of characteristics of individuals on group functioning. Cultural anthropologists while investigating many of the same topics as sociologists and psychologists, have contributed data on groups living under conditions quite different from those of modern industrial society.

Political scientists have extended their traditional interest in large institutions to include studies of the functioning of legislative groups, pressure groups, and the effects of group membership on voting. And economists have come increasingly to collect data on the way decisions to spend or save money are made in the family, how family needs and relationships affect the size of the labor force, how goals of unions affect policies in business, and how decisions having economic consequences are reached in businesses of various kinds. Since an interest in groups is shared by the various social science disciplines, it is clear that any general knowledge about the dynamics of groups has significance widely throughout the social sciences.

Findings to Social Practice

Everyone who feels a responsibility for improving the functioning of groups and the quality of their consequences for individuals and society must base his actions upon some more or less explicit view of the effects that will be produced by different conditions and procedures. Anyone who is concerned with improving the quality of work in a research team, the effectiveness of a Sunday school class, the morale of a military unit, with decreasing the destructive consequences of intergroup conflict, or with attaining any socially desirable objective through groups, can make his efforts more effective by basing them on a firm knowledge of the laws governing group life. The various professions that specialize in dealing with particular needs of individuals and of society have much to gain from advances in the scientific study of groups. One outstanding development in the more advanced societies during the past century has been the increasing differentiation undergone by the traditional professions of medicine, law, education, and theology.

Today there are people who receive extensive training and devote their lives to such professional specialties as labor-management mediation, public health education, marriage counseling, human relations training, intergroup relations, social group work, pastoral counseling, hospital administration, adult education, public administration, psychiatry, and clinical psychology- just to mention a few. The professionalization of practice in these many areas has brought about a self-conscious desire to improve standards and the establishment of requirements for proper training. The major universities now have professional schools in many of these fields to provide such training. As this training has been extended and rationalized, members of these professions have become increasingly aware of the need for knowledge of the basic findings and principles produced in the social sciences. All of these professions must work with people, not simply as individuals but in groups and through social institutions. It should not be surprising, therefore, to find that courses in group dynamics are becoming more and more common in the professional schools, that people trained in group dynamics are being employed by agencies concerned with professional practice, and that group dynamics research is often carried out in connection with the work of such agencies.

In summary, then, we have proposed that group dynamics should be defined as a field of inquiry dedicated to advancing knowledge about the na'ure of groups, the laws of their development, and their interrelations with individuals, other groups, and larger institutions. It may be identified by four distinguishing characteristics:

- An emphasis on theoretically significant empirical research,
- An interest in dynamics and the interdependence among phenomena,
- A broad relevance to all the social sciences, and
- The potential applicability of its findings in efforts to improve the functioning of groups and their consequences on individuals and society. Thus conceived, group dynamics need not be associated with any particular ideology concerning the ways in which groups should be organized and managed nor with the use of any particular techniques of group management. In fact, it is a basic objective of group dynamics to provide a better scientific basis for ideology and practice.

The Rise of Group Dynamics

Group dynamics began, as an identifiable field of inquiry, in the United States toward the end of the 1930s. Its origination as a distinct specialty is associated primarily with Kurt Lewin (1890-1947) who popularized the term group dynamics, made significant contributions to both research and theory in group dynamics and in 1945 established the first organization devoted explicitly to research on group dynamics. Lewin's contribution was of great importance, but, as we shall see in detail, group dynamics was not the creation of just one person. It was, in fact, the result of many developments that occurred over a period of several years and in several different disciplines and professions.

Viewed in historical perspective, group dynamics can be seen as the convergence of certain trends within the social sciences and, more broadly, as the product of the particular society in which it arose. The time and place of the rise of group dynamics were, of course, not accidental. American society in the 1930s provided the kind of conditions required for the emergence of such an intellectual movement. And, over the years since that time, only certain countries have afforded a favorable environment for its growth. To date, group dynamics has taken root primarily in the United States and the countries of northwestern Europe, although there have also been important developments in Israel, Japan, and India. Three major conditions seem to have been required for its rise and subsequent growth.

Supportive Society

If any field of inquiry is to prosper, it must exist in a surrounding society which is sufficiently supportive to provide the institutional resources required. By the end of the 1930s, cultural and economic conditions in the United States were favorable for the emergence and growth of group dynamics. Great value was placed on science, technology, rational problem-solving, and progress. There was a fundamental conviction that in a democracy human nature and society can be deliberately improved by education, religion, legislation, and hard work. American industry had grown so rapidly, it was believed, not only because of abundant natural resources, but especially because it had acquired technological and administrative "know how." The heroes of American progress were inventors, like Bell, Edison, Franklin, Fulton, and

Whitney, and industrialists who fashioned new social organizations for efficient mass production.

Although there had grown up a myth about the inventor as a lone wolf working in his own tool shed, research was already becoming a large-scale operation-just how big may be seen in the fact that private and public expenditures for research in the United States in 1930 amounted to more than $160,000,000 and increased, even during the depression years, to nearly $350,000,000 by 1940. Most of this research was, of course, in the natural and biological sciences and in engineering and medicine. The idea that research could be directed profitably to the solution of social problems gained acceptance much more slowly. But, even in the 1930s, significant resources were being allotted to the social sciences. The dramatic use of intelligence testing during World War I had stimulated research on human abilities and the application of testing procedures in school systems, industry, and government. "Scientific management," though slow to recognize the importance of social factors, was laying the groundwork for a scientific approach to the management of organizations.

The belief that the solution of "social problems" could be facilitated by systematic fact-finding was gaining acceptance. Thomas and Znaniecki had, by 1920, demonstrated that the difficulties accompanying the absorption of immigrants into American society could be investigated systematically; several research centers had been created to advance knowledge and to improve practice with respect to the welfare of children; by the early 1930s, practices in social work and juvenile courts were being modified on the basis of findings from an impressive series of studies on juvenile gangs in Chicago that had been conducted by Thrasher and Shaw; and, enough research had been completed on intergroup relations by 1939 so that Myrdal could write a comprehensive treatment of the "Negro problem" in America. Symptomatic of the belief in the feasibility of empirical research on social problems was the establishment in 1936 of the Society for the Psychological Study of Social Issues with 333 charter members. Thus, when the rapid expansion of group dynamics began after World War II, there were important segments of American society prepared to provide financial support for such research. Support came not only from academic institutions and foundations, but also from business, the federal government, and various organizations concerned with improving human relations.

Developed Professions

The attempt to formulate a coherent view of the nature of group life may be motivated by intellectual curiosity or by the desire to improve social practice. A study of the conditions bringing the field of group dynamics into existence reveals that both of these motivations played an important role. Interest in groups and recognition of their importance in society were apparent early among social scientists, who, according to a common stereotype, are motivated by idle curiosity. But, it should be also noted that some of the most influential early systematic writing about the nature of groups came from the pens of people working in the professions, people whose motivation has often been said to be purely practical. Before considering the social scientific background of group dynamics, we will describe briefly some of the developments within the professions that facilitated its rise.

By the 1930s, a large number of distinct professions had come into existence in the United States, probably more than in any other country. Many of these worked directly with groups of people, and, as they became concerned with improving the quality of their practice, they undertook to codify procedures and to discover general principles for dealing with groups. It gradually became evident, more quickly in some professions than in others that generalizations from experience can go only so far and that systematic research is required to produce a deeper understanding of group life. Thus, when group dynamics began to emerge as a distinct field, the leaders of some of the professions were well prepared to foster the idea that systematic research on group life could make a significant contribution to their professions.

As a result, several professions helped to create a favorable atmosphere for the financing of group dynamics research, provided from their accumulated experience a broad systematic conception of group functioning from which hypotheses for research could be drawn, afforded facilities in which research could be conducted, and furnished the beginnings of a technology for creating and manipulating variables in experimentation on groups. Four professions played an especially important part in the origin and growth of group dynamics.

Social Group Work

This profession should be mentioned first because it was one of the earliest to recognize explicitly that groups can be managed so as to bring about desired changes in members. Being responsible for the operation of clubs, recreational groups, camps and athletic teams, group workers came to realize that their techniques of dealing with groups had important effects on group processes and on the behaviours, attitudes, and personalities of those participating in these groups. Although the objective of group work included such diverse purposes as "character building," "providing constructive recreation," "keeping the kids off the street and out of trouble," and, later, "psychotherapy," it gradually became evident that, whatever the objective, some techniques of group management were more successful than others. One of the earliest experimental studies of groups concerned the effects of several leadership practices on the adjustment of boys in their summer camp cabins. The wealth of experience acquired by group workers has been systemized by Busch, Coyle, and Wilson and Ryland. Group dynamics drew heavily on this experience at the outset, and group dynamicists have continued to collaborate with group workers on various research projects.

Although group psychotherapy is commonly considered a branch of psychiatry, the use of groups for psychotherapeutic purposes has grown up in other than strictly medical settings, the Alcoholics Anonymous movement being one outstanding example.

In the development of a professional approach to psychotherapeutic work with groups, psychoanalytic theory has exerted the major, though not exclusive, influence. Freud's writing (especially his Group Psychology and the Analysis of the Ego) has set the tone, but many of the techniques for dealing with groups and much of the emphasis upon group processes have been contributed by people drawing from the field of group work-see, for example, the writings of Redl, Scheidlinger, and Slavson. A rather different tradition, although strongly psychoanalytic in its orientation, has grown up in England under the influence of Bion and a group of people associated with the Tavistock Institute of Human Relations. An important feature of this approach is the application of psychoanalytic group work to "natural" groups in the military establishment, industry, and the community.

Still another approach in group psychotherapy was established by the unusually creative and pioneering work of Moreno. His techniques of role-playing (more precisely, psychodrama and sociodrama) and sociometry were among the earliest contributions to the field and have been of great value both in group psychotherapy and in research on group dynamics. Although many of the developments in group psychotherapy and in group dynamics have been simultaneous, the early work in group psychotherapy had a clear and distinct influence on the initial work in group dynamics. And the two lines of endeavor have continued to influence each other, as can be seen, for example, in the systematic treatment of group psychotherapy by Bach.

The revolution in American public education that occurred in the first quarter of this century, influenced strongly by the writings of Dewey, broadened the conception of both the purposes and the procedures of education.

The goal of education in the public schools became the preparation of children for life in society rather than merely the transmission of knowledge. "Learning by doing" became a popular slogan and was implemented by such things as group projects, extracurricular activities, and student government.

Teachers became interested in installing skills of leadership, cooperation, responsible membership, and human relations. It gradually became apparent that teachers, like group workers, were having to take actions affecting the course of events in children's groups and needed principles to guide these events toward constructi .e ends. A similar trend was developing simultaneously in adult education, where the problems were made even more apparent by the voluntary nature of participation in adult-education programs.

There began to emerge the conception of the teacher as a group leader who affects his students' learning not merely by his subject-matter competence but also by his ability to heighten motivation, stimulate participation, and generate morale.

Although controversy over this general approach to education has persisted up to the present time, the education profession had, by the late 1930s, accumulated a considerable fund of knowledge about group life. Group dynamics drew upon this experience in formulating hypotheses for research, and group dynamicists established close working relations with educators and schools of education. Both educational practice and research in group dynamics have benefited from this association.

Administration

Under this label is a whole cluster of specialties, all concerned with the management of large organizations? Included are such specific professions as business administration, public administration, hospital administration, and educational administration. Although each of these must develop expertise in its particular sphere of operation, all share the necessity of designing effective procedures for coordinating the behaviour of people. For this reason, they share a common interest in the findings of social science. It might be expected, therefore, that systematic treatments of management would early come to recognition of the importance of groups in large enterprises and that management practices for dealing with groups would become highly developed. Actually, the historical facts are rather different. Until the 1930s, efforts to develop principles of management were remarkably blind to the existence of groups. One noteworthy exception is found in the writings of Mary P. Follett, who, after World War I, attempted to construct a systematic approach to administration, and more generally to government, in which groups were recognized as important elements. Her ideas, however, gained little acceptance.

In fact, the individualistic orientation held sway until about 1933 when the first of several books by Mayo and his associates made its appearance. These publications reported an extensive program of research begun in 1927 at the Hawthorne plant of the Western Electric Company. The initial objective of this research was to study the relation between conditions of work and the incidence of fatigue among workers. A variety of experimental variations was introduced-frequency of rest pauses, length of working hours, nature of wage incentives-with the intention of discovering their influence on fatigue and productivity. It is to the great credit of these investigators that they were alert to the existence of effects not anticipated, for the important changes actually produced by their experiments turned out to be in interpersonal relations among workers and between workers and management.

The results of this program of research led Mayo and his associates to place major emphasis on the social organization of the work group, on the social relations between the supervisor and his subordinates, on informal standards governing the behaviour of members of the work group, and on the attitudes and motives of workers existing in a group context.

The impact of this research upon all branches of administration can hardly be exaggerated. Haire has described it in the following way:

After the publication of these researches, thinking about industrial problems was radically and irrevocably changed.

It was no longer possible to see a decrement in productivity simply as a function of changes in illumination, physical fatigue, and the like. It was no longer possible to look for explanation of turnover simply in terms of an economic man maximizing dollar income. The role of the leader began to shift from one who directed work to one who enlisted cooperation. The incentive to work was no longer seen as simple and unitary, but rather infinitely varied, complex, and changing. The new view opened the way for, and demanded, more research and new conceptualizations to handle the problems.

Another important contribution to this new view of management was the systematic theory of management published in 1938 by Barnard, which was the product of his many years of experience as a business executive. Although this book did not put primary stress on groups as such, it placed human needs and social processes in the forefront of consideration. Barnard made it clear that management practice can be satisfactorily understood and effectively fashioned only if large organizations are conceived as social institutions composed of people in social interrelations. The emergence of group dynamics in the late 1930s came, then, at the very time when administrators and organization theorists were beginning to emphasize the importance of groups and of "human relations" in administration. In subsequent years, the findings from research in group dynamics have been incorporated increasingly into systematic treatments of administration and a growing number of administrators have supported group dynamics research in various ways.

Before leaving the discussion of the role of the professions in the origin and growth of group dynamics, we should note that the developments reported here had counterparts to varying degrees in other areas of social practice, many of which were not highly professionalized. Special mention should be made of the support that has come from those concerned with providing a scientific basis for work in intergroup relations, public health, the military, religious education, community organization, and speech.

Developed Social Science

In considering the conditions that stimulated the present approach to group dynamics within the social sciences, it is essential to recognize that this approach could originate only because certain advances had been accomplished in the social sciences at large. Thus, the rise of group dynamics required not only a supportive society and developed professions, but also developed social sciences. A basic premise of group dynamics is that the methods of science can be employed in the study of groups. This assumption could be entertained seriously only after the more general belief had gained acceptance that man, his behaviour, and his social relations can be properly subjected to scientific investigation. And, any question about the utilization of scientific methods for learning about human behaviour and social relations could not rise, of course, before the methods of science were well developed. It was only in the nineteenth century that serious discussions of this possibility occurred.

Comte's extensive treatment of positivism in 1830 provided a major advance in the self-conscious examination of basic assumptions about the possibility of subjecting human and social phenomena to scientific investigation; and the controversies over evolutionary theories of man in the last half of the century resulted in a drastically new view of the possibility of extending the scientific enterprise to human behaviour. Not until the last decades of the nineteenth century were there many people actually observing, measuring, or conducting experiments on human behaviour.

The first psychological laboratory was established only in 1879. One can hardly imagine how group dynamics could have come into existence before the belief had taken root that empirical research can be conducted on groups of people that important social phenomena can be measured, that group variables can be manipulated for experimental purposes, and that laws governing group life can be discovered. These beliefs gained acceptance only in recent years, though they had been advocated now and then by writers since the seventeenth century, and they are not universally held even today.

There remain those who assert that human behaviour does not operate according to laws, that important social phenomena cannot be quantified, and that experimentation on groups is impossible or immoral, or even both. William H. Whyte, Jr., in his attack on "the organization man," has spoken most eloquently for those who remain skeptical about the applicability of the methods of science to the study of man. He defines scientism as "the promise that, with the same techniques that have worked in the physical sciences, we can eventually create an exact science of man." He identifies scientism as a major component of the Social Ethic which, in his opinion, is weakening American society. And, the tragedy of scientism, he maintains, is that it is based on an illusion, for "a 'science of man' cannot work in the way its believers think it can." Were such views to prevail, group dynamics could not thrive.

The Reality of Groups

An important part of the early progress in social science consisted in clarifying certain basic assumptions about the reality of social phenomena. The first extensions of the scientific method of human behaviour occurred in close proximity to biology. Techniques of experimentation and measurement were first applied to investigations of the responses of organisms to stimulation of the sense organs and to modification of responses due to repeated stimulation. There was never much doubt about the "existence" of individual organisms, but when attention turned to groups of people and to social institutions, a great confusion arose. Discussion of these matters invoked terms like "group mind," "collective representations," "collective unconscious," and "culture."

And people argued heatedly as to whether such terms refer to any real phenomena or whether they are mere "abstractions" or "analogies." On the whole, the disciplines concerned with institutions (anthropology, economics, political science, and sociology) have freely attributed concrete reality to supra-individual entities, whereas psychology, with its interest in the physiological bases of behaviour, has been reluctant to admit existence to anything other than the behaviour of organisms. But, in all these disciplines, there have been conflicts between "institutionalists" and "behavioural scientists."

The sharpest cleavage occurred in the early days of social psychology, naturally enough, since it is a discipline concerned directly with the relations between the individual and society. Here the great debate over the "group mind" reached its climax in the 1920s. Although many people took part, the names of William McDougall and Floyd Allport are most closely associated with this controversy. At one extreme was the position that groups, institutions, and culture have reality quite apart from the particular individuals who participate in them. It was maintained that a group may continue to exist even after there has been a complete turnover of membership, that it has properties, such as a division of labor, a system of values, and a role structure, that cannot be conceived as properties of individuals, and that laws governing these group-level properties must be stated at the group level. A slogan reflecting this approach is the statement, attributed to Durkheim, that "every time a social phenomenon is directly explained by a psychological phenomenon, we may be sure that the explanation is false." In strong reaction to all this was the view, advanced most effectively by Allport, that only individuals are real and that groups or institutions are "sets of ideals, thoughts, and habits repeated in each individual mind and existing only in those minds."

Groups, then, are abstractions from collections of individual organisms. "Group mind" refers to nothing but similarities among individual minds and individuals cannot be parts of groups, for groups exist only in the minds of men. It may appear strange that social scientists should get involved in philosophical considerations about the nature of reality. As a matter of fact, however, the social scientist's view of reality makes a great deal of difference to his scientific behaviour. In the first place, it determines what things he is prepared to subject to empirical investigation. Lewin pointed out this fact succinctly in the following statement:

> Labeling something as "nonexistent" is equivalent to declaring it "out of bounds" for the scientist. Attributing "existence" to an item automatically makes it a duty of the scientist to consider this item as an object of research; it includes the necessity of considering its properties as "facts" which cannot be neglected in the total system of theories; finally, it implies that the terms with which one refers to the item are acceptable as scientific concepts (rather than as "mere words").

Secondly, the history of science shows a close interaction between the techniques of research which at any time are available and the prevailing assumptions about reality. Insistence on the existence of phenomena that cannot at that time be objectively observed, measured, or experimentally manipulated accomplishes little scientific value if it does not lead to the invention of appropriate techniques of empirical research. As a practical matter, the scientist is justified in excluding from consideration allegedly real entities whose empirical investigation appears impossible. And yet, as soon as a new technique makes it possible to treat empirically some new entity, this entity immediately acquires "reality" for the scientist. As Lewin noted, "The taboo against believing in the existence of a social entity is probably most effectively broken by handling this entity experimentally."

The history of the "group mind" controversy well illustrates these points. The early insistence on the reality of the "group mind," before techniques for investigating such phenomena were developed, contributed little to their scientific study. Allport's denial of the reality of the group actually had a strongly liberating influence on social psychologists, for he was saying, in effect, "Let us not be immobilized by insisting on the reality of things which we cannot now deal with by means of existing techniques of research." He, and like-minded psychologists, was then able to embark upon a remarkably fruitful program of research on the attitudes of individuals toward institutions and on the behaviour of individuals in social settings. Although this view of reality was too limited to encourage the empirical study of properties of groups, it did stimulate the development of research techniques that subsequently made a broader view of reality scientifically feasible. Until these techniques were in existence, those who persisted in attributing reality to groups and institutions were forced to rely on purely descriptive studies or armchair speculation from personal experience, and such work was legitimately criticized as being "subjective" since the objective techniques of science were rarely applied to such phenomena.

Development of Techniques of Research

Of extreme importance for the origin of group dynamics, then, was the shaping of research techniques that could be extended to research on groups. This process, of course, took time. It began in the last half of the nineteenth century with the rise of experimental psychology. Over the subsequent years, more and more aspects of human experience and behaviour were subjected to techniques of measurement and experimentation. Thus, for example, during the first third of this century, impressive gains were made in the measurement of attitudes. Noteworthy among these were the scale of "social distance" developed by Bogardus, the comprehensive treatment of problems of scaling by Thurstone and Thurstone and Chave, and the much simpler scaling technique of Likert. Parallel to these developments, and interacting with them, were major advances in statistics.

By the late 1930s, powerful statistical methods had been fashioned, which made possible efficient experimental designs and the evaluation of the significance of quantitative findings. These advances were important, of course, not only for the rise of group dynamics, but for progress in all the behavioural sciences. Within this general development, we may note three methodological gains contributing specifically to the rise of group dynamics.

Individual Behaviour in Groups

As noted above, research in group dynamics is deeply indebted to experimental psychology for the invention of techniques for conducting experiments on the conditions affecting human behaviour. But experimental psychology did not concern itself at first with social variables. It was only toward the beginning of the present century that a few investigators embarked upon experimental research designed to investigate the effects of social variables upon the behaviour of individuals. The nature of this early experimental social psychology has been described by G. W. Allport this way:

The first experimental problem-indeed the only problem for the first three decades of experimental research-was formulated as follows: What change in an individual's normal solitary performance occurs when other people are present? And according to Allport, the first laboratory answer to this question came from Triplett, who compared the performance of children in winding fishing reels when working alone and when working together with other children. Triplett concluded from this experience that the group situation tended to generate an increase in output of energy and achievement.

Of greater significance for the development of experimental social psychology was the work of Moede, begun at Leipzig in 1913, in which he undertook a systematic investigation of the effects of having several people take part simultaneously in a variety of the then standard psychological experiments. This work was influential in the development of social psychology primarily because Munsterberg called it to the attention of F. H. Allport and encouraged him to repeat and extend it. Allport not only conducted several impressive experiments but also provided a theoretical framework for interpreting the findings. By 1935, Dashiell was able to write a long summary of the work, comparing behaviour elicited when the subject was working in isolation and in the presence of others. Another important study of this era was that conducted by Moore in which he experimentally demonstrated the influence of "expert" and "majority" opinion upon the moral and aesthetic judgments of individuals.

These early experiments not only demonstrated the feasibility of conducting experiments on the influence of groups upon individual behaviour; they also developed techniques that are still in use. A somewhat different, but closely related, line of research attempted to compare the performance of individuals and of groups. In these studies, as illustrated by the work of Gordon, Watson, and Shaw, tasks were employed that could be performed either by individuals or by groups of people, and the question was asked whether individuals or groups did the better job. As it turned out, this question is unanswerable unless the conditions are further specified, but much was learned in seeking an answer. All this work made it much more likely that such a field as group dynamics could develop by bringing groups into the laboratory. Although these early experiments did not, strictly speaking, deal with properties of groups, they made it evident that the influence of groups upon individuals could be studied experimentally, and they made it much easier to conceive of the idea of varying group properties experimentally in the laboratory.

Controlled Observation of Social Interaction

One might think that the most obvious device for learning about the nature of group functioning would be simply to watch groups in action. Indeed, this procedure has been employed by chroniclers and reporters throughout history and has continued to be a source of data, perhaps most impressively as employed by social anthropologists in their reports of the behaviour, culture, and social structure of primitive societies. The major drawback of the procedure as a scientific technique is that the reports given by observers (the scientific data) depend to such a high degree upon the skill, sensitivity, and interpretive predilections of the observer. The first serious attempts to refine methods of observation, so that objective and quantitative data might be obtained, occurred around 1930 in the field of child psychology. A great amount of effort went into the construction of categories of observation that would permit an observer simply to indicate the presence or absence of a particular kind of behaviour or social interaction during the period of observation.

Typically, reliability was heightened by restricting observation to rather overt interactions whose "meaning" could be revealed in a short span of time and whose classification required little interpretation by the observer. Methods were also developed for sampling the interactions of a large group of people over a long time so that efficient estimates of the total interaction could be made on the basis of more limited observations. By use of such procedures and by careful training of observers, quantitative data of high reliability were obtained. The principal researchers responsible for these important advances were Goodenough, Jack, Olson, Parten, and Thomas.

Sociometry

A somewhat different approach to the study of groups is to ask questions of the members. Data obtained in this manner can, of course, reflect only those things the individual is able, and willing, to report. Nevertheless, such subjective reports from the members of a group might be expected to add valuable information to the more objective observations of behaviour. Of the many devices for obtaining information from group members, one of the earliest and most commonly used is the sociometric test, which was invented by Moreno. During World War I, Moreno had administrative responsibility for a camp of Tyrolese displaced persons, and he observed that the adjustment of people seemed to be better when they were allowed to form their own groups within the camp. Later, in the United States, he undertook to check this insight by more systematic research on groups of people in such institutions as schools and reformatories. For this purpose, he constructed a simple questionnaire on which each person was to indicate those other people with whom he would prefer to share some specified activity. It quickly became apparent that his device, and modifications of it, could provide valuable information about interpersonal attractions and repulsions among any collection of people.

The data concerning "who chooses whom" could be converted into a "sociogram or a picture in which individuals are represented by circles and choices by lines. Inspection of such sociograms revealed that some groups were more tightly knit than others, that individuals varied greatly in their social expansiveness and in the number of choices they received, and that cliques formed on the basis of characteristics such as age, sex, and race. In short, the sociometric test promised to yield valuable information about both individuals and interpersonal relations in groups. Although based essentially on subjective reports of individuals, the sociometric test provides quantifiable data about patterns of attractions and repulsions existing in a group. The publication by Moreno, in 1934, of a major book based on experience with the test and the establishment, in 1937, of a journal, Sociometry, ushered in a prodigious amount of research employing the sociometric test and numerous variations of it. The significance of sociometry for group dynamics lay both in the provision of a useful technique for research on groups and in the attention it directed to such features of groups as social position, patterns of friendship, sub-group information, and, more generally, informal structure.

Beginnings of Group Dynamics

By the mid-1930s, conditions were ripe within the social sciences for a rapid advance in empirical research on groups. And, in fact, a great burst of such activity did take place in America just prior to the entry of the United States into World War II. This research, moreover, began to display quite clearly the characteristics that are now associated with work in group dynamics. Within a period of approximately five years, several important research projects were undertaken, more or less independently of one another, but all sharing these distinctive features. We now briefly consider four of the more influential of these.

Experimental Creation of Social Norms

In 1936, Sherif published a book containing a systematic theoretical analysis of the concept social norm and an ingenious experimental investigation of the origin of social norms among groups of people. Probably the most important feature of this book was its bringing together of ideas and observations from sociology and anthropology and techniques of laboratory experimentation from experimental psychology. Sherif began by accepting the existence of customs, traditions, standards, rules, values, fashions, and other criteria of conduct (which he subsumed under the general label, social norm). Further, he agreed with Durkheim that such "collective representations" have, from the point of view of the individual, the properties of exteriority and constraint. At the same time, however, he agreed with F. H. Allport that social norms have been too often treated as something mystical and that scientific progress can be achieved only by subjecting phenomena to acceptable techniques of empirical research. He proposed that social norms should be viewed simultaneously in two ways: (a) as the product of social interaction and (b) as social stimuli which impinge upon any given individual who is a member of a group having these norms.

Conceived in this way, it would be possible to study experimentally the origin of social norms and their influence on individuals. In formulating his research problem, Sherif drew heavily upon the findings of Gestalt psychology in the field of perception. He noted that this work had established that there need not necessarily be a fixed point-point correlation between the physical stimulus and the experience and behaviour it arouses.

The frame of reference a person brings to a situation influences in no small way how he sees that situation. Sherif proposed that psychologically a social norm functions as such a frame of reference. Thus, if two people with different norms face the same situation (for example, a Mohammedan and a Christian confront a meal of pork chops), they will see it and react to it in widely different ways. For each, however, the norm serves to give meaning and to provide a stable way of reacting to the environment.

Having thus related social norms to the psychology of

perception, Sherif proceeded to ask how norms arise. It occurred to him that he might gain insight into this problem by placing people in a situation that had no clear structure and in which they would not be able to bring to bear any previously acquired frame of reference or social norm. Sherif stated the general objective of his research as follows:

> What will an individual do when he is placed in an objectively unstable situation in which all basis of comparison, as far as the external field of stimulation is concerned, is absent? In other words, what will he do when the external frame of reference is eliminated, in so far as the aspect in which we are interested is concerned? Will he give a hodgepodge of erratic judgments? Or will he establish a point of reference of his own? Consistent results in this situation may be taken as the index of a subjectively evolved frame of reference....

Moreover, "when a member of a group faces the same situation subsequently alone, after once the range and norm of his group have been established, he perceives the situation in terms of the range and norm that he brings from the situation."

Sherifs study did much to establish the feasibility of subjecting group phenomena to experimental investigation. It should be noted that he did not choose to study social norms existing in any natural group. Instead, he formed new groups in the laboratory and observed the development of an entirely new social norm. Although Sherifs experimental situation might seem artificial, and even trivial, to the anthropologist or sociologist, this very artificiality gave the findings a generality not ordinarily achieved by naturalistic research. By subjecting a group-level concept, like social norm, to psychological analysis, Sherif helped obliterate what he considered to be the unfortunate categorical separation of individual and group. And his research helped establish among psychologists the view that certain properties of groups have reality, for, as he concluded, "the fact that the norm thus established is peculiar to the group suggests that there is a factual psychological basis in the contentions of social psychologists and sociologists who maintain that new and supra-individual qualities arise in the group situations."

Social Anchorage of Attitudes

During the years 1935-39, Newcomb was conducting an intensive investigation of the same general kind of problem that interested Sherif, but with quite different methods. Newcomb selected a "natural" rather than a "laboratory" setting in which to study the operation of social norms and social influence processes, and he relied primarily upon techniques of attitude measurement, sociometry, and interviewing to obtain his data. Bennington College was the site of his study, the entire student body was his subjects, and attitudes toward political affairs provided the content of the social norms.

It was first established that the prevailing political atmosphere of the campus was "liberal" and that entering students, who came predominantly from "conservative" homes, brought with them attitudes that deviated from the college culture. The power of the college community to change attitudes of students was demonstrated by the fact that each year senior students were more liberal than freshmen. The most significant feature of this study, however, was its careful documentation of the ways in which these influences operated. Newcomb showed, for example, how the community "rewarded" students for adopting the approved attitudes. Thus, a sociometric-like test, in which students chose those "most worthy to represent the College at an intercollegiate gathering," revealed that the students thus chosen in each class were distinctly less conservative than those not so chosen. And, those students enjoying a reputation for having a close identification with the college, for being "good citizens," were also relatively more liberal in their political attitudes.

By means of several ingenious devices, Newcomb was able to discover the student's "subjective role," or self-view of his own relationship to the student community. Analysis of these data revealed several different ways in which students accommodated to the social pressures of the community. Of particular interest in this analysis was the evidence of conflicting group loyalties between membership in the college community and membership in the family group and some of the conditions determining the relative influence of each? Coming to the social level, we can push our problem further. What will a group of people do in the same unstable situation? Will the different individuals in the group give a hodgepodge of judgments? Or will there be established a common norm peculiar to the particular group situation and depending upon the presence of these individuals together and their influence upon one another? If they, in time, come to perceive the uncertain and unstable situation which they face in common in such a way as to give it some sort of order, perceiving it as ordered by a frame of reference developed among them in the course of the experiment, and if this frame of reference is peculiar to the group, then we may say that we have at least the prototype of the psychological process involved in the formation of a norm in a group.

In order to subject these questions to experimental investigation, Sherif made use of what is known in psychology as the auto kinetic effect. It had previously been shown in perceptual research that if a subject looks at a stationary point of light in an otherwise dark room, he will soon see it as moving. Furthermore, there are considerable individual differences in the extent of perceived motion. Sherifs experiment consisted of placing subjects individually in the darkened room and getting judgments of the extent of apparent motion. He found that upon repeated test the subject establishes a range within which his judgments fall and that this range is peculiar to each individual. Sherif then repeated the experiment, but this time having groups of subjects observe the light and report aloud their judgments. Now he found that the individual ranges of judgment converged to a group range that was peculiar to the group. In additional variations, Sherif was able to show that:

When the individual, in whom a range and a norm within that range are first developed in the individual situation, is put into a group situation, together with other individuals who also come into the situation with their own ranges and norms established in their own individual sessions, the ranges and norms tend to converge.

Newcomb's study showed that the attitudes of individuals are strongly rooted in the groups to which people belong, that the influence of a group upon an individual's attitudes depends upon the nature of the relationship between the individual and the group, and that groups evaluate members, partially at least, on the basis of their conformity to group norms. Although most of these points had been made in one form or another by writers in the speculative era of social science, this study was especially significant because it provided detailed objective, and quantitative, evidence. It thereby demonstrated, as Sherifs study did in a different way, the feasibility of conducting scientific research on important features of group.

Groups in Street Corner Society

The sociological and anthropological background of group dynamics is most apparent in the third important study of this era. In 1937, W. F. Whyte moved into one of the slums of Boston to begin a three and one-half year study of social clubs, political organizations, and racketeering. His method was that of "the participant observer," which had been most highly developed in anthropological research. More specifically, he drew upon the experience of Warner and Arensberg which was derived from the "Yankee City" studies. In various ways, he gained admittance to the social and political life of the community and faithfully kept notes of the various happenings that he observed or heard about. In the resulting book, Whyte reported in vivid detail on the structure, culture, and functioning of the Norton Street gang and the Italian Community Club. The importance of these social groups in the life of their members and in the political structure of the larger society was extensively documented.

In the interpretation and systematization of his findings, Whyte was greatly influenced by the "interactionist" point of view that was then being developed by Arensberg and Chappie, and that was subsequently presented by such writers as Chappie, Bales, and Homans. The orientation derived by Mayo and his colleagues from the Western Electric studies is also evident in Whyte's analysis of his data. Although he made no effort to quantify the interactions he observed, Whyte's great care for detail lent a strong flavor of objectivity to his account of the interactions among the people he observed. His "higher order" concepts, like social structure, cohesion, leadership, and status, were clearly related to the more directly observable interactions among people, thus giving them a close tie with empirical reality.

The major importance of this study for subsequent work in group dynamics was threefold:

- It dramatized, and described in painstaking detail, the great significance of groups in the lives of individuals and in the functioning of larger social systems.
- It gave impetus to the interpretation of group properties and processes in terms of interactions among individuals.
- It generated a number of hypotheses concerning the relations among such variables as initiation of interaction, leadership, status, mutual obligations, and group cohesion. These hypotheses have served to guide much of Whyte's later work on groups as well as the research of many others.

Experimental Manipulation of Group Atmosphere

By far the most influential work in the emerging study of group dynamics was that of Lewin, Lippitt, and White. Conducted at the Iowa Child Welfare Research Station between 1937 and 1940, these investigations of group atmosphere and styles of leadership accomplished a creative synthesis of the various trends and developments considered above. In describing the background of this research, Lippitt noted that the issue of what constitutes "good" leadership had come to the fore in the professions of social group work, education, and administration and he observed that, with the exception of the Western Electric studies, remarkably little research had been conducted to help guide practice in these professions. In setting up his theoretical problem, he drew explicitly on the previous work in social, clinical, and child psychology, sociology, cultural anthropology, and political science. And, in designing his research, he made use, with important modifications, of the available techniques of experimental psychology, controlled observation, and sociometry.

This work, then, relied heavily upon previous advances in social science and the professions, but it had an originality and significance which immediately produced a marked impact on all these fields. The basic objective of this research was to study the influences upon the group as a whole and upon individual members of certain experimentally induced "group atmospheres," or "styles of leadership." Groups of ten- and eleven-year-old children were formed to meet regularly over a period of several weeks under the leadership of an adult who induced the different group atmospheres. In creating these groups, care was taken to assure their initial comparability; by utilizing the sociometric test, playground observations, and teacher interviews, the structural properties of the various groups were made as similar as possible; on the basis of school records and interviews with the children, the backgrounds and individual characteristics of the members were equated for all the groups; and the same group activities and physical setting were employed in every group.

The experimental manipulation consisted of having the adult leaders behave in a prescribed fashion in each experimental treatment, and in order to rule out the differential effects of the personalities of the leaders, each one led a group under each of the experimental conditions. Three types of leadership, or group atmosphere, were investigated: democratic, autocratic, and laissez faire. In the light of present-day knowledge, it is clear that a considerable number of separable variables were combined within each style of leadership. Perhaps for this very reason, however, the effects produced in the behaviour of the group members were large and dramatic. For example, rather severe forms of scapegoating occurred in the autocratic groups, and at the end of the experiment, the children in some of the autocratic groups proceeded to destroy the things they had constructed. Each group, moreover, developed a characteristic level of aggressiveness, and it was demonstrated that when individual members were transferred from one group to another, their aggressiveness changed to approach the new group level.

An interesting insight into the dynamics of aggression was provided by the rather violent emotional "explosion" which took place when some of the groups that had reacted submissively to autocratic leadership were given a new, more permissive leader. As might be expected from the fact that this research was both original and concerned with emotionally loaded matters of political ideology, it was immediately subjected to criticism, both justified and unjustified. But the major effect on the social sciences and relevant professions was to open up new vistas and to raise the level of aspiration. The creation of "miniature political systems" in the laboratory and the demonstration of their power to influence the behaviour and social relations of people made it clear that practical problems of group management could be subjected to the experimental method and that social scientists could employ the methods of science to solve problems of vital significance to society.

Of major importance for subsequent research in group dynamics was the way in which Lewin formulated the essential purpose of these experiments. The problem of leadership was chosen for investigation, in part, because of its practical importance in education, social group work, administration, and political affairs. Nevertheless, in creating the different types of leadership in the laboratory, the intention was not to mirror or to simulate any "pure types" that might exist in society. The purpose was rather to lay bare some of the more important ways in which leader behaviour may vary and to discover how various styles of leadership influence the properties of groups and the behaviour of members. As Lewin put it, the purpose "was not to duplicate any given autocracy or democracy or to study an 'ideal' autocracy or democracy, but to create set-ups which would give insight into the underlying group dynamics." This statement, published in 1939, appears to be the earliest use by Lewin of the phrase group dynamics. It is important to note rather carefully how Lewin generalized the research problem.

He might have viewed this research primarily as a contribution to the technology of group management in social work or education. Or he might have placed it in the context of research on leadership. Actually, however, he stated the problem in a most abstract way as one of learning about the underlying dynamics of group life.

He believed that it was possible to construct a coherent body of empirical knowledge about the nature of group life that would be meaningful when specified for any particular kind of group. Thus, he envisioned a general theory of groups that could be brought to bear on such apparently diverse matters as family life, work groups, classrooms, committees, military units, and the community. Furthermore, he saw such specific problems as leadership, status, communication, social norms, group atmosphere, and intergroup relations as part of the general problem of understanding the nature of group dynamics. Almost immediately, Lewin and those associated with him began various research projects designed to contribute information relevant to a general theory of group dynamics. Thus, French conducted a laboratory experiment designed to compare the effects of fear and frustration on organized versus unorganized groups. Bavelas undertook an experiment to determine whether the actual behaviour of leaders of youth groups could be significantly modified through training.

Later, Bavelas suggested to Lewin the cluster of ideas that became known as "group decision." With America's entry into the war, he and French, in association with Marrow, explored group decision and related techniques as a means of improving industrial production, and Margaret Mead interested Lewin in studying problems related to wartime food shortages, with the result that Radke together with others conducted experiments on group decision as a means of changing food habits. Group dynamics is a field of inquiry dedicated to advancing knowledge about the nature of groups, the laws of their development, and their interrelations with individuals, other groups, and larger institutions. It may be identified by its reliance upon empirical research for obtaining data of theoretical significance, its emphasis in research and theory upon the dynamic aspects of group life, its broad relevance to all the social sciences, and the potential applicability of its findings to the improvement of social practice.

It became an identifiable field toward the end of the 1930s in the United States and has experienced a rapid growth since that time. Its rise was fostered by certain conditions that were particularly favorable in the United States just prior to World War II. These same conditions have facilitated its growth here and in certain other countries since that time. Of particular importance among these has been the acceptance by significant segments of society of the belief that research on groups is feasible and ultimately useful. This belief was initially encouraged by a strong interest in groups among such professions as social group work, group psychotherapy, education, and administration. It was made feasible because the social sciences had attained sufficient progress, by clarifying basic assumptions about the reality of groups and by designing research techniques for the study of groups, to permit empirical research on the functioning of groups.

By the end of the 1930s, several trends converged with the result that a new field of group dynamics began to take shape. The practical and theoretical importance of groups was by then documented empirically. The feasibility of conducting objective and quantitative research on the dynamics of group life was no longer debatable. And the reality of groups had been removed from the realm of mysticism and placed squarely within the domain of empirical social science. Group norms could be objectively measured, even created experimentally in the laboratory, and some of the processes by which they influence the behaviour and attitudes of individuals had been determined. The dependence of certain emotional states of individuals upon the prevailing group atmosphere had been established. And different styles of leadership had been created experimentally and shown to produce marked consequences on the functioning of groups. After the interruption imposed by World War II, rapid advances were made in constructing a systematic, and empirically based, body of knowledge concerning the dynamics of group life.

Dynamics of Disability Programmes

The dynamics of the disability programs have been shaped over the years by many events. Economic conditions, demographic changes, public opinion, and resulting congressional and Administrative actions have had a significant impact on program experience. This chapter reviews the historical development and growth of the disability programs administered by the Social Security Administration (SSA) for the working age population in the 45 years since the inception of the Social Security Disability Insurance (SSDI) program in 1956 and in the 30 years since the Supplemental Security Income (SSI) program in 1972. The chapter further discusses some of the main factors—economic and noneconomic, intrinsic and extrinsic to the program—that have shaped these programs over the years. These include legislative initiatives and judicial decisions, the demographic composition and characteristics of the population, the types of impairments of applicants, incentives and outreach, and the changing nature of work.

Although the decision of an individual to apply is an important variable in the program size, the program's eligibility requirements affect its ultimate size. Moreover, the stringency or leniency of program implementation impacts the size and cost of the program and also the probability of a person's applying. Growth in the initial awards (or allowances) often is attributable to some of the same factors that are associated with growth in applications during that period. A better understanding of the dynamics of the disability programs is essential to enhance the ability to predict the future growth and cost of the program. In the 1970s when the disability programs were growing rapidly, econometric research studies using aggregate time series techniques were undertaken to understand the role of the various factors in this growth. Recent rapid growth in the programs again has focused attention on the need to undertake a rigorous research program to estimate the extent of disability in the United States and to determine the potential need for disability benefits in the twenty-first century.

Unfortunately, analysts have been faced with a paucity of current information since the late 1960s and 1970s when SSA conducted three surveys of disability and work. These surveys obtained information on impairments and various socioeconomic factors that were useful in the analysis of disability programs. Likewise, any legislative and/or administrative initiatives to increase control over the program size and to improve the processing of claims should be based on research aimed at understanding the relative roles of the various variables that impact on disability programs administered by the SSA. Some of these factors may be within the control of the Congress and the Administration, while others may be outside their purview.

The need for disability insurance was recognized in the late 1930s when the Social Security Act was enacted. For many years, Congress and the Administration were hesitant to enact such a program because of concerns about the difficulties in deciding whether a particular person is disabled and in containing costs and predicting future program growth. These concerns have remained to the present day. However, a Social Security Disability Insurance program was enacted in 1956 to provide cash benefits to a person unable to engage in substantial gainful activity (SGA) ($780.00 per month in 2002) by virtue of a medical impairment that was expected to result in death or be of long-continued or indefinite duration.

The Act gave states responsibility for initial disability determination, acting under contract with the federal government. Reflecting the concerns about containing costs, it limited disability benefits to individuals 50–64 years old and did not extend benefits to the dependents of disability beneficiaries. A separate disability insurance tax rate and trust fund were established to allow close monitoring of program costs. The first payments were made in 1957. At that time, SSDI was thought of as a source of early retirement benefits mainly for men who had worked most of their lives but became disabled with chronic diseases of aging close to the normal age of retirement.

Period of Growth

Over the years the SSDI program has steadily, if not uniformly, expanded its coverage and support levels. The program grew rapidly in the early 1960s and through the middle of the 1970s. Several amendments to the Social Security Act extended the qualifying requirements for disability benefits. In 1958, benefits were extended to dependents of beneficiaries.

The 1960 amendments extended benefits to all qualified persons under 65 years of age. These alterations changed the concept of SSDI from being an alternative to retirement to an alternative to working. The legislative amendments of 1965 made the definition of disability more liberal by requiring only that the impairment be expected to result in death or to last for at least 12 months. The 1967 amendments eased the insured status requirements for persons under age 31, allowing a substantial number of young beneficiaries to enter the rolls. These amendments led to an increasing proportion of younger and relatively healthier beneficiaries.

The required waiting period before receiving benefits was reduced from six to five months in 1972. The level of SSDI benefit amounts was increased in the early 1970s and automatic cost-of-living adjustments were enacted. Also in 1972, Medicare coverage was extended to persons who had received disability benefits for two years. By the mid-1970s these changes had resulted in higher replacement rates of prior earnings, making it more financially attractive for people to apply for benefits and for beneficiaries to remain on the rolls.

These changes defined a much larger pool of persons potentially qualified for entitlement. The early 1970s experienced a rapid increase in the number of applications and awards. During the period 1960–1975, the number of applications grew rapidly from about 418,000 in 1960 to nearly 1.3 million in 1975. During the same period the number of awards grew from about 200,000 in 1960 to almost 600,000 in 1975. In relative terms, the number of applicants grew from 8.6 to 15 per 1,000 persons insured in case of disability from 1960 to 1975.

In 1970, Congress enacted legislation establishing the Black Lung Program and in 1972 enacted legislation establishing the Supplemental Security Income program for the aged, blind, and disabled (P.L. 92-603).

These programs, especially SSI, had a major impact on the growth and management of disability programs administered by SSA. The SSI is a nationwide federal assistance program administered by SSA that guarantees a minimum level of income for needy aged, blind, and disabled persons (SSA, 2001b). SSI benefits are provided on the basis of need to eligible individuals to the extent that their needs are not met by other sources; insured worker status is not required. SSI replaced the means-tested assistance programs administered by the states—Old-Age Assistance, Aid to the Blind, and Aid to the permanently and Totally Disabled—with a program of uniform benefits and eligibility criteria across states. The definition of disability and blindness for adults was the same as that used for SSDI, and as with SSDI, state Disability Determination Services (DDSs) have the responsibility to process initial disability claims.

The five-month waiting period before the start of benefits under SSDI does not apply to SSI recipients. Whereas SSDI beneficiaries are transferred to the Social Security retirement program, SSI recipients may remain on the rolls even after they are 65 years of age. SSI recipients also are eligible for Medicaid. Benefit payments under the SSI program started in January 1974. About 1.3 million disabled persons who were receiving welfare payments under the state programs were transferred to the SSI rolls in 1974. During 1972–1974, processing disability redeterminations for continuing eligibility of former state welfare recipients for SSI disability payments and for new disability claims under the new SSI program resulted in additional workloads for processing disability claims. The SSI program requires applicants under the age of 65 to apply first for benefits from all other programs, including SSDI that may partially or fully offset SSI benefits. This provision, combined with the increased publicity and active outreach efforts that accompanied implementation of this new program, as well as pressures on limited staff resources of administering the new programs, may have contributed to the sharp increase in applications and new awards under both SSI and SSDI from 1972 to 1976.

The recession of 1974–1975 placed additional burden on the two programs. Applications for benefits continued to increase and terminations declined. Disability benefit allowances were increased during this period, first in 1970 and again in 1971 and 1972, making it more financially attractive for people to apply for disability benefits and for beneficiaries to remain on the rolls rather than return to work. In 1974 when the SSI payments started, 1,503,000 persons aged 18–64 received federally administered SSI payments; by the end of 2000 there were 3,744,000 SSI recipients 18–64 years of age. Processing this large workload with limited staff resources led to administrative expediencies in the requirements for processing disability claims. Central Office reviews of DDS decisions for quality assurance fell from 100 percent to about 5 percent in 1972, and they were conducted after, rather than before, payment of benefits began. Most reviews were deferred, and only obvious decision errors were returned for correction.

The legislative changes, increased benefit levels, changes in program administration, and the economic downturn of the early 1970s probably contributed to the sharp increase in the disability incidence rate (number of new SSDI benefit awards per 1,000 workers insured in case of disability) from 4.8 in 1970 to a high of 7.1 in 1975. At the same time the termination rate (proportion of beneficiaries whose benefits were terminated) declined from 174 per 1,000 beneficiaries in 1970 to 132 per 1,000 in 1975. Terminations of SSDI benefits occur as a result of death, conversion of disability benefits to old age and survivor benefits upon attainment of normal retirement age (currently 65), or recovery (beneficiary no longer meets the standards used to define disability, either because of medical recovery or return to work). More than half of the decline from 1970 to 1975 in termination rates was due to lower medical recovery rates.

Period of Retrenchment

The rapid growth in disability rolls during this period renewed past concerns about SSA's ability to control program growth and the unpredictability of program expenditures. This situation led to legislative and administrative changes in the program in the late 1970s and early 1980s, slowing the increase in disability program growth. The legislative amendments in 1977 reduced the income replacement rates in SSDI, particularly for younger beneficiaries. The 1980 amendments mandated reviews of 65 percent of allowed claims in the ensuing three years prior to the start of any payment. They also required a vastly increased process of review of the eligibility of existing disability beneficiaries. The 1980 amendments also limited the total amount of monthly Social Security benefits that could be paid to a disabled worker and his family by enacting replacement rate caps, further modified the calculation of benefits for younger disabled workers, and added work incentives. In 1981, Congress eliminated the minimum Social Security benefit for new beneficiaries.

SSA also refined its regulations and guidelines changed the instructions and training to state Disability Determination Services to make eligibility criteria and evidentiary requirements more stringent, made quality assurance reviews more stringent, and increased the number of continuing disability reviews (CDRs). These actions had a dramatic impact on applications for benefits and initial award decisions. The proportion of claims awarded benefits by the DDSs declined from 46 percent of the claims in 1975 to 31 percent in 1980, and terminations rose to almost 143 per 1,000 beneficiaries by 1980. The rate of applications also declined from 15 per 1,000 insured workers in 1975 to 12.6 in 1980. Although the economy was in decline, the number of new awards dropped sharply and the number of persons discontinued for "medical and return-to-work recovery" reasons increased (SSA, 2001d).

Period of Slow Growth

These legislative and administrative changes and resulting practices faced strong resistance both in the courts and in state governments, and led to widespread criticism in the media. Negative publicity over the large numbers of beneficiaries—particularly the mentally impaired—being removed from the disability rolls led to a reconsideration of the changes in disability programmes. By 1984, another reversal in attitudes occurred followed by another round of legislative and administrative changes. SSA placed an administrative moratorium on the conduct of CDRs. A series of congressional hearings were held highlighting the plight of beneficiaries removed from the rolls. Several legislative and judiciary actions undid many of the stringent policies that had produced the retrenchment during the late 1970s and early 1980s. Court cases and class action suits increased dramatically, and many persons were returned to the rolls through court appeals. Congress enacted the Social Security Benefits Reform Act of 1984.

Its provisions included more liberal standards for mental impairments that emphasized the individual's ability to perform substantial gainful work, consideration of combined effects of multiple impairments in the absence of a single severe impairment, requirement for proof of medical improvements before termination of benefits, and use of SSA's regulatory standards to evaluate the effect of pain on disability. Court decisions on class action suits during the middle 1980s resulted in placing more emphasis on the opinion of treating physicians in the disability determination process, the role of pain as a disabling factor, and evaluation of a person's functional limitations in addition to the medical condition.

Once again, both applications and awards began to rise. The initial allowance rate that had declined to a low of around 31 percent of applications in 1980 and 1981 increased steadily during 1985–1989 and remained at about 35–44 percent during 1985–1990.

The final implementing regulations revising the eligibility criteria for mental impairments were published in 1986, resulting in dramatic increases in the number of benefits awarded on this basis. The number of awards to individuals with disabilities based on AIDS or HIV infection contributed to this increase. The termination rates also declined significantly as a result of SSA's moratorium on CDRs and their subsequent reinstatement under new and less stringent standards. During the latter half of the 1980s, after the brief increase in the late 1980s associated with adjudicating a large number of cases under the new regulations for mental impairments, applications and incidence rates for disability benefits remained fairly stable.

Growth in the 1990s

Although the legislative and administrative climate was relatively stable after 1985, applications and awards for disability benefits once again began to climb rapidly in 1989 and into the 1990s. Most of the increase in awards followed the sharp increase in applications for benefits accompanied by a small increase in the initial allowance rates. The economic downturn in 1990 and 1991 may account for part of this increase. Applications for SSDI benefits rose by 8.4 percent in 1990 over the previous year followed by another 13 percent increase in 1991. This growth resulted in an increase in the incidence rate from 3.7 per 1,000 in 1989 to 4.5 in 1991, a 21.6 percent increase over the two-year period. In recent years, well in excess of a million disabled workers have applied for SSDI benefits each year reaching 1.3 million in 2000. More than 600,000 disabled workers were awarded benefits in 2000. In contrast, the number of persons whose benefits have been terminated was around 460,000 in that year. With the exception of the late 1970s and early 1980s, the proportion of

SSDI beneficiaries whose benefits have been terminated has declined steadily from the earliest years of the program, from 132 per 1,000 beneficiaries in 1975 to nearly 143 per 1,000 in 1980, to 115.6 in 1990, and to about 91 per 1,000 in 2000. Most terminations occur as a result of death or conversion. The trend in terminations has been declining. Two significant factors contribute to this trend— lower death rates as a result of people living longer and a reduction in the average age of beneficiaries.

The change in the number of persons 18–64 awarded SSI disability benefits and the total number of recipients over time is similar to the dynamics observed in the SSDI program. The rapid increase in the total number of SSI participants in the early 1990s is a function of the growth in the number of disabled persons among SSI applicants and the poor economy as the 1990s began. The growth in the number of disabled adults is complicated and not fully understood. The reforms of the early 1980s and the outreach efforts in the 1980s also resulted in increases in the SSI program. With the strong economy of the late 1990s, a modest decline in SSI program participation was noted. However, because relatively few persons leave the SSI rolls, the total number of recipients has risen steadily since the 1980s, with the exception of a slight decline in the late 1990s.

Factors Contributing to Recent Growth

As stated above, applications and awards for disability benefits in both the SSDI and the SSI programs increased significantly in 1989 and into the 1990s. The reasons for this recent increase are complex and are not fully understood. A combination of many factors may have contributed to this growth—some may be related to the broader socioeconomic and demographic environment and others may be associated with programmatic actions and court decisions. Many of the same factors have had a role in the programs' growth since their inception and are contributing also to the recent growth of the disability programs of SSA. Some of these factors are discussed briefly below.

Demographic Trends

The number of persons who apply for and receive benefits is influenced by the size, composition, and characteristics of the potentially eligible population. The composition of the SSDI and SSI populations has changed dramatically since the programs' inceptions. The size of the insured population for disability insurance has grown primarily because the working age population has grown (and an increasing number of women have entered the labor force). Between 1980 and 2000 the population of workers 20–64 years of age insured in the event of disability grew from 56.6 million to 71.6 million for men and from 37.4 million to 62.5 million for women (SSA, 2001d). The working age eligible population is projected to increase in the coming years as the baby boom generation ages and reaches 40–50 years of age, when chronic disease and disabilities are more likely to occur.

The composition of the SSI population also has undergone a fundamental change since the program began in 1974. In the early years, nearly 60 percent of the recipients were aged. Over the years, the number of aged beneficiaries has declined significantly until today they comprise about 30 percent of the SSI rolls—about 20 percent of these are eligible based on age and 11 percent on the basis of disability. Today about 80 percent of SSI recipients are eligible on the basis of disability; 56 percent of these are 18–64 years of age (SSA, 2001b). The beneficiary population, especially in the SSI program, is diverse. Throughout the 1990s, the proportion of SSI awards each year for adults 18–64 who are noncitizens has ranged from 7 to 8 percent of the total (SSA, 2001b). The largest numbers come from Viet Nam, Mexico, and Cuba. Many of them have limited or no work experience and limited English proficiency (SSA, 2000).

The law provides uniform standards for citizenship and residency. However under certain circumstances, "qualified aliens" are eligible for SSI (some permanently and others for up to seven years). To qualify for SSI, someone who is not a U.S. citizen must be a qualified alien and meet one of certain additional requirements such as: a person lawfully admitted for permanent residence in the United States, a refugee, asylum seekers, or a person subjected to battery or extreme cruelty or whose child or parent has been subjected to such battery; or is a "qualified alien" who was lawfully residing in the United States and receiving SSI as of August 22, 1996, or who was living in the United States on August 22, 1996, and subsequently became blind or disabled (U.S. House of Representatives, 2000; SSA, 2001b). Legislative amendments in 2000 (P.L. 106-386) extended eligibility to noncitizens, regardless of their immigration status, as refugees if they are determined to be "victims" of "severe forms of trafficking in persons" (SSA, 2001b).

Age and Gender

The increases in applications and awards and a decrease in the number leaving the program have resulted in a dramatic growth in the number of beneficiaries on the rolls. This growth is due, at least in part, to an increase in the number of persons in the relatively younger ages entering the disability programs with fewer life-threatening impairments, resulting in increasing the duration of entitlement. The average age of persons awarded disability insurance benefits has been declining for both men and women, with a consequent increase in the duration of benefits. The average age of men awarded SSDI benefits declined from 54.5 in 1960 to 51.2 in 1980 and 49.6 in 2000, while the average age of women awarded SSDI benefits declined from 52.5 in 1960 to 51.1 in 1980 and 48.7 in 2000. In 1960 less than 1 percent of men and women who were awarded SSDI benefits were under 30 years of age, but by 2000, 6.8 percent of the men and 5.8 percent of the women were in this age range when awarded benefits. Similarly, the proportion of both men and women who were between 30 and 39 years of age when awarded benefits approximately doubled, while the proportion between ages 40 and 49 when awarded benefits also increased.

In contrast, the proportion of men 50 to 64 years of age when awarded benefits decreased from about 75 percent in

1960 to nearly 57 percent in 2000; the proportion of women in this age group awarded benefits decreased from 70 percent in 1960 to almost 55 percent in 2000. As increasing number of women have entered the labor force, the proportion of beneficiaries who are women has increased. Thus, in 1960, 78 percent of the 455,000 SSDI disabled worker beneficiaries were men and 22 percent were women, but by 2000, of the approximately 5 million SSDI disabled worker beneficiaries, the proportion who was men had declined to 56.6 percent and the proportion of women had increased to about 43 percent (SSA, 2001d).

Impairments

In the early years of the SSDI program, a much larger proportion of benefits were awarded on the basis of chronic diseases of aging. In recent years, as a result of legislative changes and court decisions, an increased number of awards have been based on impairments that occur much earlier in life such as mental disorders, including mental retardation. In 1981, 11 percent of SSDI disabled worker beneficiaries 18–64 years of age were awarded benefits on the basis of mental disorders including mental retardation compared with 24 percent in 2000, an increase of 118 percent. A similar distribution of impairments is noted for SSI working age beneficiaries, with 31 percent receiving benefits in 2000 because of mental disorders other than mental retardation and another 21 percent receiving benefits because of mental retardation.

Between 1981 and 2000, the proportion of SSDI benefit awards based on circulatory conditions, the top ranked condition in the earlier year, declined by 52 percent. The proportion of persons awarded benefits on the basis of musculoskeletal conditions increased by 41 percent between 1981 and 2000. By 2000, musculoskeletal conditions had eclipsed circulatory conditions as the most common set of conditions associated with the award of SSDI benefits. One possible explanation is the aging of the baby boom generation cohorts (1946–1964) who are currently entering the ages of highest incidence of arthritis and back disorders. In addition, rates of cardiovascular disease have declined over the past 10 to 15 years.

Outreach Efforts

As mentioned in the previous section, mandated outreach activities to enroll persons in the SSI program contributed to growth in the programs in the early and mid-1970s, when a nationwide effort was launched to enroll eligible persons in the new SSI program that was enacted in 1972 and implemented in 1974. During the late 1980s, Congress again mandated a number of SSI outreach activities to facilitate applications by needy individuals with severe disabilities. Beginning with earmarked appropriations in 1989, SSI outreach activities became a priority for SSA. In addition to its own effort, SSA promoted outreach through a series of grants to the private sector. Some who applied for SSI were found to have enough covered work experience to qualify for disability insurance benefits concurrently with SSI.

Cost Shifting by States

In times of poor economy, cuts made in state and locally funded general assistance and other welfare programs result in shifting the burden from state and local programs to federal programs. Welfare agencies routinely refer persons to SSA's disability programs. During 1989–1992, such cost shifting may have contributed to the acceleration of applications and awards particularly in the SSI programs. Deinstitutionalization of persons with mental disorders and mental retardation and other disabilities who were previously cared for in and financed by state hospital systems also led to an increase in the SSI claims.

Legislative and Regulatory Changes and Court Decisions

As in the early years of the programs, legislative and regulatory changes and court decisions continue to play a crucial role in extending or restricting the scope of the disability programs. For example, Congress and the courts required revision of the medical and functional criteria and new evidentiary requirements used in determining eligibility for disability benefits. In 1984, Congress required SSA to review and update the Listings of Impairments and related regulations resulting in significant increases in awards of benefits for mental impairments in the late 1980s.

The 1996 legislation dropped drug abuse and alcoholism as a contributing factor material to finding disability. The Welfare Reforms and legislative changes with respect to qualifying noncitizens for SSI benefits also led to changes in applications for benefits. Court decisions have had a major impact on the programs by modifying and liberalizing the adjudication standards. The publicity created by court cases increased public awareness and perception of easier standards, which in turn may have led to growth in applications for benefits.

Structural Changes in the Labour Market

Structural shifts in the economy have an uncertain impact on workers with disabilities and can influence the types of impairments that result in work disability. For instance, the shift from manufacturing to service industries and occupations and the emergence of new terms of employment have been emerging over the past several decades. The changing demands of work also limit employment prospects for individuals whose social and adaptive functioning is impaired by mental disorders. The current labour market places emphasis on cognitive and technical skills, advanced education and the ability to communicate and interact with others. People with disabilities, especially those with mental impairments, have poor employment prospects in such a market. Rupp and Stapleton (1995) argue that business cycle effects overwhelm the effects of economic restructuring. Their study found a negative effect of restructuring for the SSDI only, but it was small and not replicated for other program categories; they found no significant long-term effect of economic restructuring. Although the short-term effect of economic restructuring may increase applications for benefits, the long-term effect may be to decrease applications because workers in service sector jobs are less susceptible to disabling injuries, at least as far as physical impairments are concerned.

Changes in Economic Conditions

As in the 1970s, the economic downturn of 1990–1991 contributed to the rapid increase in applications and awards in the disability programs. In times of poor economy and high unemployment, low-wage workers with disabilities are more adversely affected than others in the workforce. Lack of training, unavailability of adequate alternative employment and prospects of losing medical coverage lead to increased applications for disability benefits. In the 1980s, despite poor economic conditions at the time, applications and awards declined as a result of programmatic changes in the SSDI and SSI programmes.

Labour Market Dynamics

In 1960, almost all working age (18–64) men were in the labor force, while only a minority of women of these ages were in the labor force. Since then, labor force participation rates among men fell, dramatically so among men 55–64 years of age, the decade prior to entitlement to full Social Security retirement benefits. At the same time, labor force participation rates among women have increased. In 1960, 66.8 percent of all working age persons were in the labor force. Primarily because of the substantial increases in employment among women, the overall labor force participation rate among working age persons increased to 79.0 percent as of 1998, or by more than 18 percent in relative terms.

In 1960, 93.2 percent of all working age men were in the labor force. However, male labor force participation rates fell dramatically, particularly after 1970, before stabilizing in the last few years. By 1998, only 86.3 percent of all working age men reported being in the labor force, a decline of 7 percent in relative terms. The employment picture among women is the reverse of that observed among men, with substantial increases in labor force participation rates among women. Thus, between 1960 and 1998, labor force participation rates among all working age women rose from 42.7 to 72.0 percent, or by 69 percent.

Employment patterns among persons with disabilities reflect these overall trends among men and women. Among all working age persons with disabilities, labor force participation rates decreased from 48.6 to 41.5 percent between 1983 and 1999, a decline of 14.6 percent. This overall decrease is the net effect of a huge decrease among men with disabilities—from 60.0 percent in 1983 to 44.9 percent in 1999, or by 25.2 percent—and a slight increase among women with disabilities from 38.0 percent in 1983 to 38.5 percent in 1999. Compared to men without disabilities, men with disabilities experienced a larger relative decrease in labor force participation rates (25.2 versus 1.2 percent, respectively). Compared to women without disabilities, women with disabilities experienced a much smaller relative increase in these rates (1.3 versus 11.7 percent, respectively). This is consistent with the hypothesis that persons with disabilities, like those facing discrimination on the basis of age, gender, or race, are prone to a last hired, first fired phenomenon.

Labour Market for Persons with Disabilities

Although among all working age persons, including men (and even extending to men 55 to 64 years of age), labor force participation rates have increased in the last few years, two recent studies indicate that persons with disabilities have not shared in this increase, while another study finds no change. Thus, although labor force participation rates among persons with disabilities reflected the trends affecting all workers over the past two decades, there is now at least equivocal evidence that, despite the passage of the Americans with Disabilities Act of 1990 (ADA), the employment picture among persons with disabilities diverged from that among the remainder of the working age population at the end of the 1990s. Studies conducted in recent years have suggested that the ADA may have unintentionally harmed rather than helped workers with disabilities.

The ADA was enacted to remove barriers to employment for people with disabilities by banning discrimination and requiring employers to provide accommodations. However, the costs of complying with the Act and fear of litigation may reduce the demand for their labor and undo its intended effect. Bound and Waidmann (2001) using the Current Population Survey (CPS) data from 1989 to 1999 found little evidence indicating much of a role for the ADA, but argue that increases in Social Security disability benefits played an important causal role in the growth of the population on disability rolls and can account for the decline in employment of working age men with disabilities during the period. Others also have indicated that the increasing program generosity and worsening labor market conditions increase the option value of disability applications. The literature on employment among persons with disabilities suggests that their labor force participation rates appear to reflect more general labor market dynamics.

Consistent with this observation, during the slack labor markets in the 1970s and late 1980s, there were substantial increases in the number of people applying for Social Security Disability Insurance benefits. The impact of any one factor on the demand for and provision of disability benefits is difficult to determine. In addition to the factors already discussed above, other factors also may have led to the growth of the disability programs at different times. These include record low termination rates of beneficiaries, public perceptions about the ease of qualifying for benefits, and access to medical care and its role in influencing choice between work and acceptance of disability benefits. As stated earlier in the chapter, the disability rolls are projected to grow over the coming decades as the baby boom generation reaches the ages of increased likelihood of developing disabilities.

This increase in workloads will make it increasingly important for SSA to have clear and workable policies, rules, and guidelines to operate its programs and to project future growth. The gradual increase in full retirement age from 65 to 67 years also means that disabled workers may remain on the rolls for two additional years before converting to Social Security retirement. An improved understanding of the dynamics of the programs and the factors that influence them is required. At this time, little is known with certainty about what contributes to disability trends and to what degree. Ongoing and future research using new data sources, such as the data that will be generated by the National Study of Health and Activity and other SSA administrative files, should provide relevant information about disability program participation and cost and other related policy issues.

Moreover, as aptly stated by Burkhauser et al. (2001), "no studies have been able to satisfactorily disentangle the impact of demand side factors related to the passage of the ADA or changes in the mix of jobs in the economy in the 1990s from supply side factors related to changes in the ease of access to SSDI and SSI benefits or to a reduction in the share of jobs that provide private health insurance, which would discourage work among the population with disabilities." Research is needed to delineate the magnitude of the various effects in order to understand the causes of recent declines in employment among people with disabilities. Only then can policies be developed to reverse the trend.

7

Dynamics of Social Work

Social science follows of necessity from the rapid development of the solidarity of the social world. The earthquake in San Francisco shakes the financial centers of London and Berlin. The miseries of Mexico afflict the citizens of the United States. The outbreak of the plague in Singapore turns the people of New Orleans into rat catchers. The roar of cannon in France awakens the echoes of exploding shrapnel in South Africa and Kiau Chau. The closing of the Dardanelles increases the price of bread in Chicago and Pekin. The fierce desperation of Germany not only destroys the lives of a million of her foes, but condemns a hundred innocent citizens of the United States to instant execution. The devastation of Belgium starts a beneficent golden stream of ten million dollars a month in America. St. Paul's declaration applied to the Christian church, "None of us liveth to himself and none dieth to himself," has today a world-wide application.

As physical science materializes in corporations, transportation lines, and factories, so social science in its various branches develops concretely in associations, institutions, and public policies. Thus the science of theology is applied in the activities of churches, schools, missions, and Christian associations; the science of medicine is the foundation for hospitals, health departments, and preventive medicine; the science of criminology has led to the remarkable developments of modern penology, and the science of psychology is rapidly revolutionizing public policies in the treatment of the insane, the feeble-minded, and the delinquent.

Social science reveals the sources and the causes of human ills; social workers apply that science not only to the immediate relief of suffering but to the development of individuals and families, and to practical efforts for the removal of the causes and the extirpation of pauperism, vice, and crime.

We are to discuss this morning social work. By this term is meant the associated effort of those who seek to promote justice and happiness in behalf of their fellow members of society.

Subjectively, the distinctive mark of social work is the associated effort of all the forces of society which make for human welfare, working together; individuals, churches, schools, social settlements, charitable and philanthropic societies, government, all co-operating to the same end. Objectively, social work takes account of the fact that its objects are members of society and that their welfare is vitally associated with that of the whole community. To again enlarge the significance of one of St. Paul's statements respecting the church:

"Whether one member suffereth, all the members suffer with it." The destructive effects of contagious diseases, intemperance, vice, or sloth can not be restricted to their victims alone; others inevitably suffer likewise.

The Thesis

The purpose of this address is to declare and illustrate this thesis: The moving force and essence of all true social work is spiritual, o social work is worthy of the name which does not spring from a spiritual purpose and which does not terminate in a spiritual result.

The word spiritual, in this address, is used to signify, in the words of the Standard Dictionary: "Pertaining to the soul or inner man; relating to or affecting the immaterial nature of man, especially that higher principle of man's is which is distinguished from the animal soul." The truth of this thesis will readily be conceded with reference to those social activities which are commonly known as religious work; the work of the church, the Sunday school, the young men's Christian association, and the various temperance organizations. It will also be conceded, probably, that all forms of educational work are essentially spiritual; the theological seminary, the college, the academy, the military school, the vocational school, the public school. All forms of education call for leaders of consecration and unselfish devotion, and fail of their proper influence unless they establish character in their pupils; unless they develop and confirm the virtues of temperance, industry, integrity, courage, and altruism.

But our thesis is not only true of religious and educational work, it is equally true of all other forms of social work; social settlements, good housing, public playgrounds, public health, social hygiene, charity, and correction. In all of these fields it is now recognized that we must have leaders who are not inspired by the desire for gain or prestige or promotion, but who are moved by the same spirit of consecration and devotion which we expect of the clergyman or the missionary, and that work in those lines as well as in religion and education is fruitless unless it produces an actual spiritual result. The entertainment of groups of young people in clubs and playgrounds has little value unless they are inspired to right thinking, fair play, good citizenship, and clean living. The compulsory cleanliness of the prison, the almshouse, or the tenement is of little use unless the individual can be inspired with the purpose not only of physical cleanliness but of moral cleanliness as well. Model tenements soon become nuisances unless their occupants learn to enjoy wholesome environment and better living. It is vain to feed the tramp or to replenish the pantry of the improvident family unless they can be inspired with some measure of hopefulness, self-respect, and exertion. It is worse than useless to confine the drunkard or the petty thief in prison for a few days or weeks, only to return him, unchanged, to the same environment from which he came. There must be developed in him the fixed purpose of reformation and the power to resist temptation. It is hopeless to undertake the cure of the insane if all of their surroundings and their treatment are such as lead only to helplessness, lethargy, and despair.

Recognition of the spiritual element as the essence of social work has already made far-reaching changes in its forms and methods; but, at the outset, it must be distinctly understood that the application of this principle thus far is by no means universal.

We still have many institutions which are formal, mechanical, and materialistic; but in every form of social work there is actual progress in humanizing and spiritualizing its operations; and it is this progress which we are to record. This new conception has already created new standards and has enlisted new types of men and women. Within my recollection it was thought that anyone would do to take charge of social work. The superintendency of almshouses, prisons, institutions for children, and such offices as superintendent of the poor or secretary of a child-helping society were refuges for people who needed a job; superannuated clergymen, worn-out school teachers, unsuccessful business men, and hungry politicians filled these responsible places. It is now becoming understood that we need for these places men and women who are competent, alert, trained, and conscientious.

Agents of relief societies and superintendents of private institutions were often chosen because of their zeal and their general good intentions rather than for experience and practical efficiency. Today we find in the list of social workers such people as Jane Addams, whose name has become a household word throughout the world; Julia Lathrop, who was chosen by President Taft and confirmed by President Wilson as chief of the Children's Bureau at Washington, D. C.; Dr. Charles R. Henderson of the Chicago University, who laid down his life in efforts for the unemployed; Dr. Graham Taylor, the splendid head of the Chicago Commons and leader in Civic Reform in Chicago. A true institution is an organism.

It grows, not by outward accretions but by an inward vital principle. It is animated and controlled by a living spirit which is peculiar to itself, which determines its character and measures its power. Money can not make a genuine institution. It may increase its resources and enlarge its opportunities, but it can create nothing. Let us now consider the practical application of the spiritual method to dependents. By dependents we mean people of normal mind who, because of age, disease, misfortune, or incompetency are unable to provide for themselves and are obliged to depend upon public or private aid.

The early ideals of the care of dependent people were spiritual. When people lived on farms and in villages, the problems of poverty and orphanage were met in a neighborly way. Everyone knew the situation and needs of his neighbors, and in case of distress the need was instantly and cheerfully met by those nearest at hand, and out of their own poverty they poured forth lavishly. When the need was beyond the resources of the individual neighbor, the churdji assumed the responsibility.

The church built orphanages, hospitals homes for the aged, and asylums for the insane, and the inspiration was spiritual. As society became complex, as cities were built, as neighbors ceased to know each other, as the well-to-do drew off into select groups and suburbs of their own and the poor began to inhabit tenement houses and slums, the spiritual method became less prevalent.

Benevolent people organized relief societies; the public built almshouses and appointed poor masters. Officialism and party politics intruded upon the field of charity. Almshouses were purposely made forbidding discouraging the lazy and the vicious, and there old people who were victims of misfortune and disaster, worthless and idle vagabonds, little orphaned children, idiots and insane people, were herded together in misery.

Children in orphanages were dressed in uniforms and meagerly fed, marched in long lines with shaven heads and listless mien, governed by perfunctory matrons and inefficient caretakers. About forty years ago there was an awakening of the public conscience under the lead of such women and men as Mrs. C. R. Lowell and Dorothea Dix, William P. Letchworth, Oscar Craig, Robert Treat Paine, Andrew Elmore, Frederick Howard Wines, and General Roeliff Brinkerhoft, which led to a new conception of the duty of the community toward the unfortunate.

As a result there has been a gradual decline of the almshouse population in the United States. The insane have been removed to hospitals prepared for their especial care. The keeping of children in almshouses has been forbidden by law. Farm colonies are being established for able-bodied vagrants, and public employment agencies are being organized to provide opportunity for those who are able and willing to work. There is a growing disposition to admit to almshouses only those who are disabled by infirmity and then to provide for them as comfortably as circumstances will permit. Instead of county almshouses we have "county infirmaries" in Ohio and "county asylums" in Indiana. The city of New York has provided on Staten Island comfortable and well-conducted cottages for old people who, after a life of industry, are obliged to accept a public refuge.

This beneficent principle is working even more efficiently in private agencies for dependents. Churches of different denominations are establishing homes for the aged where decent people can be provided for in their old age without the necessity of going to a public almshouse. Relief societies no longer restrict their activities to doling out meager gratuities and old clothes.

Such societies as the New York Association for Improving the Condition of the Poor and the St. Louis Provident Association are adopting constructive methods and are seeking to preserve and improve family life. Within the past thirty-five years there have grown up throughout the United States a multitude of charity organization societies or associated charities.

They started with the motto, "Not alms but a friend." They spend their efforts chiefly to help the poor to help themselves. They are working for improved housing, improved sanitary conditions, good milk, the establishment of public markets, improved opportunities for recreation. They enlist volunteers as friendly visitors and endeavor to establish the human touch between the poor and those who seek to befriend them. They extend relief when necessary, but material relief is a secondary function. Their chief mission is to develop a spirit of courage, hopefulness, self-reliance, and self-help.

Sometimes, like the members of South End House in Boston, they live in ordinary tenement houses; sometimes they live in one common building. But in either case they seek to share in the lives of those among whom they live and to promote good citizenship, civic spirit, education, artistic culture, wholesome recreation, good health, and happy domestic life. They build houses in which are established clubs for men and women, boys and girls; kindergartens; evening classes; gymnasia, and so forth. Some social settlements, lacking leadership, have failed to realize their purpose; but many of them have become a vital force in the community for the promotion of the public welfare centers for the fusion of foreign nationalities and for the promotion of patriotism and civic righteousness. One needs only mention Chicago Commons and Hull House in Chicago; Henry Street Settlement, Greenwich House, and Waverley House in New York; South End House and Peabody House in Boston, to realize how far reaching the influence of social settlements has become.

The great leaders in this movement have obtained a tremendous grip on the community because they deal intelligently with the vital elements of human life and human character. Thus far the social settlement idea has made but little progress in small cities and rural communities, though a few have been established and more are sure to follow. In my judgment the most useful and practical social settlement is the home of an educated, intelligent Christian family who, instead of removing to some favoured suburb, voluntarily locate among the poor and there live a normal, wholesome, and happy life, neighboring with those about them and sharing with them their books, music, merriment, and good will, and giving demonstrations in their daily home life of economical buying, good cooking, sensible dressing, artistic furnishing at small expense, and of the proper rearing and training of children.

The influence for good of such a family in a poor district is incalculable. This idea is not theoretical; it has been carried out in multitudes of cases. I will mention two examples which have come under my personal observation. Mrs. Harris Barrett of Hampton, Virginia, established, years ago, such a social center in her own house. She and her husband, though possessed of very limited means, built on one end of their large lot a cottage in which are held mothers' clubs, boys' clubs, girls' clubs, classes in art and domestic work, and social gatherings. On the same grounds the children of the neighborhood have play space and room for individual gardens. Miss Anna Jones, a public school principal in Kansas City, Missouri, has living in her own house a little group of teachers, a physician, and a nurse who have become a power for social betterment in the district in which they live. The application of the spiritual principle has produced remarkable results for dependent children. For generations, the orphan asylum plan of dealing with the dependent child was the prevailing method in the United States. When a child was left homeless by the death or default of his natural protectors, it was thought that a substitute should be provided for the natural home and the idea prevailed that the substitute could be made better than the original article. Thus grew up the orphan asylum system of bringing up homeless children in institutions from infancy to young manhood and womanhood.

A good argument can be made in favor of the orphan asylum system. It is said that in the ordinary home of poverty it is impossible for the child to have a fair chance. The home is insanitary, the food is insufficient, the parents are incompetent and in many cases vicious and cruel, the surroundings are demoralizing and the child is forced into undesirable associations. In a well-managed institution there can be maintained perfect sanitary conditions, good ventilation, suitable food, sufficient clothing, and wholesome influences.

If necessary, the child's food can be prescribed by a physician and weighed out for him at every meal. He is constantly under the influence of selected caretakers. He never plays truant, he never misses the evening study hour, he never runs with the gang. His religious, moral, intellectual, and vocational instruction can be gauged to his needs with precision. Under these circumstances it is asked: "How can a good institution fail to produce a better product than the home of ignorance, vice, or intemperance?" The answer is, "Institutionalism." Institution life is contrary to child nature. It is artificial and unnatural. The cooking is done by steam, the washing is done by steam, the house is heated by steam; the bell rings for the child to get up in the morning, for him to say his prayers, for him to go to meals and back from meals, to go to church and back from school all day long the bell! What does that mean? It means that someone else is planning his life for him, that someone else is doing his thinking for him.

The graduate of the orphan asylum lacks initiative. He does not know how to spend or to save money. He has no knowledge of human life or human nature and when the time comes, as it must come, for him to take his place in society, he is at a disadvantage. In some orphan asylums we find children with shaven heads and uniform clothing marching listlessly in long lines, eating an endless repetition of a prescribed dietary served in thick dishes, with iron cups and repulsive oilcloth table covers and uncomfortable benches. In such institutions life is barren, inhuman, and abnormal. It is not surprising to learn that many of their graduates fail to succeed.

The best orphan asylums have long recognized this evil and have sought to overcome it. Such institutions as the Chicago Orphan Asylum, the Rose Orphan Asylum at Terre

Haute, Indiana, the Protestant Orphan Asylum at Cleveland, the Rochester Orphan Asylum, the New York Orphanage at Hastings-on-Hudson, New York, and the Hebrew Sheltering Guardian Society at Pleasantville, New York, are seeking to adapt their work to the personal needs and development of their pupils. They reproduce, as far as possible, the conditions of family life. They teach the children the use of money. They keep them in touch with their friends out in the world. They give them efficient training in the school of letters and the vocational school, and they watch over their children with fostering care after they leave the institution.

There are still many superintendents of the old-fashioned type and the lives of their children are artificial, unnatural, and sometimes unhappy; but there are many of an entirely new spirit, like the superintendent of the Cleveland Orphan Asylum, himself an orphan boy, who has a keen realization of the feelings and the needs of his children; or like the superintendent of the New York Orphanage, an eminent educator, who creates for his children an atmosphere of love and joyous living. He weaves the whole life of the child into his education and makes school life a daily festival.

He pays his children wages, teaches them to spend, to give, and to save, and finds ways by which their lives may expand according to their natural endowments. His whole life is an expression of the fatherhood of which his wards have unfortunately been deprived. We have orphanages like the Hebrew Sheltering Guardian Asylum where the children are divided into families, each family in its own cottage with its kitchen, living room, and a group of older people. In this asylum the neglected children from the Ghetto of New York, coming from homes of wretchedness, have developed the spirit of hope and courage and aspiration.

These children, who would never have entered the doors of a high school, pass the examinations of the State Board of Regents and graduate from the high school in nine years from their entrance into the primary school, receiving, at the same time, a more thorough vocational education than is given in any other school with which I am acquainted. These orphanages and others of similar spirit are slowly revolutionizing the institutional work of the United States. Unfortunately institutions of this type are as yet comparatively few in number. In the twentieth century orphan asylum the superintendent is a man or woman of culture, with the instincts of a high-grade school teacher. The children live in cottages containing from 12 to 30 children. Each cottage has its own kitchen, dining room, and living room, with a housemother who is in close personal touch and sympathy with the members of her family. The dining room, the kitchen, and the living room resemble as closely as possible those of an ordinary family.

There is a carefully chosen library supplied not only with books but with games. The children give parties to the children of other cottages, keep pets, build rabbit hutches and playhouses, earn a little money and learn to spend it. The children either attend a good public school or have schools of their own which are equal in their curriculum and instruction to those of the best public schools. They are instructed in some practical vocation, and when they leave the orphanage, remain under the friendly watch-care of its officers until they are fairly established in life. On the other hand, the influence of the spiritual movement in the care of the dependent child is doing away with orphanages. The building of such institutions has-been checked. In Massachusetts and Indiana many orphan asylums and children's homes have been closed and have gone out of business. Home life for orphan and dependent children is secured by placing them in carefully selected family homes.

This method is widely prevalent throughout the United States. It has been especially developed in states like Massachusetts, Pennsylvania, Indiana, and Iowa. In some states, as in Michigan and Minnesota, state schools for children have been provided from which they are distributed, after a brief stay, to carefully chosen family homes. The evils of institutionalism are realized not only by social students but by many institution people. In 1909 there was held in the city of Washington a remarkable conference to which were invited 200 delegates representing every state in the Union and every form of work for neglected children. At that meeting there was unanimously adopted a significant platform, which began as follows:

"Home life is the highest and finest product of civilization. It is the great molding force of mind and of character. Children should not be deprived of it except for urgent and compelling reasons. Children of parents of worthy character, suffering from temporary misfortune and children of reasonably efficient and deserving mothers who are without the support of the normal bread-winner, should, as a rule, be kept with their parents, such aid being given as may be necessary to maintain suitable homes for the rearing of the children. This aid should be given by such methods and from such sources as may be determined by the general relief policy of each community, preferably in the form of private charity, rather than of public relief. Except in unusual circumstances, the home should not be broken up for reasons of poverty, but only for considerations of inefficiency or immorality." The fact that this resolution was unanimously adopted in a conference including many representatives of orphan asylums, children's homes/ and other institutions, makes the action exceedingly significant. It was a united declaration of the friends of dependent children in favor of the family home as the natural and preferable abiding place for the dependent child. It was an emphatic recognition of the sacredness of family life and of a new unwillingness to separate children from their parents simply because of poverty. The spirit of this declaration has found expression in the passage in many states, during the past five years, of mothers' pension laws, which are intended to obviate any necessity or excuse for separating good mothers from their children. These laws are crude and imperfect, as yet, but they stand for a principle which commands the assent of every lover of childhood and of family life.

Implications for Education

The contrasting situation between scientific rationality and hermeneutic reasonableness shows not only the relation between natural sciences and human sciences, but also, in some sense, exemplifies the contrast between Western culture and Chinese culture. Scientific rationality, as a well-structured procedural control over phenomena manifested through the interaction between empirical experiments and logico-mathematic formulations, is embodied in Western modern natural science and technology, especially in their success and efficacy for the explanation and technical control natural phenomena. The demand for reasonableness, especially in the hermeneutic activities of the human sciences, requires that the human mind refer to some kind of totality, either that of the experience of our self or that of existence. This is characteristic of Chinese culture and its main systems of thought such as Confucianism, Taoism and Buddhism. Both have their cognitive and their practical implications which must be taken into consideration in the educational process.

Now we are witnessing a deepening world process in which, as F.S.C. Northrop said, "The East and the West are meeting and merging. The epoch which Kipling so aptly described but about which he so falsely prophesied is over." On the other hand, the interaction and the balance between the natural and human sciences are much emphasized in the intellectual milieu and in the educational process. A key to the mutual understanding between Eastern and Western culture and to the formation of a kind of complementarity between natural sciences and human sciences consists in exploiting the nature and dynamism of both scientific rationality and hermeneutic reasonableness. The consequences of this for education will be considered at the end of this.

Cognitively speaking, scientific rationality envisages a systematic broadening of our knowledge through control procedures of circumscribed validity. For example, in the case of the natural sciences, theories are presented either through steps of generalization or as outcomes of creative imagination, and are then extended to new domains of experience. But, since the main theoretical instrument of the natural sciences is theoretical language, the progress of natural sciences depends much upon the construction and development of theories whose validity it is also important to control. This is normally done by the procedures of experimentation which consist of identifying a specific phenomenon in order to gain what K. Popper called either corroboration or falsification of the theory in question.

Since the above procedures are operational in nature, the cognitive side of scientific rationality is much related to its practical side and is deeply involved in action. The formal reasoning and even calculation of the logical structure of theories have transformed the abstract structure of meaning in language, just as operations during experimentation change the organization or state of affairs in space and time. Generally speaking, the practical side of scientific rationality could be analyzed by the mutual relationship between means and end, under the constraint of calculation and experimentation. This kind of rationality could be termed, on the one hand, strategic rationality, when in calculation it envisages logical connections between possible actions. On the other hand, it could be termed instrumental rationality, when in experimentation it judges the problem of whether one action is rational or not according to the efficiency of a certain means to attain its end.

Generally speaking, the development of Western modern sciences, especially natural sciences, is based on the interaction between scientific theories and controlled experiments, both conceived as human constructs, the one as rational constructs, the other as empirical constructs. On its rational side, modern science is constituted by scientific theories which essentially are logico-mathematically structured propositions. On its empirical side, modern science is characterized by its well-controlled systematic experimentation. Both aspects go hand in hand to serve the advancement of science, but this interaction always must be checked by theoretical deduction and meta-scientific reflection. In his *Critique of Pure Reason*, Kant seems to have grasped well the complementary interaction of these two aspects of modern science:

Without sensibility no object would be given to us,

without understanding no object would be thought. Thoughts without content are empty, intuitions without concepts are blind. It is, therefore, just as necessary to make our concepts sensible, that is, to add the object to them in intuition, as to make our intuitions intelligible, that is to bring them under concepts.... Only through their union can knowledge arise. In applying Kant's words to the case of scientific knowledge, the *sensible object* would refer to data gathered through well-controlled experimentation, while the *intelligible concepts* could be understood as constitutive of those logically structured scientific theories. Only their interaction could constitute scientific knowledge as such.

Compared with Western modern science, Chinese traditional science in general seems to be weak or even lacking in scientific rationality. First, it did not have a logico-mathematic structure for theory construction, nor had it ever reflected upon its own linguistic structure to the point of elaborating a system of logic for the formulation and control of its scientific discourse. Mathematics, although highly developed, was used only for describing data, not for formulating theories. Lacking in logical mathematical structures, Chinese quasi-scientific theories were presented principally through intuition and speculative imagination. This might have the advantage of being able to penetrate the totality of life and environment, but it lacked the rigor of logical control.

Second, empirical data in Chinese traditional science were established through detailed but passive observations, with or without the aid of instruments. But it seldom attempted any systematically organized experimentation or any active artificial control of perception. Finally, it did not have a tradition of epistemological reflection and philosophy of science, as was the case of European modern science. Let us take, for example, the case of Confucianism. Apparently, Confucian learning seems to have emphasized the accumulation of empirical knowledge, on the one hand, and their intelligible unity, on the other. B. Schwarts is correct when he says, "To Confucius knowledge does begin with the empirical cumulative knowledge of masses of particulars, then includes the ability to link these particulars first to one's own experiences and ultimately with the underlying unity that binds this thought together." But further reflection shows that this Confucian conception of interaction between empirical knowledge and its intelligible unity does not constitute a scientific rationality.

First, concerning the empirical side of Confucian learning, Confucius did not have in mind sensible data gathered by technically controlled process. What he stressed consisted rather in the concrete and factual knowledge of the institutions, the code of behaviour, the achievement of an idealized culture (that of the Chou dynasty for example), and the components of the environment of our life. This extended from knowledge of names of birds, animals, and trees to that of the meaning of a religious rite. This empirical knowledge concerns mostly the meaningful world of man rather than the meaningless world of nature, which, in Confucius's eyes, was to be reorganized in terms of codes congenial to human nature rather than being controlled by mere technical processes.

Second, concerning the rational side of Confucian learning, there seemed to be no emphasis on a rigorous logico-mathematical structure for discourse. One thing Confucius did propose which was connected with the rationality of discourse was his emphasis upon correctness of names. This concerned mostly language and its relation to reality, but was not proposed by Confucius as a semantic theory for concerned terms in themselves, but only as used in human speech and actions. Therefore it had some pragmatic significance in the social rather than in the logical arena, for it referred to a social code of behaviour, rather than to any concept of definition in the sense of Aristotelian logic.

Mathematics was never considered by Confucians to be the measure of rationality, not to mention taking it as necessary for constructing meaningful discourse. The only exception was perhaps Shao Yung who gave a very high place to number, seen by him as the manifestation of Tao; but this was a metaphysical rather than a scientific position. Anyhow, mathematics was not highly valued in itself, which may be explained by the primacy of a social orientation in Confucianism. As J. Needham suggests, "Mathematics was essential, up to a certain point, for the planning and control of the hydraulic engineering works, but those professing it were likely to remain inferior officials." This explains partly the unimportance of mathematical discourse in Confucianism. A more internal reason might be that mathematics was considered as a technique of calculation and an instrument for organizing and describing empirical data, not as the objective structure of reality and discourse.

Third, concerning the mode of interaction between empirical knowledge and the intelligible ground of its unity, Confucianism did not conceive an interactive relation in the mode of deduction/falsification or induction/verification. For Confucianism, the mode of unity was a kind of mental integration referring to the ultimate ground—Tao—through the process of ethical praxis. Praxis here was not interpreted as the technical application of theories to control concrete natural and social phenomena. It was understood rather as active involvement in the process of realizing what is properly human in the life of an individual and a collectivity. The status of science and technique must be reconsidered in the context of this ethical praxis.

From the above analysis, it becomes clear now that Chinese learning is not scientifically rational, though it is reasonable in a hermeneutic sense. To be scientifically rational, one must control the gathering of empirical data through technical process, formulate theories in logico-mathematical structure and establish their correspondence through interactive processes. But to be reasonable we must refer to the totality of our existence and its meaningful interpretation by human life as a whole. Confucianism and Chinese learning as a whole tried always to be reasonable, while neglecting their potentiality for scientific rationality.

Human sciences are hermeneutic in nature; the function

of reason found there is that of reasonableness, rather than of rationality. Hermeneutic reasonableness has both cognitive and practical implications. On its cognitive side, hermeneutic reasonableness concerns the dimension of meaning: the meaning of a literary or artistic work, the meaning of behaviour, the meaning of a social institution, the meaning of a certain culture, etc. The model of this cognitive activity is that understanding and interpretation are universal for mankind in that they could be extended to any form of relationship of man with the totality of the world. In understanding the meaning of a text, we have to refer to the totality of myself and the totality of the relationships I have with the world. In some sense, this has to begin from myself as the subject of my experience and understanding in order to reconstitute the meaning of a text. This echoes Husserl's position that the constitution of meaning refers inevitably to the intentionality of the one who understands.

The basic procedure of hermeneutics consists first of all in positing an interpretive hypothesis and then validating it by the text (or the work, the behaviour, etc.) in question. The criteria of this hermeneutic knowledge are not that of falsification, as Popper would suggest, but rather of subjective saturation. In other words, the more an interpretive hypothesis can generate satisfaction in our heart concerning the meaning of a work of art for example, the more acceptable to us is this hypothesis. On its practical side, hermeneutic reasonableness determines all actions concerned with subjective choice and subjective involvement in meaning, constituting, for example, those concerned with the creation and appreciation of works of art, with the realization and evaluation of moral intention, and even those political actions concerned with deciding the historical orientation of a certain social group.

The above first or cognitive aspect of hermeneutic reasonableness, although it refers to the totality of one's Self and the relation between the Self and the world, is nevertheless quite limited to human-centered orientation. But the second or practical aspect of hermeneutic reasonableness has a more speculative tendency for it concerns more the totality of Being, not limiting itself to the core of human subjectivity, human experience and human meaningfulness. Heidegger's *Seinsdenken* and Whitehead's speculative philosophy are of this kind. They refer to the totality of being or of cosmic experience in order to reveal the ontological dimension of our meaning constitution. Speculative philosophy is the endeavor to frame a coherent, logical, necessary system of general ideas in terms of which every element of our experience can be interpreted. By this notion of 'interpretation' I mean that everything of which we are conscious, as enjoyed, perceived, willed, or thought, shall have the character of a particular instance of the general scheme.

Up to this level hermeneutic reasonableness could be seen as the effort of reason itself to attain an integrated and integral understanding of itself, in which there are not yet the distinctions between theory and praxis, knowledge and action, thought and being, subjectivity and objectivity. On the contrary, all these distinctions must find their justification in this ultimate effort of reason is and it considered as the self-differentiation of auto-comprehending reason. It is from this integrating and yet original self-comprehension that the most profound movements of Being are motivated. Starting from here we have the distinction between the cognitive and the practical aspects of reason, but the nature of self-comprehending reasonableness itself is both cognitive and practical.

Hermeneutic reasonableness, therefore, is caught in the tension between the reference to the totality of one's self and the reference to the totality of the realm of existence. On this level, Chinese philosophy is quite similar to Western philosophy in demanding a necessary reference to the totality in order to show the function of reasonableness in human reason. For example, Confucianism insists upon the need to refer to the totality of human existence, whereas Taoism points out the need to escape the "human, all too human" tendency of humanist philosophy and to refer rather to the totality of existence exemplified by the concept of Tao. Let us explain this point in more detail.

First, in contrast to the rationality of modern Western science, Confucianism is a system of reasonable ideas which refers ultimately to the totality of human existence and its realization as the horizon within which the meaning of human actions, and even that of natural phenomena, is to be determined. In the case of classical Confucianism, this system of ideas was constituted essentially of Jen (), Yi () and Li (). Jen could be seen as the dynamic interconnectedness of one's self with other men, with nature and even with heaven. It is the ultimate ground and the transcendental foundation of men's ethical life. It is our subjectivity as well as our intersubjectivity, and is manifested especially in and through our moral awareness. From Jen, the Confucians derive Yi, which represents moral norms, moral obligations, moral judgements, or sometimes our consciousness of these obligations and even the virtue of acting always according to moral norms. From Yi the Confucians would derive Li which represents the code of behaviour, religious and political ceremonies and social institutions.

Both Yi and Li represent the "ought to be" of human existence, whereas Jen represents the Being of human existence. The rule-governedness of human nature is not to be understood in the light of natural laws, nor to be reduced to them. On the contrary, it is to be understood in accordance with the "to be" and the "ought to be" of human beings as expressed in the conceptual framework of Jen, Yi and Li. Even the laws of nature have to be reinterpreted by, and integrated into, the dignity of human nature as defined by these systems of ideas. Arthur F. Wright seems to have grasped this Confucian reasonableness when he says: "Confucianism of all ages viewed the natural and human worlds as an organism made up of multitudinous interconnected parts.... But man was the principle agent of both harmony and disharmony."

Confucian reasonableness refers to the totality of the human agent and his or her relation with the world. But it is quite different with Taoism, especially that of Lao Tzu and Chuang Tzu, which is a vehement critique of Confucianism.

In the eyes of Taoists, Confucianism emphasizes deliberate actions taken with anthropocentric self-consciousness, and in so doing, it forgets the spontaneity of man and his roots in Tao. Lao Tzu proposes instead a mindless spontaneous creativity springing from Tao itself as the real solution. For him, without Tao's creative support and the spontaneous character of Teh, the Confucian system of transcendental philosophy—which grounded Li in Yi and Yi in Jen—tends to degrade and degenerate. Thus, Taoist reasonableness refers ultimately to the Teh, and to the source of all creativity, the Tao, as representing the totality of all totalities.

Lao Tzu pushed the meaning of Tao to its speculative extreme. The concept of Tao became, thereby, neither the ways followed by human beings, nor the way out of a social, political and even spiritual crisis, but the Way itself, the Ultimate Reality or the Being of all beings. Here the concept of Being differs from the negative connotation it has in Hegel's Logic (mere beingness), as the most impoverished ontological determination, robbed of any positive aspect whatsoever. Instead, it represents something like Heidegger's self-manifesting Being.

This is not even a concept, because treating Tao as a concept reduces it to a mere conceptual being, or *ens rationis* with ontic status. That is why Lao Tzu said, "The Tao that could be told of is not the eternal Tao; the name that can be named is not the eternal name."

The case of Taoist philosophy shows that reasonableness, as the function of reason understanding itself in reference to the totality of being, is also an exploitation of reason to its limits to attain thereby self-understanding in knowing its own limitation. This is the ontological basis of all spirit of critical reflection. Taoist philosophy, as a philosophy referring to the totality of Being, and Confucianism, as a philosophy referring to the totality of human existence, exemplify two complementary aspects of hermeneutic reasonableness.

The basic situation of our times could be characterized as one of dynamic tension between, on the one hand, the overwhelming influence of modern science and technology and the processes of universalisation which they promote, and, on the other hand, the awakening of historical consciousness leading toward the uniqueness of each historical tradition and the concern for the meaning of human life. Under this global situation, the educational process, especially at the level of higher education, suffers many serious problems. To a philosopher, the most crucial of the problems appear as follows.

First, with the inevitable process of specialization and the operational character of modern science, scientists tend not to be aware of the philosophical meaning of what they are doing. The rationality of their research activities is not sufficiently understood and self-aware. Second, under the overwhelming influence of modern science and technology, the human sciences suffer from the disadvantage of being forced to take natural sciences as the model of their scientific character, while having fewer resources for their own self-development and fewer opportunities to influence the public sphere of society. Third, with the rapidly developing complexity of the problems which humankind now faces, interdisciplinary research and interdisciplinary training are necessary for today's higher education. But the philosophical meaning of the interdisciplinarity, especially its relation to the function of our reason is not clearly defined.

From the first section above, we know that the operation and development of modern science depend much upon scientific rationality. Scientists must understand that this has both cognitive and practical aspects. Cognitively speaking, scientific rationality is an operationally controlled interaction between the theoretical construct as constituted in a logico-mathematical way and the empirical construct as constituted in the experimentation process. Practically speaking, scientific rationality is both strategic and instrumental in character; its limitations are also determined by this.

Our analysis in the second section seems to indicate that, in the educational process, natural science education must be balanced by education in the human sciences. These are historical in character in the sense that their goal is to achieve self-understanding through the study of textual objects given to us through historical tradition (for example, classical texts). Thus, Confucian, Taoist and Buddhist texts are means by which the Chinese people can come to understand themselves. The implication for education is that, on the one hand, the reading of essential textual objects in one's own cultural tradition, and their correct as well as creative understanding should constitute an important part of the educational process of each country. On the other hand, since the understanding of, and openness to, other cultural traditions and other ways of existence are essential to the development of reason, the reading of important texts of other cultural traditions also should be properly emphasized in the educational process.

Openness to different cultures and a comparative vision are important for education and even for research activity. This combination of self-understanding and mutual understanding must not be neglected due to a notion of incommensurability, for any one who wants to prove the incommensurability between two traditions or two different texts presupposes thereby that he understands both. Finally, interdisciplinarity in its essence aims at better coordination between different levels of rationality and between rationality and reasonableness. Every scientific discipline is involved in either one or both. An individual or a school, in undertaking this kind of coordination, has to realize both scientific rationality and hermeneutic reasonableness, cognitively as well as practically.

This is especially important in the teaching process because sometimes interdisciplinary research becomes entangled as each concerned discipline becomes defensive of its own method and rationality. Sometimes too it is difficult to listen to and to understand the jargons of other disciplines. But in coordinated interdisciplinary teaching, each professor should explain clearly to the students the state of the art in his or her own discipline. Comparative work with a common audience helps bring different disciplines into mutual understanding, and thereby contributes to interdisciplinary research. Today, both in education and in research, we face a common situation. On the one hand, teaching and research in the natural sciences, and even in some hard social sciences, over-emphasize positive knowledge and recognize nothing but scientific rationality. This attitude has bad effects also on teaching and research in the human sciences. On the other hand, research in the meaning of literary works and works of art emphasizes more the subjective meaning/constructing process.

Both activities stand in opposition to such an extent that they constitute a separation as between two cultures. No one is concerned for the dimension of totality in order to prepare better grounds for the coordination of the rationality of the physical sciences and the reasonableness of the human sciences. The reform of education should endeavor to realize in each discipline self-understanding of its rationality, to penetrate through different levels of rationality and reasonableness, and to achieve self-understanding on the part of reason of all its possibilities. The function of reason must not be divided unknowingly, but must be self-understood in both its integrity and its integration.

8

Theory of Standards

The world of technical standards making is a global but arcane and diverse society of experts and their various interests are engaged in setting standards for virtually every aspect of our modern industrial/information society. Standards making engages tens of thousands of individuals that travel widely and confer on a vast variety of issues, mostly technical but more and more often bridging into the policy realm as we move into an increasingly technology-dependent social and commercial environment (e.g., privacy, quality, environmental management, consumer policy, etc.). But, standards making is wholly a social practice that has gradually developed through pragmatic commercial and social necessity—not through any theoretical impetus. It found its modern origins in the demands of trade, commerce and manufacturing brought by the industrial revolution.

Metrology standards (e.g., weights, measures, etc.) were a necessity of early exchange, transportation and trade; and the introduction of mass production depended completely on industrial standardization of components, measurements and materials. Standards have also been used for political economic purposes of exclusion, domination or protection. Eastern European railroad gauges were deliberately chosen to be incompatible across certain borders for strategic purposes of impeding potential military invasion. In more modern times, television broadcasting standards were deliberately chosen to stake out trade blocks and avoid domination by outside manufacturers or transmitters.

Today, the globalization of economic and industrial production and the dramatic acceleration of the pace of technological development have severely stressed the conventional institutions and formal practices upon which standardization depends. These institutions traditionally depended on income from publishing standards have found their economic basis undermined by the internet and the ascendancy of electronic document distribution. They have also found themselves somewhat eclipsed, particularly in certain industries such as information technology, by private consortia and forums that have been able to move more rapidly and more responsively to the demands of accelerated markets, mobile capital and shortened product lifetimes. Another stress exacerbated by globalization has been certain regional, cultural and institutional differences in views and traditions about the basic role of standardization in a market economy.

As a European Commission official recently expressed this conflict, "In Europe Standards are not just documents thrown into the market to compete with each other...as if they were merely a 'product'." In view of these stresses, if a firm theoretical basis can now be established for this practice of standards making, it is possible that it might be broadened and improved and its stresses resolved or accommodated to the benefit of both commerce and democracy. Several bodies of theory suggest significant contributions toward establishing such a theory of standards. These bodies of theory offered here include Policy Science with its framework for identifying common interests and its heuristic methodology; Studies of Technology and Society (STS) and its theory of Social Constructivism; and Public Sphere theory and its study of deliberative democracy and discursive practice. These bodies of theory can be used to approach the concept of standards from three disciplinary perspectives: policy, technology and implementation. This chapter proposes such an interdisciplinary approach to formulating a general theory of standards and identifies certain key elements of such a theory.

Theory and Research

The academic discourse today on standards focuses on technical, curricular and instrumental dimensions. Hesser and Czaya have described the academic debate today as concentrating "...on standards and their implications for competitive policy, international trade and company strategies." The literature of the disciplines of Business Management, Engineering Sciences and Law has treated standards in entirely instrumental and industrial process oriented terms. The social science disciplines of Sociology, Philosophy, Political Science and Communication Studies have almost entirely overlooked the phenomenon of technical standardization per se. This chapter attempts to reach into the literature of these latter disciplines and identify fundamental theoretical approaches and concepts that can offer explanatory insights and analytical tools to advance the study of standardization practice, recognizing that any study of standards theory must take an inherently interdisciplinary approach.

The discipline of Political Science contributes a fundamental body of theoretical methodological thought to our analysis of standards making practice: Policy Science and its Central Theory as developed by the late American political scientist, Harold Lasswell. The Policy Science approach to the analysis of policy issues is a heuristic one—a method of inquiry that serves by pointing out places to look for the discovery of the relevant elements and their interrelationships. These places to look are categorized primarily into the 1) Decision Process, 2) Social Process, and 3) Problem Orientation, but also include identification of the Common Interest and recognition of the Maximization Postulate—that each actor is predisposed to complete acts in ways that are expected to leave the actor better off than if they had been completed differently—and of the recognition that any analysis cannot be value free and therefore, Human Dignity must be a central value of the analysis, and that the perspective of the investigator cannot be ignored. Policy Science also recognizes the importance of looking at issues contextually, broadly enough and from multiple viewpoints.

The Decision Process is specialized to the shaping and sharing of power. Such power represents one of an array of eight values, each of which are driven by the maximization postulate. Each participant in the decision process may perceive power, as well as the other values, from a different perspective. These participants and their various perspectives, situations, base values, strategies and outcomes sought are analyzed below in the Social Process. The Decision Process heuristic divides the decision process into a sequence of parts including, in order, intelligence, promotion, prescription, invocation, application, termination and appraisal. In the case of universal service, we begin with the prescription, invocation and application.

Each participant in the Decision Process perceives the situation from a different perspective and with unique base values. The term participant is intended to include both those actively engaged in the discourse and those effected by or having some interest in the result (i.e., stakeholders). The Social Process heuristic examines these participants and their various perspectives, situations, base values, strategies or outcomes sought. An important part of this Social Process has to do with institutional practices. A practice according to Lasswell is a pattern of perspectives and operations that are typically specialized to the shaping of a class of values. He further defines a perspective as the identities, demands and expectations of those involved in the practice. Operations are behavioural routines such as externalized or internalized acts, or acts of resource or sign manipulation.

From analysis of the Decision Process and the Social Process, the Problem Orientation can become clearer—in other words, the particular problem which the policy project has set out to address can be clearly identified. The Problem Orientation heuristic examines the goals, trends, conditions, projections and alternatives related to the policy or standardization issue and its context. The goals of any particular policymaking (or standardization) project are often embedded in its prescriptions (e.g., laws, policies, standards, etc.) but may not be well articulated; although ultimately they seek to pursue fulfillment of some stated or unstated policy goal on the part of some participant(s). The stated policy goals may be different from the actual policy outcomes or from the desired policy goal. For example, as in the case of telecommunications, standards can be established with the goal of ostensibly stabilizing a market and guaranteeing service quality but to some participants, the real goal may be to embed intellectual property or to legitimate monopolies. Lasswell would find the principal intellectual test of the policy scientist to understand the power of decision. In terms of methodology, he would recommend the empirical and pragmatic approach of studying standards making, by making standards rather than by detached ethnographic observation.

A tradition variously known as STS (Studies of Technology and Society; or earlier, Science, Technology and Society; or most currently as Socio-historical Technology Studies), emerged from the disciplines of Philosophy and Sociology and contributes several useful theoretical concepts to inform our analysis of standards making practice: Social Constructivism, Relevant Social Groups, Interpretive Flexibility, Socio-technical Ensembles, and theories of technical change.

Social Constructivism

In the Social Construction of Technology (SCOT) model, participants comprising various Relevant Social Groups view and, through their interactions with each other, constitute technologies and technological artifacts through a process of Interpretive Flexibility. "In this descriptive model, an artifact does not suddenly leap into existence as the result of a momentous act by a heroic inventor; rather, it is gradually constructed or deconstructed in the social interactions of Relevant Social Groups." Formal standards bodies could be seen as constitutive of such Relevant Social Groups.

Interpretive Flexibility

Interpretive Flexibility is the process by which various Relevant Social Groups attribute meaning and utility to such artifacts; and by which artifacts may find applications very different from those envisioned by the original inventors or developers. Such is the case of the telephone, the radio and television.

Socio-technical Ensembles

In reaction to the traditional positivistic approaches of policy and economic analysis, and to the reductionism of technological determinism, STS scholars find both technical and social elements in a dialectical interaction with the final analysis that, "The technical is socially constructed and the social is technically constructed." Since technical standards are socially constructed through the dynamic of standards bodies, these theories explaining the operation of Sociotechnical Ensembles and their Relevant Social Groups can contribute to a basis for a theory of standardization. Social Constructivism offers a theoretical platform on which to construct a theory of standards, and the standards arena offers a place to realize the goal of the constructivist project. Bijker suggests such, noting, regulations and norms are a traditional steering instrument, but they are almost always used with a mechanistic stimulus-and-response perspective on technology... regulations and norms can be studied as activating and supporting networks of firms and other relevant social groups that are involved in the construction of a technology.

It is largely in these deliberative bodies that decisions are made about what form new technologies will take as they diffuse into the marketplace. Also, the formal standards bodies constitute one of the few arenas (at least in the U.S.) where competitors can legitimately gather (without invoking antitrust complaints) to confer and seek a common interest because it largely institutionalizes rules of democratic openness, fairness, and due process. Standardization practice is international, voluntary and non governmental and, in theory if not always in practice, embodies the essential ideals of the public sphere.

Theories of the Public Sphere

The discipline and tradition of Political Philosophy

contributes three fundamental theoretical models which inform our analysis of standards making practice: discourse ethics, the concept of the public sphere and the theory of communicative action, developed by the contemporary German philosopher Jürgen Habermas.

Discourse Ethics

Standards making can be seen as a form of discourse ethics within the context defined by Habermas. In his model of discourse ethics, Habermas finds a dialogically derived middle ground between the universalistic and rationalistic but monologic Kantian ethics and the situational/contextual Aristotelian ethics based on social practice and pursuit of desired virtue. The essence of discourse ethics is that universal ethical principles and the relation between the justification and application of norms can be socially constructed from rational discourse based on language. In this model, Habermas extends the enlightenment project, committing to the proposition that negotiated norms of truth and good can be determined through consensus and group will, especially if procedural principles of rational discourse, which include what he calls "ideal speech," can be adhered to.

The Public Sphere

Standards making can also be seen as a form of the public sphere embodied in a specific social practice. The public sphere, as Habermas conceives it, is that conceptual public space where private individuals come together to engage in rational discourse on matters of mutual concern. It is essentially the forum for discourse ethics and crucially depends upon his principles of ideal speech or rules of argumentation. Such principles include freedom of access, equal rights to participate, truthfulness on the part of participants, absence of coercion, etc. Inherent in the idea of the public sphere is the notion that, given the principles of ideal speech, reasonable men will be able to reach a common consensus or substantial agreement on issues of mutual interest.

A particularly significant myth of modern post industrial

society is that public policy formation is the sole domain of government. In contemporary discourse, a primary distinction is drawn between the public sector and the private sector with the public sector being synonymous with government. What is completely missing in this dichotomy is the concept of the public sphere, described by Habermas as that space which exists between the civil society and the state, where public policy was traditionally developed both in ancient Greek society and in modern western society beginning with the enlightenment. Enlightenment theories of democratic government and its institutions were developed in an active public sphere, through public debate among private individuals and which had nothing to do with the government of the time—in fact they often sought to replace it. Habermas stresses that a true public sphere can only exist apart from government (which has unfortunately been referred to as the public sector) for in a democracy, government is a result of its deliberations.

In the late 20th century, perhaps due to the complexity, isolation and preoccupation of modern life, we have unconsciously acquiesced, increasingly delegating the challenging task of public policy formation to governmental and bureaucratic institutions, to the point where such is assumed to be the proper government role and consequently no longer the proper role or responsibility of private parties operating in a public sphere. As proposed earlier, privately (i.e., not convened by government) constituted standards bodies potentially comprise a form of revitalized public sphere in the context of modern technological society, and no other institution seems better suited to dealing with certain difficult and important global technical and public policy issues.

Communicative Action

In his theory of communicative action, Habermas further develops these ideas. He proposes to resolve the conflict between private and public autonomy (i.e., individual rights vs. collective rights) which he attributes to individual and collective subjectivity, by introducing the concept of intersubjectivity whereby the conflicting subjective interests are worked out through a discursive formation of public opinion and which recognizes the equal validity of public and private rights. Habermas measures democratic legitimacy not in terms of majority decision-making but by the discursive quality of the process of deliberation that lead to such decisions. In standards making practice, in contrast to lawmaking and usual democratic governance, simple majority decision is not considered adequate, and only a consensus can result in a viable standard. In this sense, perhaps standards making practice is potentially one of the best examples of communicative action available in modern society.

Habermas' term for the rational discursive process by which normative disputes are resolved to mutual satisfaction is "practical discourse." He proposes three sets of rules applying to three levels of argumentation on which practical discourse depends: 1) participants must speak the same natural language according to the same general conventions, 2) participants must desire to reach agreement and must defend only what they believe to be true, and 3) participants must only offer arguments that could command assent and not merely seek a desired behaviour or outcome.

In this third level, he draws the distinction between strategic action concerned only with external outcome (e.g., possibly employing rhetoric, political influence, threats, bribes, coercion, etc.) and communicative action concerned with a prevailing "force of the better argument." Strategic Action introduces distortions into the ideal speech process. Standards making practice has long sought to institutionalize these same rules of argumentation based on communicative action, perhaps with some measure of success.

The concepts described above are further integrated and developed by Habermas in his latest work, Between Facts and Norms, where he examines the structure and processes of judicial, legislative and political institutions from the philosophical perspective of discourse theory, ethics the public sphere and communication. These vital social institutions and processes are concerned with establishing what "is" and what "ought to be", as are the institutions and processes of standardization.

The formal standards making process today is constituted around a set of rules and procedures that essentially mirror Habermas' concept of ideal speech and his rules of argumentation. The operational directives of the international standards bodies (e.g., ISO, IEC, JTC1, ITU, IEEE, etc.) and most national or regional bodies (e.g., ANSI, CENELEC, etc.) all embody principles of fairness, adherence to procedures of due notice, openness, inclusion of stakeholders, and decision by consensus that are consistent with the model of ideal speech. In this sense, formal standards making practice has been characterized as a form of revitalized public sphere within the context of modern technological/industrial society.

Inarguably, standards making practice is subject to a number of forms of distortion. Before it can fully function as a public sphere, it must address such issues as stakeholders' identification, scope of participation, the role of expertise, and public access. The extent to which the actual practice lives up to the principles of ideal speech and theory of communicative action is an interesting question which bears further examination. Two additional bodies of theory which inform this question are 1) theories of rhetoric from the discipline of Communication Studies and 2) institutional analysis from Political Science.

Theories of Rhetoric

Rhetoric is concerned with the study and practice of purposive human communication, spoken and written, and it is perhaps the oldest discipline, originating with ancient Greeks and long considered central to being educated. Rhetoric is about persuasion—and the institutions of law (i.e., legislation and adjudication) and other norms (i.e., standardization) are also about persuasion. Habermas' banishment of "strategic action" from the public sphere has not gone unquestioned. Hauser presents an extensive critique of Habermas, proposing an expanded rhetorical model of the public sphere, in which he observes that Habermas' reliance on ideal speech in the public sphere and thus on "...participants' competence and the rational validity of their discourse, ...excludes many arenas in which public dialog occurs," and, "...establishes criteria for communication that are insensitive to its essential rhetorically."

Hauser calls for a rhetorical model of the public sphere that envisions rather a "web of discursive spheres" that comprise a civil society in which members "...engage one another in ongoing dialogues that continually confront public problems, constitute publics, and challenge within and across domains for the formation of public opinion." Although Hauser is referring to society at large, the rhetorical character and embedded ideological beliefs evident in standards discourse present practical difficulties to standards committee participants not in agreement with the dominant discourse; and it is clear that an atmosphere of rational discourse is not always a practical reality. To this, Habermas would likely reply that such discourse does not adhere to the rules of ideal speech and does not really constitute communicative action. But what is to be done? The standards making practice does constitute a global "web of discursive spheres" or publics and perhaps the "rules" need to at least recognize rhetorical practices so that they can be effectively separated from the rational ones.

Institutional Analysis

Since all normative practices are formed around or form institutional structures, how those structures are constituted can then influence how the practices proceed and can limit or shape the discourse taking place in them. Much of the theory described here so far (e.g., social construction of technology, policy science, democracy, etc.) speaks to standardization in the terms of culture and social values. In contrast, Steinmo has taken an institutionalist approach, examining the role of institutional structures differentiating from that of culture in shaping the outcome of deliberative processes.

In the context of his study of American approaches to welfare legislation vs. other western nations, he identifies ways in which institutional fragmentation and the power of elites "...profoundly shapes who can effectively participate in politics, how they must be organized and what is possible to achieve—irrespective of our ideologies or values." The mechanisms Steinmo identifies are particularly useful in understanding the historical and institutional differences between the structure of standardization found in the U.S. and that in Europe and they shed useful light on the issue raised by the EC Commissioner cited earlier. The problem is not only cultural but institutional in nature.

This has proposed a beginning approach to the establishment of a general theory of standards drawing on theoretical and methodological frameworks from three separate disciplines. From political science and Policy Science we obtain a general method of analysis for standardization projects and problems. From sociology and Studies of Technology and Society, we obtain a general understanding of the role of standards in the interplay of technology and society and the basic processes of technological change. From Philosophy and Communication Studies, we obtain a theoretical framework within which to situate the standards making process itself.

For example, a further area of exploration is suggested by the field of Communication Studies and specifically the work of Walter Ong who has examined the ancient study of rhetoric and the implications of communication technologies for how ideas, society and culture are constructed. The study of rhetoric offers further fundamental analytical and theoretical insights into the discursive practice of standards making.

Other communication scholars such as Harold Innis and Marshall McLuhan have also investigated the interaction of communication technology and culture, and these ideas have been further developed (and somewhat radicalized) by postmodernist sociologist Jean Baudrillard. The philosopher and historian, Michel Foucault has studied how discourse and discursive practices become institutionalized—a topic rich in implications for standardization practice. Many other fruitful areas in the social sciences remain to be explored as we begin to form a general theory of standards.

Family- social Institution

To provide a safe lifestyle and environment for the perpetuation of the human race, the institution of marriage was created by various societies based upon an agreement by a man and woman to become husband and wife. Within this system of dealing with responsibilities and safeguards of property rights and family lines, the family unit of husband, wife and children born to them, establish, preserve and maintain morals. They also cultivate, improve and perpetuate our civilization, legal, social and ethical codes both explicitly and implicitly.

Among these codes is consideration for the sex drive of men and women. It is understood that marriage provides a place of private sexual activity between husband and wife. That same environment also provides a place of family activity when children are born of this husband and wife's sexual activity. Societies throughout history, as a whole, have upheld and maintained the concept that marriage is a powerful commitment between a man and a woman to become husband and wife. That commitment has peripheral legal and personal responsibility factors.

While the actual dynamics of marriage functions have changed throughout the centuries, as have perceived public needs, opinions and practices, the concept of a man and a woman as husband and wife bonding together in love, forming a family unit, with the potential of having children born of the marriage, has not changed. The beginning of marriage as a necessary social institution was first recognized from a religious point of view. This view has gradually shifted to that of a civil point of view, while still retaining the original religious influences.

During this time of shifting from religious to include civil influences, there has been a period of attempts to redefine marriage as an individual's right to happiness and as a contract between two persons of same community standing. The "make me happy" concept of marriage has resulted in an approximate 50 per cent divorce rate, with the typical marriage lasting about seven years. In addition to that there have been tremendous shifts of concepts of sexual activities outside of marriage, child custody rights and the psychology of properly raising children in today's society.

The "same community standing" mentality fostered by belief in equal political, economic, social, and civil rights for all people attempted to eliminate the historically unequal difference between the sexes which was felt to contribute to an unhealthy and unbalanced relationship in marriage. This resulted in trying to reduce marriage to a mutual contractual obligation to be observed by both parties to the marriage.

The response from the religious community, and many in the civil community, has been to continue to defend the traditional man and woman, husband and wife sexual relationship in the institution of marriage, with all the responsibilities and safeguards as the norm for humanity. In addition, a veritable volley of historical, legal, biblical, religious, political, social, economic, traditional and cultural arguments, accompanied by statistical reports, have been presented to influence lawmakers and public opinion. The purpose of this barrage of alleged "information" are attempts to "prove" that changing the definition and function of marriage will result in positive or negative social values, that same-sex "marriages" are, or are not, simply a natural evolutionary phase of society, that same-sex parenting of children is, or is not, psychologically unhealthy for them, that divorce rates have stabilized, or risen spectacularly in those places where same-sex marriages are sanctioned by government.

Also, that recognition of same-sex unions as "marriages" eliminates, or does not eliminate, a perceived social inequality. The list goes on and on, but will, in most cases, turn out to be a variation of one of the above issues. There are also strong attempts to equate racial discrimination and discrimination against same-sex marriages. The purpose is to then categorize the homosexual and lesbian "marriage" discrimination as a civil rights issue. Arguments are advanced that homosexual and lesbian lovers have been among us for many, many years and have not been an adverse effect upon society. The opposite could also be noted, namely that there is no particular benefit associated with the sexual activities of homosexual and lesbian lovers. Other arguments are that bisexual persons can marry persons of the opposite sex. The point of this logic remains undefined.

How this gender issue is attempting to become a civil rights issue is illogical. Persons of any and every sexual orientation are as free as everybody else to marry anyone of the opposite sex, which is the essence of traditional marriages. After all the fireworks-oriented semantical arguments and carefully contrived statistical (mis)representations have grown cold, hopefully also the emotions will become less heated on both sides. What has to be determined is a basic value analysis: what's this thing for, really. And what does it cost? Then, what else will do the same job, and what does *it* cost? Heterosexual marriage between a man and a woman makes them husband and wife. As stated before heterosexual marriage provides a safe lifestyle and environment for the perpetuation of the human race. Marriage was created by various societies as a system of dealing with responsibilities and safeguards of property rights and family lines, and the family unit, including children born to them. Moral, civilization, legal, social and ethical codes are preserved and maintained by the institution of marriage.

Specifically, marriage has and will continue to include penetration of a woman's vagina with a male penis, which among other things has the potential of causing pregnancy and babies, which brings new life upon this earth. To stipulate that a plastic or rubber device shaped like a penis, or that mutual oral stimulation or anal intercourse to achieve an orgasm is the basis of marriage is preposterous. This is, at best, usage of sex toys and indulgence in sexual foreplay, a "pretend" kind of substitute for sex organs, which in heterosexual marriage sexual activity will culminate in "penetration of a woman's vagina with a male penis, which among other things has the potential of causing pregnancy and babies, which brings new life upon this earth."

A man engaging in sexual activity with another man or a woman engaging in sexual activity with another woman has no potential for bringing a baby, a new life, into this world. There is no family environment: only two people of the same sex doing sexual things with each other. If that's what they want to do to feel sexually fulfilled, that's their choice. As long as they do so in privacy, just as all sexual activity should be in a private place. It's not a matter of condoning or condemning their sexual behavior. It has to do with accepting the fact that it happens as a part of real life.

People have been doing that for years and years and years and will no doubt continue. But to attempt to redefine "marriage" as including two homosexual males, or two lesbian women indulging in this "pretend" kind of substitute for sex organs using sex toys and foreplay, whose sole object is to induce a pleasurable orgasm—totally devoid of the potential of bringing new life upon this earth—is outrageously ridiculous. To those who think it's logical to redefine marriage in that manner, you have to question your very own motivation to do so. High on that motivation list are political agenda's, followed by misguided and prejudiced reformers, rebellers and rejects of every known category and then some that aren't yet known.

To accord the status of "marriage" to any two men or any two women desiring to be stimulated by the other to orgasm will raise the cost of social and healthcare benefits for the American people to a staggering amount of money, which should be better spent in other areas of our society. As citizens, do we really concern ourselves with how other countries make decisions about what marriage really is? Do you really want to redefine marriage as a "make me happy" feel-good social game? Do you really want a "same community standing" contractual obligation between *any* two human beings? Consider the high cost of so redefining marriage. Are you really prepared to pay the cost to do so? Think about it. There is no viable option for the institution of marriage in this country.

If America's citizens allow lawmakers to so redefine marriage it will serve only to create two differing societal values. It will, in effect, polarize Americans into two different camps, which gives further cause for each side to increase attacks on the other side. Think about it: a very small minority of persons further divided against an overwhelming majority who believe in the traditional concept of marriage. In such an environment, the only thing that will thrive is further persecution of this small minority by the overwhelming majority.

Disasters, from this perspective, are *interpreted as normal events* largely originating within identifiable historical and structural conditions. Like other social problems, understanding the private troubles experienced requires the capacity to shift abstraction levels and examine relevant public issues.

And sometimes the analysis must transcend the public concerns of any given era and identify latent juxtapositions of social trends and structural conditions that will ignite in future areas of conflict, instability, and human hurt. This orientation provides a *context* for drawing upon the insights seen by others who have selected different areas of human travail for study ranging from crime to race relations to poverty and so on. As with analyses of these areas, however, there is no inherent bias toward the negative. Disasters do at times, and for some much of the time, *have positive consequences*.

What this perspective forces the analyst to specify, however, is a definition of the value judgments that are being made to declare any given behavior as "positive" or "negative." Hence, the cultural context of the definer is made explicit and may be contrasted with that of others whose circumstance and value position may differ. So-called "good business practices" that some would define as "unethical" illustrate a type of analysis that similarly permits enhanced understanding of the historical contexts and ideologies that foster classrooms of children who will become suicide bombers within the next few years.

The same can be said for the thousands of American citizens who will be injured or killed because of domestically birthed gang violence. The same can be said for the billions of young girls from centuries past, like millions today, whose personal security requires unquestioning obedience and *loyalty* to unjust systems rooted in patterns of inequality, abuse, and intolerance.

Clearly, this orientation presses analysts to ask *new research questions* not just about "routineness" but also many other important matters. In what ways, and with what consequences, is disasters "non routine"? What additional differences, and of course similarities, can be identified when disasters are compared to other social problems? In what ways are these processes similar, and different, across the range of society's existent today and over centuries past? If the society is the patient, as a social problems perspective assumes, what is being said to disaster researchers as they pursue their craft?

It didn't take long; however, as my pen pushed my thinking as it commonly does, to realize the severity of my impaired vision. The challenge goes far beyond future social problems textbooks. And the information flow must be multidirectional. As we reach out more frequently to bring our "goods" to others working within different academic and professional settings, we too will grow in unanticipated ways. Sometimes it will be because of questions or criticism. But other times it will be because someone else has had a creative insight about a statistical method or conceptual framework that helped them understand some aspect of crime, or how certain elementary school classrooms traumatized students trapped therein.

If we are open to such ideas, new ways to thinking about disasters and hazards will stimulate growth. To the degree that we encourage isolation and separateness, our growth will be constrained. Thinking through the numerous linkages afforded within social problems perspectives will stimulate such growth among disaster researchers.

Recent writings by Wismer et al. 2003, Enarson et al. 2003 and many others have pressed all of us to think harder about the meaning of "social vulnerability". Patterns of risk are shaped by social processes that usually reflect the contours of power and privilege. Does the risk of living in a flood prone area parallel the pathway that results in the death of a hate crime victim whose sexual orientation is despised by his killers? And do either of these risks merit the amount of public expenditures currently being allocated daily to ensure that all airline passengers remove their shoes before boarding? We often hear rhetoric about funding decisions for disaster mitigation and preparedness programs being based on threat assessments. But what range of threats is really being assessed by those holding and directing the flow of dollars? And when we return to the orientation proposed by Hart (2006), and ask about the real sources of insecurity confronting *all* American citizens, not just the well off, the linkage to social problems perspectives becomes much clearer.

For it has been within these frameworks, enriched by basic sociological studies of crime, poverty, sexism, racism, ageism and the like, that our understanding of *root causes of social problems* has been most enhanced. Increasingly, we must frame our research agendas within crossnational and historical contexts. The pollutants of Love Canal fame did not arrive there like the 1999 tornado that hit Moore, Oklahoma. And the woman who was beaten badly by a spouse, whose sense of frustration with flood relief run- arounds and cleanup fatigue boiled over, is every much a victim as those temporarily living in a Red Cross shelter. But we must dig deeper and ultimately confront the realities of "the power elite" and their roles in the changing distributions of risk and patterns of victimization.

While most may prefer to stay within the confines of flood studies, for example, even if they accept the challenge of cross-societal analysis, even they must confront the human caused nature of flooding be it reflections of timber harvesting, failed levee and dam construction or maintenance, unregulated upstream development, or just stupidity. Others must venture into the less charted waters of conflict disasters and their root causes. Record levels of arms production and sales, expanded military training facilities, and the like, are linked directly to the economic security of many, not just those at the top. How such economic interdependencies fuel policy decisions within both the public and private sector require scrutiny. For it is within such structural arrangements that the root causes of the most violent disasters are to be found. One need not accept the strategy or the value set of the "environmental justice movement", for example, but it might very well be a good place to start.

And so is the further reflection on the implications of the conclusions reached by Thomas Paine in his initial essay on the "Rights of Man" (original publication, 1791). For example, ponder the relevance of these words to an analysis of "root causes" of disaster. "Every war terminates with an addition of taxes, and consequently with an addition of revenue; and in any event of war, in the manner they are now commenced and concluded, the power and interest of Governments are increased. War, therefore, from its productiveness, as it easily furnishes the pretence of necessity for taxes and appointments to places and offices, becomes a principal part of the system of old Governments; and to establish any mode to abolish war, however advantageous it might be to Nations, would be to take from such Government the most lucrative of its branches."

Since the creation of FEMA in 1979, the profession of emergency management has experienced acceleration in its long-term evolution. From two university degree programs in 1996, by a decade later over 100 were operating. Additionally, over 50 programs were introducing students to aspects of homeland and defense security. I noted these earlier and my concern about the current capacity and interest of faculty in critical examination of emergency management policy. I believe firmly that the social problems perspective on disaster that I have herein proposed would assist these faculty, and subsequently, those practicing within this profession to develop a *more strategic perspective* on their profession. By explicitly recognizing and better understanding the mix of social trends and structures within which their agencies are embedded, ranging from the local community to the international context, they will better be able to provide the leadership and technical expertise reflected in the vision statements of their professional associations (e.g., International Association of Emergency Managers, IAEM).

And they will better be able to grasp the policy implications of broad historical analyses like Barry's (2005) analysis of military troop movements and emergent quarantine efforts that resulted in both the rapid spread of the 1918 influenza virus and poorly implemented mitigation policies. Furthermore, an understanding of how social processes and structures, interact with environmental realities like those described by Jared Diamond (2005) in his theoretical framework of societal collapse, can provide emergency managers with the breadth of knowledge essential for more informed policy review and creation.

"When people are desperate, undernourished, and without hope, they blame their governments, which they see as responsible for or unable to solve their problems. They try to emigrate at any cost. They fight each other over land. They kill each other.

They start civil wars. They figure that they have nothing to loose, so they become terrorists, or they support or tolerate terrorism." Disasters are nonroutine social problems. At least that is one way of viewing conjunctions of historical conditions and social definitions of physical harm and social disruption. It is not the only way, nor does it preclude other definitions and perspectives. But it is a perspective that offers some unique insights, integrative mechanisms, and linkages to both substantive areas of study and the future practice of emergency management.

Bibliography

Althusser, Louis, 1971, *Lenin and Philosophy and Other Essays* trans. Ben Brewster, London: New Left Books.

Anderson, Elizabeth, 1999, "What is the Point of Equality?" *Ethics*, 109/2: 287-337.

Barnes, Barry, 1995, *The Elements of Social Theory*, Princeton, N.J.: Princeton University Press.

Bhaskar, Roy, 1979, *The Possibility of Naturalism*, Brighton: Harvester.

Blake, Michael, 2001, "Distributive Justice, State Coercion and Autonomy", *Philosophy and Public Affairs*, 30/3: 257-296.

Bloor, David, 1997, *Wittgenstein, Rules and Institutions*, London: Routledge.

Bratman, Michael, 1987, *Intentions, Plans and Practical Reason*, Cambridge, Mass.: Harvard University Press.

Cohen, G. A., 1978, *Karl Marx's Theory of History: A Defence*, Oxford: Clarendon Press.

Durkheim, Emile, 1992, *Professional Ethics and Civic Morals*, C. Brookfield (tr.), London: Routledge.

Durkheim, Emile, 1964, *Rules of Sociological Method*, New York: Free Press.

Elster, Jon, 1989, *Nuts and Bolts for the Social Sciences*, Cambridge: Cambridge University Press.

French, Peter, 1984, *Collective and Corporate Responsibility*, New York: Columbia University Press.

Giddens, Anthony, 1976, *New Rules of Sociological Method*,

London: Hutchinson.

—, 1984, *The Constitution of Society: Outline of the Theory of Structuration*, Cambridge: Polity Press.

Erving Goffman, 1961, *Asylums*, Chicago: Aldine Publishing.

Grice, Paul, 1989, "Utterer's Meaning, Sentence-meaning and Word-meaning", in P. Grice, *Studies in the Way of Words*, Cambridge, MA: Harvard University Press.

Harre, Rom, 1979, *Social Being*, Oxford: Blackwell.

Lewis, David, 1969, *Convention: A Philosophical Study*, Harvard University Press.

Miller, Seumas, 2001, *Social Action: A Teleological Account*, New York: Cambridge University Press.

—, 2003, "Institutions, Collective Goods and Moral Rights", *ProtoSociology*, 18-19: 184-207.

Mayntz, Renate, 2004, "Mechanisms in the Analysis of Social Macro-Phenomena", *Philosophy of the Social Sciences*, 34/2: 237-259.

Parsons, Talcott, 1968, *The Structure of Social Action*, New York: Free Press.

—, 1982, *On Institutions and Social Evolution*, Chicago: University of Chicago Press.

Radcliffe-Brown, A. R., 1958, *Method in Social Anthropology*, N. Srinivas (ed.), Chicago: University of Chicago Press.

Rawls, John, 1972, *A Theory of Justice*, Cambridge, MA: Harvard University Press.

—, 1999, *The Law of Peoples*, Cambridge, MA: Harvard University Press.

Ruben, David-Hillel, 1985, *The Metaphysics of the Social World*, London: Routledge and Kegan Paul.

Ryan, Alan, 1970, *The Philosophy of the Social Sciences*, London: Macmillan.

Schotter, A., 1981, *The Economic Theory of Institutions*, Cambridge: Cambridge University Press.

Scott, Richard, 2001, *Institutions and Organisations*, London: Sage.

Searle, John, 1995, *The Construction of Social Reality*, London: Penguin.

Sokal, Alan, 1996, "Transgressing the Boundaries: Toward a Transformative Hermeneutic of Quantum Gravity", *Social Text*, 46-47: 217-252.

Spencer, Herbert, 1971, *Structure, Function and Evolution*, S. Andreski (ed.), London: Michael Joseph.

Tuomela, Raimo, 2002, *The Philosophy of Social Practices: A Collective Acceptance View*, Cambridge: Cambridge University Press.

Turner, Jonathan, 1997, *The Institutional Order*, New York: Longman.

Walzer, Michael, 1983, *Spheres of Justice*, New York: Basic Books.

Warwick, D.P., 1981, "Ethics of Administrative Discretion", in J.L. Fleishman *et al.* (eds.), *Public Duties: The Moral Obligations of Public Officials*, Boston: Harvard University Press.

Weber, Max, 1949, *The Methodology of the Social Sciences*, Glencoe, Illinois: Free Press.

Index